Know Your Rights

Your Guide To The Law

Louise Carmichael

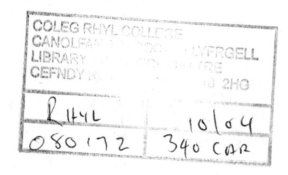
Published by Robert Frederick Ltd, 4 North Parade, Bath BA1 1LF

First published 2003

Produced by Louise Carmichael for Librios Publishing Ltd, 21 Catherine Street, London
WC2B 5JS. www.librios.com.

ISBN 0-7554-1726-7

Important note
This book is not intended as a substitute for specialist legal advice. Readers are strongly
advised to take professional advice before acting in any matter that may involve the law.
This book has been written on the basis of information and law current as at 1 April
2003. The author and Librios Publishing Ltd have done their utmost to ensure that all the
information in this book is correct to the best of their knowledge. The author, producers
and publisher cannot assume legal responsibility for the accuracy of any particular
statement in this work. No responsibility for loss or damage occasioned to any person
acting or refraining from action as a result of the material in this publication can be
accepted by the author, the producer or the publisher.

Contents

	Introduction	**5**
1	A roof over your head	**7**
2	Buying and selling	**38**
3	Your relationships	**58**
4	The law and young people	**80**
5	Your health	**102**
6	Accidents and injuries	**115**
7	When someone dies	**132**
8	Offences against property and the person	**151**
9	At work	**165**
10	Motoring	**200**
11	Leisure and travel	**219**
12	Pets and other animals	**249**
13	Immigration, nationality and identity	**258**
14	Navigating the legal system	**285**
15	Further reading and useful addresses	**307**
	Index	**316**

Introduction

The law is a notoriously complex field. Lawyers train for years before entering practice, and they spend huge amounts of time keeping up with the unprecendented mountains of new legislation produced by our government. This book is designed as a general guide for ordinary people, and is written as far as possible in plain English.

The book is divided into chapters, each roughly covering an area of our lives: work, leisure, travel, property, etc. It has been organised with a view to accessing the information in it quickly and easily, rather than as a book to read from start to finish. The index is probably the first point of access, but the reader will also find cross-reference boxes throughout, leading her to information on related subjects. Key legal terms are listed at the end of each chapter. It can be very difficult to define legal concepts in a few words, so the author has given a general definition only, so that readers become familiar with legal jargon, and it becomes less of a stumbling block when talking to legal professionals. The key terms sections cross-refer back into the relevant chapter, acting as a mini-index to the subject. In addition, the boxes are used to highlight warnings to the reader. These point out particular spots in which she might get into difficulty when tackling a legal problem.

Chapter 15 lists a large number of organisations that can provide specialist information, practical support and advice to members of the public.

Warning!

There is a well-known saying that 'the man who is his own lawyer has a fool for a client'. Laws change, and they may be interpreted differently depending on the details of individual situations. While a general book such as this can pack in a lot of information, it can only draw a rough sketch of some broad areas of the law.

For these reasons, it is vital to get specialist legal advice from a qualified professional before acting in any matter. There are two excellent sources of free advice in the UK: the chain of Citizens Advice Bureaux (see page xxx), which has offices more or less in every town, and an excellent website offering reams of information; and the Community Legal Service (see page xxx), which publishes easy-to-understand booklets on many issues relating to the law and your rights. In addition, many solicitors offer short assessment interviews free of charge.

Acknowledgements

The author would like to thank Martin Barr and her colleagues at Librios Publishing for their support and advice during the writing of this book. She would also like to express her gratitude to Michael for providing a haven of tranquility in which to work and for never failing to produce food, firewood and encouragement when most needed. Thank-you.

1 A Roof Over Your Head

One of our most basic needs in life is shelter, and acquiring and maintaining the roof over our head and those of our family is one of the most expensive items in most people's budgets. This chapter looks at many issues to do with the place in which we live. It starts with the different ways in which the law regulates rented accommodation, what your rights are as a tenant and what are the rights of your landlord in such matters as rent, the end of your agreement, repairs to the property and rights of access. Next, it looks at buying and selling property and the different rights you may have under leaseholds, freeholds and the proposed new commonholds.

Renting a place to live

While many people these days own the houses or flats they live in, a significant number rent the roof over their head. Renting is defined in law by a contract (written or verbal) between two people – the tenant and the landlord. To be valid, the agreement must include the landlord allowing you exclusive use of all or part of a property for your 'quiet enjoyment', and you must agree to pay the rent (or render 'services' that can be valued as rent) and to vacate the premises when the agreement comes to an end.

Rental agreements

The law calls most rental agreements 'leases', and those who rent under leases are tenants. However, some rental agreements are 'licences', and the renting party is therefore known as the licensee. Confusingly, some people who own their own homes actually only own a lease, albeit a long one, and are therefore, in law, tenants, but they are also often known as leaseholders. For more information on long leases (leaseholds) see pages 20–23.

Several different types of agreement are recognised by the law, and each one carries different terms, but some rules apply to all of them. These include what a tenant must do if he or she wishes to end a tenancy, the general procedure for eviction of an unwanted tenant, rules on deposits, who is responsible for repairs, the landlord's rights of access and the issue of harrassment.

When a tenant wishes to end an agreement

The tenant's right to end an agreement depends on the type of agreement he has. If the agreement is for a fixed period (six months, for example), and he wants to leave before the end of the fixed term, he must give at least a month's notice, and the landlord can ask that the rent for the rest of the period is paid. In some cases, landlords will waive this if a new tenant is found and the landlord doesn't lose any payments. Some fixed-term agreements include a clause that tenants may leave without paying the balance of the rent if sufficient notice is given.

If the period of the agreement is not fixed, the tenant may leave without being liable for extra rent as long as he gives a reasonable amount of notice.

Eviction

In general, when a person enters into a tenancy agreement with a landlord, he implicitly agrees to leave the property either at the end of the tenancy or when either party serves the appropriate notice. If a landlord gives a tenant lawful notice to leave and the tenant does not duly depart, the landlord can go to court to begin 'possession proceedings', that is, a legal action to take back possession of the property. The aim of the possession proceedings is to decide whether to issue a possession order. If the answer is yes, and the order is served on the tenant, and if he still does not leave, the landlord can ask the court to send bailiffs to have the tenant removed. The amount of time this takes, the rights of the landlord, and the opportunities the tenant has to challenge the landlord's case or influence the court in another way (for example, by having the possession order delayed until arrears of rent can be paid), depend on the type of agreement in place between the landlord and tenant. See pages 10–18 for detailed information on each type of tenancy.

Deposits

Most landlords ask their tenants for a deposit at the start of a tenancy agreement. The agreement should include a statement that the deposit has been paid (a receipt), what it could be used to cover (damage to the property, for example), and when it will be returned to the tenant. Some landlords keep deposits in interest-bearing accounts, and offer to pay the tenant interest at the end of the tenancy, but this, unhappily, is by no means the norm, and it is not a legal requirement.

Repairs and renovations

In general, the landlord is responsible for repair work to any rented accommodation, particularly to the common parts. But much depends on the contract that has been agreed. However, landlords have a number of responsibilities regardless of which type of agreement is in force. They must:

◆ keep the outside of the building and any 'common parts' (for example, halls and staircases) in good repair
◆ maintain all sanitary, heating and hot water systems
◆ maintain all electrical and gas equipment and installations (except those supplied by the tenant) and ensure all drainage systems are in good repair
◆ ensure that all gas appliances are tested annually by a registered engineer, and supply a copy of the engineer's report to the tenant

If you feel your accommodation is in such a state of disrepair that it is unsafe, or poses a risk for your health, contact the Environmental Health office of your Local Authority. If you have difficulty getting your landlord to make repairs or undertake necessary maintenance work, your local Citizens Advice Bureau will be able to advise on how to proceed in your particular circumstances.

Some tenants like to decorate and improve their accommodation. In general, they can only do so with the consent of the landlord, and there is no obligation on the landlord to pay the cost of any work the tenant undertakes (although many do). However, the landlord is not entitled to raise the rent on the basis that the tenant's improvements have increased the rental value of the property.

Landlord's rights of access

It is implied in any tenancy agreement that the tenant essentially takes possession of the property under the terms of the agreement, and has a right to its quiet enjoyment without being bothered by the landlord. A landlord has a right to enter a property to make repairs or to ensure that there is no damage. However, he must give the tenant a reasonable period of notice, usually 24 hours, and he must arrange to visit the property at a reasonable hour of the day. The only exception to this is if there is an emergency.

Harassment

Most landlords are exemplary in their dealings with their tenants, fostering an amicable relationship. But some are not. No landlord has the right to use bullying tactics to force a tenant to leave, even if the rental agreement is over. Harassment can include:

- threats against the person or possessions
- actual damage to possessions or person (which would, of course, be another matter altogether)
- demands for access to the property at short notice and/or at unreasonable hours
- any kind of behaviour which the victim finds unreasonable, inappropriate or offensive.

In order to strengthen your case against a bullying landlord, keep a record of every event as it takes place, including your responses. Also, keep any correspondence between you and your landlord. You may need to produce them in court.

Types of rental agreement

Rental agreements are in general divided into three categories: private rentals, council rentals and housing association rentals. If you are renting from a private landlord (either an individual or a company), your agreement with the landlord will fall into one of the following categories:

- protected tenancy (sometimes called a 'regulated' tenancy)
- assured tenancy
- assured shorthold tenancy
- licence.

If you are renting from a council or housing association of one kind or another, you may have one of the above arrangements or you may have a 'secure' tenancy.

Your rights as a tenant, and the rights of your landlord depend on which kind of agreement you have, and tenancy agreements generally cover such things as how much rent can be asked, when it can be raised, whether the landlord can ask you to leave, and if he does so and you don't leave, what steps he has to take in order for him to get the court to evict you.

Protected tenancies

People whose tenancy agreement started before 15 January 1989 most probably have this kind of agreement, and it gives the tenant the most rights against the landlord of any of the forms of agreement in the private sector. You may be a protected tenant if:

◆ your agreement started before 1989
◆ your landlord is not resident and does not come into your property on a daily basis, for example to clean or service the property (and does not ask someone else to do this on his behalf)
◆ your tenancy is not a 'company let', i.e. a company rents from the landlord and then allows an employee to live in the property on a licence agreement (see page 15)
◆ your accommodation is not 'bed-and-breakfast'
◆ your accommodation is not a holiday let or student accommodation.

If your tenancy began before this date and you are not sure of your status as a tenant, or you are a protected tenant and your landlord asks you to sign a different kind of tenancy agreement, seek advice – your rights as a protected tenant are very valuable indeed.

Ending a protected tenancy

It is quite difficult in legal terms for landlords to move protected tenants from their property should they wish to do so. Landlords must be able to show that they have one of 17 reasons expressly stipulated by the law. In law these reasons are called 'grounds', and are divided into two groups: mandatory reasons and discretionary reasons. If the landlord wants the tenant to leave, he must first give a certain minimum period of notice, either two weeks or two months. He must then apply to the court for a possession order and give one of the 17 reasons. If his reason falls into the category of 'mandatory' reasons (and, of course, they have to be proved, and the tenant can challenge the landlord in court), the court has no choice but to rule that the tenant must leave. If he gives one of the 'discretionary' reasons, the court does not necessarily have to grant his request, but must be satisfied that the landlord's notice to quit is reasonable.

Mandatory reasons could include:

◆ non-payment of rent; in this case, the tenant may be given an opportunity to pay the arrears before making or enforcing the possession order

◆ the property was formerly the home of the landlord, and he gave you notice that this was the case, and he now wants to return, or his family want to return

◆ the mortgage company that is financing the property wants to repossess it

◆ the landlord wishes to redevelop the property

◆ the tenant has died and the person in residence in the property does not have the right to inherit the tenancy (see pages 134–135 for more on this).

Discretionary reasons might include:

◆ the tenant is frequently late with the rent

◆ the property has been used for immoral or illegal activities

◆ the tenant or someone living with her has been convicted of criminal activities in the local area

◆ the tenant, someone living with her, or a visitor, is causing a nuisance to neighbours and others in the area

◆ the original tenancy was based on false information given by the tenant

Neighbourhood problems

For information on how the law deals with antisocial behaviour in housing and with disputes between neighbours see chapter three.

- the landlord's furniture has been damaged
- the tenancy was arranged in association with the tenant's employment by the landlord, and that person is no longer employed.

If you are a protected tenant and you are asked to leave by your landlord, seek specialist advice immediately. A good place to start would be your local Citizens Advice Bureau or law centre.

Protected tenancies: rent increases

Protected tenancies are covered by fair rent legislation. This means that a tenant with this kind of agreement can ask the Rent Officer at their local authority to assess the property and set what is considered to be a fair rent. The rent could be raised or reduced by the Rent Officer, and in either case the tenant or the landlord can appeal against the decision. If the Rent Officer opts to increase the rent, the landlord must give the tenant notice before starting to charge at the higher rate.

Assured tenancies

Tenancies dating from between 15 January 1989 and 27 February 1997 may be either assured tenancies or assured shorthold tenancies. If the tenancy agreement includes a notice telling the tenant that this is an assured shorthold tenancy, then so it is. If the landlord never made a declaration of this type, and it is not clear from the written contract what was intended, then it is an assured tenancy.

Assured tenancies can occur if the landlord is in the private sector, but also if the landlord is a housing association of some description (see page 17). If the agreement is a company let, if the landlord is also resident in the property or if he provides services such as food or cleaning (as for protected tenancies (see page 11)), the agreement will not be an assured tenancy.

Ending an assured tenancy

Assured tenants are protected from eviction in much the same way as protected tenants, and if you have this kind of agreement and your landlord asks you to leave, you should seek advice immediately.

Assured tenancies: rent increases

If the tenancy agreement is for a fixed period of time (perhaps six months), the landlord cannot raise the rent during that period unless the contract says specifically that the rent will rise. The landlord is entitled to raise the rent after a year, but he must give adequate notice. He is also entitled to raise the rent if the agreement is renewed after the fixed period.

If the agreement is not for a fixed period (i.e. gives no end date), the landlord is entitled to raise the rent at any time. If the tenant disagrees with the rise, the Rent Assessment Committee at the local authority can be asked to assess the rent, and will compare it with average rents for similar kinds of property in the local area.

Assured shorthold tenancies

Most tenancy agreements that were begun after 28 February 1997 are assured shorthold tenancies. In a few cases, they may be assured tenancies (see above), but there would be a declaration of this in the agreement if this were the case. Again, in a few cases, contracts begun before this date may be assured shorthold tenancies.

An assured shorthold tenancy is an agreement that lasts for a minimum fixed period. It can be renewed after the end of the initial period for a further period of time.

Ending an assured shorthold tenancy

During the 'assured period' (usually six months, but sometimes

---

Discrimination when renting

The discrimination laws ensure that in general men and women are treated equally – or at least that there is a remedy if we feel we haven't been treated the same as a person of the opposite sex, or of a different nationality or race, or someone able-bodied when we have a disability. One exception does exist, however. It's perfectly legal for a person who is taking a lodger to state whether the lodger should be male or female. This applies if the lodger is going to be sharing a room or rooms (not including a staircase or hallway) with the landlord. Even in this case, though, it is not lawful for a landlord to discriminate on grounds on race or nationality, or disability.

the parties agree that the period will be a year or more), the landlord may not evict the tenant for any reason. After the assured period is over, the landlord can ask the tenant to leave. Indeed, some landlords include with their standard assured shorthold tenancy contracts a separate notice to quit dated so that it comes into force at the end of the period. If the tenant does not do so, the landlord can ask the court for an eviction order and does not need to give any reasons at all for the eviction. A fast-track method of doing this is available. The landlord may simply write to the court with details. The court may then issue an eviction order without any need for a court hearing. So this kind of tenancy offers fewer rights for the tenant than other forms.

Assured shorthold tenancies: rent increases

In general, the rules for rent increases in assured shorthold tenancies are the same as for assured tenancies (see pages 13–14), and the tenant may challenge any rent increase by contacting the Rent Assessment Committee of the local authority. However, the period of time during which a challenge can be made depends on the date on which the tenancy agreement began, and because the landlord can evict so easily, it would be wise to get specialist advice before rocking the boat by challenging the rent officially.

Licenses

Licences offer the tenant the least protection of all forms of tenancy agreement. They are generally used when a person is renting space in the landlord's own home, or when a person takes accommodation either free or at a very low rent instead of wages for the job they do (e.g. a school caretaker or farm worker).

Ending a licence agreement

If the licensee shares the accommodation with the landlord, there is no protection against eviction whatsoever. 'Reasonable' notice to quit must be given, but doesn't need to be in writing. If the licensee does not share the accommodation with the landlord, the landlord must give written notice to quit on a specific legal form. If after the notice period has run out the licensee has not left, the landlord can go to court for a 'possession order', and will be granted one with no questions asked.

Licences: rent increases

The landlord is entitled to charge any rent at all, and the licensee does not have the right to challenge the rent legally. The landlord is entitled to raise the rent at any time during the agreement (unless the agreement specifically states otherwise, and this would have to be negotiated between the landlord and the licensee). However, the landlord should give reasonable notice of the rent increase.

Secure tenancies

Most people who rent accommodation from their local council have secure tenancies. This means that they are tenants for life, and they can pass on the right to remain in the property to a spouse, for example, when they die (see page 134–135). There are some exceptions to this, the most important of which is those council tenants with 'introductory tenancies'. This form of tenancy gives the tenant a probationary period, during which the council has the right to evict him if he proves to be undesirable.

Ending a secure tenancy

Secure tenancies are similar to protected tenancies, in that the landlord (in this case, the council) must give the tenant notice that it wants him to leave the property. The council can evict the tenant if he refuses to leave. The council must tell the tenant that it is going to court, and must show the court that it has a good reason to evict. See the list on page 12 for the types of reasons the council may use to have a secure tenant evicted. If the council is using 'discretionary' reasons to have a tenant evicted, it must show that it has offered the tenant suitable

Joint tenancies

If two people are named on the tenancy agreement, this is known as a joint tenancy. This complicates the rules, especially when the agreement gives the tenant extensive rights to stay in the accommodation. If you have a joint tenancy agreement, and one of you wishes to leave, or some other change occurs, you should not do anything before seeking specialist advice.

alternative accommodation, and that it is reasonable to evict on these grounds.

If any member of a tenant's family (or cohabiting partner) has been forced to leave the property because of the tenant's violence or threats of violence, the tenant can be evicted immediately.

Secure tenancies: rent increases

The council is entitled to increase the rent at any time, and there is no simple way in which council tenants can challenge such increases. The council must give reasonable notice that the rent is being increased.

Council tenancies and repairs

The council, as landlord, is responsible for repairs to council property. If the council fail to make appropriate repairs at the appropriate time, it is hard to force them to do so. However, some tenants' associations are able to apply to manage their own properties, and this could be a way of getting over the problem. If you believe your property is in such a poor state that it is endangering your health, you may be able to take the council to court under environmental health legislation. If you think you have a case, a good place to start for information would be your local Citizens Advice Bureau or local law centre.

Social housing

Much of Britain's social housing stock has been passed over in recent years by the councils who used to own it on behalf of the local community to private organisations. In addition, much of the building and management of new social housing is now being undertaken by outside organisations. These organisations may be housing associations, co-operatives or housing trusts, and some may be charities. Many are classified as 'registered social landlords' (RSLs). A tenancy agreement with one of these RSLs is likely to be either a secure tenancy (see page 16) or an assured or assured shorthold tenancy (see page 13–15), and in general the tenant's rights are the same as if they were renting in the private sector.

Council tenants: the right to buy

Many council and housing association tenants have the right to buy the property they live in. They must be secure tenants, and must have lived in their property for more than two years. Those who live in houses are entitled to buy the freehold (see page 22), and those living in flats are entitled to buy a 125-year lease (see pages 20–21).

Property ownership

UK law currently allows for two different types of home ownership: leasehold and freehold. Each brings with it obligations and responsibilities as well as rights. The process of buying and selling leaseholds and freeholds, called conveyancing, is complex, especially where it includes a loan to finance the transaction. All parties involved in such transactions (mortgage advisors, surveyors, estate agents, conveyancers) have duties and responsibilities in law, and the purchaser (the buyer) or the vendor (the seller) may be able to seek redress if these duties and responsibilities are not honoured.

Freeholds

Much of the property in the UK is owned freehold (although some is leased for extremely long periods to leaseholders, see pages 20–23). As far as the law is concerned, freehold relates to land rather than buildings, but most people think of buying buildings when they contemplate purchasing their home freehold. The purchase of most houses, for example, is in fact the purchase of the freehold to the land on which the house stands.

Freeholds are owned forever, and they can be bought and sold or bequeathed to someone else in much the same way as other possessions, but the regulations concerning the trade in freeholds and their use are rather more complicated than for, say, a three-piece suite.

Owning the freehold does not mean that the freeholder has an absolute right to do what he wants with the property. The freehold may include restrictions on the use of the property called 'covenants', and other people may have specific rights over the land, called 'easements'.

There are two types of covenant: positive covenants and restrictive (negative) covenants. Positive covenants force a party to carry out certain actions. Freeholds may not include any positive covenant that persists forever. A specific purchaser may agree to a positive covenant to carry out a specific action, but this responsibility is not passed on to the next purchaser. Restrictive covenants, on the other hand, prevent the freeholder carrying out certain actions, and in general restrict the rights of the owner. An example of a restrictive covenant is the 'zoning' of property, by which certain property is to be used only for residential, and not industrial purposes.

Easements are rights that neighbours or other people have over the land. Common easements include:

◆ a right of way
◆ a right to light
◆ a right to have drains pass under the land
◆ a right to support (e.g. a neighbouring freeholder may not demolish his house if it means a neighbouring house will become unstable).

Easements and covenants are listed at the Land Registry (see page 311), and some are backed up by separate legislation. When buying a freehold, the conveyancer should point out anything unusual that might lead to a claim against the new owner.

It is possible to agree restrictive covenants or easements with neighbours or other interested parties. You may wish to sell your neighbour a new right of way (perhaps to a garage he has built at the end of his garden), but any agreement of this sort should be drawn up by a solicitor and registered in the proper manner for it to become an entitlement in perpetuity.

In addition to restrictive covenants, positive covenants and easements, other parties may have some legal right to determine

---

Rights of way: warning!

In the UK, if a person has been openly crossing a piece of land for 20 years or more, the law recognises that person's right in some cases to continue doing so, bringing a right of way into being. It is most important, therefore, to stop other people using your land by erecting a barrier such as a gate with a notice exerting your rights as the owner. For information on what to do about trespassers, see page 159.

how you use your freehold property. This is most particularly true of the community at large (usually in the form of the local authority), which can, among other things:

- enforce hygiene regulations
- enforce regulations on nuisance (see page 73)
- control the types of buildings erected on the land and regulate changes of use
- compulsorily purchase the land
- restrict the type of fuel you burn
- enforce the power of the police and others to enter the property
- claim any 'treasure trove' (see page 25) found on the land on behalf of the Crown, and any oil, gold or silver.

Any mortgage lender will also have rights over a mortgaged property; in particular, the right to repossess the property should the mortgage payments not be met. See page 32 for more on mortgage agreements.

Leaseholds

Leaseholds are essentially very long tenancy agreements. They can be bought and sold in a similar manner to freeholds, and can also be passed on through inheritance. This means that to all intents and purposes, leaseholds represent to most people a form of ownership. However, there is a landlord, in the person of the freeholder, and even though the leaseholder (also called the lessee or tenant) may have paid an enormous fixed sum to buy the leasehold, there is still rent to pay (called ground rent, and sometimes a very small amount); and there may also be a service charge.

When first granted (i.e. sold by the freeholder to the first leaseholder) leaseholds can be anything over 25 years, but are often 99 years or even 999 years. But the main difference between owning property that is leasehold and owning a property freehold is that a leasehold will one day expire, and the entitlement to possession will revert to the landlord. The length of time that the leasehold has still to run affects the value of the property, and some leaseholders with leases that are less than 65 years or thereabouts have seen their property become difficult to sell or drop in value. However, recent legislation has meant that leaseholders may be able to get their leases extended (see page 23) and may even be able to buy the freehold from the existing freeholder and thus take control of the building in common with other residents (see page 23–24).

Most leaseholds relate to flats in a converted house or in a block, but houses on some new estate developments are sold leasehold, although this is becoming rarer following legislation. In brief, the lease bought gives the leaseholder the right to exclusive possession of the property (say, a flat in a block of 10), and the use of 'common parts', such as gardens, staircases and hallways for the period of the lease. The leaseholder is responsible for the upkeep of the part of the building of which she has exclusive possession, and the landlord is in general responsible for keeping up the common parts and the exterior. The landlord usually charges an annual service charge to pay for this work, and for the services of any manager (called a managing agent) employed by the landlord. Many leaseholders find it useful to form into a group such a tenant's association in order to present a single voice to the landlord and in order to be able to claim some legal rights.

Service charges and managing agents

One of the most common areas of conflict between landlords and their leaseholders is in the area of service charges. While many landlords carry out their duties in a reasonable and timely manner, some are less assiduous. So there are various rules regulating the actions of landlords or their managing agents in the charging of service charges and in carrying out work, both major and minor. They are derived from several pieces of legislation and they include the following principles:

Sub-letting leasehold property

Leaseholders have the right (unless their lease specifically forbids it) to let their property to someone else. Of course, they cannot let the property for longer than the period of their own leasehold, and they cannot let the property to the freeholder. There are usually restrictions on sub-letting arising from an agreement with a mortgage lender, and leasholders who have a mortgage should never let their property without checking the mortgage agreement, and, if necessary, informing the mortgage lender.

- ◆ the landlord must give the leaseholders an address in the UK where legal documents can be sent
- ◆ the landlord should not make a profit – service charges are for the upkeep of the building
- ◆ the landlord should inform the leaseholders how he arrived at the figure for the service charges
- ◆ leaseholders are entitled to see receipts and accounts
- ◆ the landlord must hold service charges in trust, and not, for example, use the funds for work relating to other buildings, or for personal use
- ◆ the landlord cannot demand excessive amounts from leaseholders
- ◆ leaseholders must be given notice of any major works
- ◆ if the work planned is to cost more than £50 per flat multiplied by the number of flats or £1,000 whichever is the greater, then the landlord must get at least two estimates (which the leaseholders can demand to see)
- ◆ when a new managing agent is being appointed by the landlord, the leaseholders have the right to know who he intends to appoint, what duties the managing agent will be asked to carry out, and they have the right to let their opinions on the proposed managing agent be heard
- ◆ if a managing agent is already employed by the landlord, the leaseholders are entitled to a formal list of the agent's duties, to comment on the way in which the agent has been carrying out those duties and to make their opinion known as to whether they want the agent to continue
- ◆ in certain circumstances, leaseholders are entitled to have an independent audit of the management company's accounts carried out to ensure that the management of their building is as efficient and effective as possible.

The right to buy the freehold

In 1967, legislation enabled house-owners with leases and certain other kinds of house tenants to purchase the freehold. Recent legislation has now made it possible for groups of leaseholders in flats to buy the freehold to their building, a process known in law as 'enfranchisement'. A single leaseholder may not do this; only a group of leaseholders may do so, and only under certain conditions:

- ◆ if the landlord is resident in the block, and the block has less than five flats, the leaseholders do not have the right to buy the freehold.
- ◆ 90% or more of the building must be residential
- ◆ two-thirds or more of the flats in the building must be leasehold
- ◆ a total of at least two-thirds of the leaseholders in the building, accounting for at least half of the flats in the block, must agree to take part in the purchase.

If the landlord wishes to sell the freehold, he must, in all but a few cases, give the leaseholders first refusal to buy it. If he sells to someone else and does not inform the leaseholders, they have the right to buy the freehold from the new owner at the price paid. If the leaseholders do not accept the landlord's price for the freehold, and he then sells it to someone else at a lower price, the leaseholders may purchase it from the new owner at the price paid.

Arranging the joint purchase of a freehold is a tricky business, and the least of your worries will be getting everyone in your group to agree! Any group of leaseholders planning to do so should obtain specialist advice from the outset, particularly in the valuation of the freehold.

Extending the lease

Under legislation enacted in 1993, owners of leaseholds may renew them for a further 90 years under certain conditions:

- ◆ the lease must be for more than 21 years
- ◆ the leaseholder must be using the property as his main residence and must have done so for a total period of three years in the last 10
- ◆ the lease must be on a low rent.

Again, take professional advice if you are considering extending your lease in this way.

Commonholds

At the time of writing, the government was considering a new type of ownership, called commonhold, which would enable all the owners in a building to take part in its ownership and upkeep. In theory, all those owning the flats in a building would own a freehold for their particular space, ensuring that they were entitled to own it in perpetuity. A 'commonhold association', similar to a company and subject to special legal rules and regulations, would be set up to manage the common parts of the building. All the commonholders would be members of this association, and it would have to be registered with the Land Registry. While this new proposal dispenses with the landlord, however, it does not mean that flat-owners will stop having to pay service charges!

Shared ownership

It is possible to buy property jointly with one or more other people. In fact, in these days of high property prices, some people find it impossible to afford to buy unless they join up with someone else and pool their resources. Usually this is a spouse or other family member, but it could be a cohabiting partner or a friend. There are two types of multiple ownership:

◆   joint tenancies, or
◆   tenancies-in-common.

Joint tenants own the property in equal shares. If one of them dies, the other automatically acquires the other part of the property. This is the case with married couples, for example. In contrast, co-habiting partners do not have these automatic rights even if they have lived with their partner for many years and have a demonstrably stable family relationship.

Where there is a tenancy in common, the owners each own a certain agreed proportion of the property independently of the other owner or owners. If one of the owners wishes to sell, he may legally sell to someone else independently of the other owners and without their permission. If one owner dies, the property passes to whoever is the beneficiary under his will or according to the rules of intestacy (see page 134–135). Because any tenant-in-common is entitled to dispose of his part of the

Property rights of co-habitees

For information on where co-habitees stand in the property-ownership stakes, see page 70.

property independently, it is virtually essential that people considering purchasing property together in this way draw up a legal document outlining the agreements between them as to the proportion of the property each owns and how to go about disposing of the property.

Squatters' rights

Squatting is the occupation of vacant land or buildings without the legal right to do so. Squatters take up residency without a legal agreement with the owner (written or verbal), and without paying rent. If a squatter has occupied property for 20 years or more, he is entitled to become the legal owner of the property. This very rarely happens in practice, but it could be that one landowner shifts a boundary without his neighbour noticing, thus surreptitiously annexing land his neighbour is not using.

This is very different from breaking into property, which is a criminal offence, and the police may be called to remove people who have entered a property by breaking in. If a property owner finds trespassers on the property, he should take immediate action by calling the police while the evidence of the offence (broken windows or locks, for instance) still exists.

Squatters generally enter unprotected vacant property and they may not be removed without a court order. A fast-track method exists to enable property owners to acquire a court order, known as an interim possession order. Squatters are served with this order and must leave within 24 hours, otherwise the police can be called to arrest and remove them as trespassers. This offence carries a prison sentence and/or a fine.

Treasure trove

In the UK, anyone discovering treasure must report the find to the coroner with 14 days of its discovery or within 14 days of the realisation that what has been found might be considered treasure. The coroner will decide whether the treasure has been deliberately concealed, in which case it is called 'treasure trove' and belongs to the Crown. If the coroner rules that it has simply been lost, the finder may have a right to it. In some cases, those who find treasure trove may be paid compensation.

In order to qualify for an interim possession order, the property owner must apply to the court as soon as he becomes aware that squatters are present. This process, however, does not apply if the squatters are occupying land rather than buildings. In this case, the property owner must apply for an eviction order in the usual way.

Buying and selling property

It is often said that buying or selling property is one of the most stressful experiences we can undergo. This may be because the financial stakes are generally so high that choosing the right moment to buy or sell and the right property to buy is of vital importance, but it may also be because the legal requirements can be very complex and people involved in a property transaction usually need the services of professionals such as surveyors and conveyancers. The internet and book shops are awash with advice on how to go about buying and selling property, but here there is only space to outline some of the legalities relating to each step in the process.

Property sale: the process

In general, the following steps are carried out in the following order:

- ◆ the vendor (seller) usually approaches an estate agent to have his property valued and put on the market. He will enter into an agreement with the agent either to act as sole agent or as one in a multiple agency (see page 30).
- ◆ the agent takes the particulars of the property from the vendor and publishes them, usually advertising the property in the local press, online and/or in a high street window.
- ◆ the purchaser (buyer) decides what kind of property she is looking for and in what area, and, most importantly, what she can afford to pay taking into account her income and likely outgoings. She would usually at the outset approach a number of mortgage lenders (if necessary) to get a preliminary agreement on a loan.
- ◆ the purchaser views the property and, if she wants to buy it, makes an offer to the estate agent who must pass

it on to the vendor. The offer may be for any price, but is often at or under the price asked by the agent. Offers should be made in writing, and the words 'subject to contract' should be written at the start of the document.

◆ if the vendor accepts the offer, the purchaser may be asked to place a small deposit as a sign of good faith (no more than £500 would be reasonable), although this is not always the case. At this stage, the agent may ask the purchaser for a certificate from the possible mortgage lender affirming that the purchaser is likely to get the loan she requires should the sale go ahead. If the vendor does not accept the offer, some negotiation may take place.

◆ when the vendor has accepted the offer, the purchaser and the vendor instruct their conveyancers (usually, but not always, a solicitor). The vendor's conveyancer sends the purchaser's conveyancer details of the deeds to the property and a draft contract for the sale. The vendor's conveyancer also provides the purchaser's conveyancer with a number of official forms giving information about any disputes, notices, alterations to the property and a list of what fixtures and fittings are included in the sale. The purchaser's conveyancer undertakes a local authority search to check whether there are any plans that might affect the value of the property (e.g. to build a motorway nearby).

◆ at the same time as this legal work is taking place, the mortgage lender will probably send a surveyor to the property to check that it is worth the price that the purchaser has agreed to pay. In addition, all purchasers are advised to arrange their own survey to check the structure of the property and its general condition (see page 33–34).

◆ if the legal work and the surveys yield satisfactory results, and the finance is in place, the parties may progress to the point of exchanging contracts. Each party (or their conveyancers) sign identical contracts, and these documents are then exchanged. A deposit of a minimum of 5% of the purchase price (but more usually 10%) is paid by the purchaser to her conveyancer, who passes it on to the vendor's conveyancer. Once the contracts have been exchanged and the deposit paid, neither party can withdraw without incurring penalties. If the purchaser withdraws, the vendor is usually entitled to keep the whole of the deposit. If the vendor withdraws, the purchaser may sue for compensation. At the point of exchange, the purchaser becomes responsible for the property, and would be well-advised to have buildings insurance in place from that point on.

◆ a completion date is agreed, upon which the balance of the price is to be paid and the vendor is to vacate. The period of time between contract and completion varies, but it typically takes between 14 days and a month.

◆ after the contracts have been signed, the purchaser's conveyancer carries out some final checks at the Land Registry. The purchaser finalises arrangements for the loan if necessary, and her solicitor draws up a deed of transfer. A few days before the completion date, the purchaser transfers any funds due to her conveyancer, including Stamp Duty and outstanding legal fees.

◆ when the day of completion finally arrives, the outstanding balance on the purchase price is paid to the vendor's conveyancer, and the purchaser's conveyancer is sent the deeds to the property. The vendor pays his estate agent and his conveyancer. The keys are handed over, the vendor vacates and the purchaser takes possession of the property.

◆ after completion, the purchaser's conveyancer registers the transfer of the property at the Land Registry and eventually the new owner receives a copy of the details entered into the register.

Of course, as people are fond of saying, there's many a slip twixt cup and lip, and all sorts of problems and delays may arise, particularly if there is a chain of purchasers and vendors, all needing to wait until their opposite partner in the transaction can complete on their own transactions.

Some new laws are in the pipeline to help the process move more quickly, although these seem to be long in coming, considering that they are similar to the laws of Scotland and many other European countries. The proposals include requiring the vendor to provide a 'seller's pack', including a survey and other documentation, which will speed the legal checking stages along, and in theory make the process cheaper and less risky for purchasers.

Using an estate agent

Most people who wish to sell property use an estate agent to handle the sale. In an increasing number of cases, people work without an estate agent, and internet advertising is becoming an increasingly successful way of publicising a property. If the sale is of a freehold, the vendor is not in a hurry to sell and the property market is buoyant, working without an agent can present few problems, with the added benefit that the vendor does not have to pay agent's fees.

For purchasers, the most important thing to remember is that the agent is usually acting on behalf of the vendor, and is trying to get the best possible deal for that party. This includes getting the best possible price from the purchaser who is most likely to complete the transaction. As a purchaser, do not be lulled into thinking the estate agent is on your side!

Some estate agents offer other services, including arranging mortgage loans and carrying out surveys. Neither the vendor nor the purchaser can be forced to take any other services as a 'bundle', and the agent must not discriminate in favour of purchasers or vendors who do so. In addition, an agent who offers the purchaser extra services must tell the vendor he is

Gazumping

Gazumping takes place when a vendor has accepted one purchaser's offer, but then reneges on his acceptance when he receives a higher offer from someone else. This can involve the original purchaser in wasted fees and in some cases a lot of heartache. Surprisingly, gazumping is not illegal.

New legislation, including the requirement for a non-returnable deposit at an earlier stage in the process, may help to stop gazumping. However, until this comes into force, a purchaser may be able to persuade a vendor to enter into a pre-contract 'lock-out' agreement in which he agrees to take property off the market and promises not to entertain any further offers.

doing so, and if the purchaser takes up that offer, the agent must inform the vendor.

Agency agreements

Estate agents are, in the vast majority of cases, employed by the vendor. When the agent is asked to supply this service, a written agreement should be drawn up between the parties, and before signing, the vendor should make sure he understands the document and agrees to all the terms.

Agency agreements can be divided into three different types: sole agency, sole selling rights and multiple agency.

In sole agency agreements the vendor agrees that this agent is the only agent with the right to market the property. If someone whose business is not to sell property makes the sale (i.e. the vendor finds a purchaser through word of mouth), then the agent is not entitled to the commission.

If the vendor gives the agent sole selling rights, then regardless of who makes the sale, the vendor will have to pay the commission to the agent.

In a multiple agency deal, the vendor asks several agents to market the property and the agent that finally makes the sale gets the commission.

In an agency agreement, the vendor may come across the term 'ready, willing and able purchaser'. If these terms are written into an agreement, it means that if the agent finds a purchaser who wants to enter into a contract, has the money to do so and will do so immediately, the vendor must pay the commission, even if he pulls out prior to the signing of the contract.

An agency agreement should also contain information on how long the agreement lasts. An open-ended agreement may leave you tied up with an agent who is not getting results, and unable legally to get other agents involved. Check on what grounds you are able to cancel the contract.

Payments to estate agents

As with all service contracts, get a firm quote from the agent. This is usually given as a percentage of the eventual selling price. If the agent asks for expenses, the vendor is entitled to a statement of how the expenses will be calculated. Estate agent fees are usually paid on completion, but note that the vendor will usually become liable to pay on exchange of contracts. So if the transaction fails after the contract is signed, the agency fee may still be payable. If the agreement is to find a 'ready, willing and able' purchaser, the fee becomes payable as soon as this person is found.

Estate agents: conflict of interest

Estate agents must tell the vendor if a prospective purchaser is himself, a member of his family or a business colleague. Equally, if the property on sale belongs to the estate agent, a member of his family or a colleague, he must make the purchaser aware of this.

Details of the property

Estate agents usually proceed by drawing up a leaflet detailing some particulars of the property. Purchasers must not rely on these particulars as being an accurate description of the property: a disclaimer at the bottom of the leaflet almost always tells the purchaser that the estate agent accepts no liability if the purchaser relies on a piece of information that subsequently turns out to be a mistake.

As with all buying and selling transactions, it is a criminal offence to knowingly make a false description of the thing being sold. While it is not a legal obligation to point out problems with the property, the agent and the vendor must not make statements that are false if asked a direct question.

Passing on offers

The estate agent is legally obliged to tell the vendor when he receives an offer above the minimum you agree between you, even if you have already accepted an offer. If you find he has not made you aware of all the offers, to your detriment, you may be able to take him to court and claim compensation.

Service contracts

Estate agents are providers of a service, just like conveyancers, solicitors and plumbers. Many provide an efficient service and conduct themselves in a professional manner. But if you are not happy with the way your estate agent has acted, you may be able to cancel the contract or refuse to pay part of the fees due. See pages 45–47 for more on how to decide whether you are entitled to cancel a service contract.

A ROOF OVER YOUR HEAD

Arranging a mortgage

Many purchasers need to take out a loan in order to pay the full price of the property. Such large amounts require security, and purchasers generally have to offer the property they are buying. Legally, the lender hands over the money in return for a 'charge' against the property, which means that if the purchaser fails to keep up the payments, the lender can take possession of the property. The term 'mortgage' refers to this right, rather than to the loan itself.

Mortgage lenders may be banks, building societies or other financial institutions. In addition, an army of mortgage brokers is ready to match mortgage lenders with prospective borrowers and take a commission from the lender.

The choice of mortgage 'product' can be bewildering. All mortgage lending institutions are regulated by the Financial Services Authority, which has a code of practice by which mortgage lenders should give borrowers clear information and advice about their products, although the code is not always followed. So prospective borrowers should never sign an agreement that has not been fully explained.

Many mortgage agreements include various responsibilities that fall on the borrower. They may include:

◆ not treating the property in such a way that its value decreases

◆ not making any major changes to the property without informing the mortgage lender

◆ not letting the property out or taking a lodger without informing the mortgage lender

◆ not using the property for any purposes other than as a residence (including not working from home or carrying on any business) if the agreement stipulates

◆ arranging and paying for insurance to cover the buildings, and in some cases arranging and paying for life insurance to cover outstanding loan repayments in the event of the borrower's death.

Default and reposession

Any property on which there is a mortgage is at risk of repossession should the mortgage payments not be made. Indeed, mortgage lenders have the right to possess a property on which they have made a loan at any time. In practice though, lenders only exercise this right in cases where the payments are not being met. Further, most mortgage lenders do as much as they can to help those who are having difficulty making their payments, and this includes giving the borrower a reasonable period of time in which to make up the arrears. However, if all else fails, the mortgage lender may seek repossession. To do this, the lender needs to apply to the court for a possession order, and it is up to the court whether to grant this order forthwith or whether to put off doing so in order for the borrower to have an opportunity to pay the arrears.

If a property is repossessed and sold, the lender has an obligation to get the best possible price for the property. If the price for the property is greater than the outstanding loan, the borrower is paid the excess.

In all cases where a borrower has difficulty making payments, or when the value of the property on the open market falls below the value of the loan outstanding and the owner wishes to sell, borrowers are advised to take advice either from the lender or some other financial adviser as soon as possible.

Surveying the property

All purchasers are advised to have a qualified surveyor carry out a survey on any property they are serious about buying, even though the mortgage lender may also have carried out a survey of some sort. Surveys are useful because they provide peace of mind for the purchaser. A purchaser must be reasonably well-informed about the condition of any property bought and cannot seek redress from the buyer later if a problem comes to light that would have been exposed by a survey. In addition, prospective

Discrimination and your mortgage

The discrimination laws cover many aspects of our lives. When arranging a mortgage, for example, the company offering the mortgage must treat men and women alike. So, if it is the woman in a couple who earns the higher income, the mortgage must be calculated on her income rather than on that of her male partner. Equally, mortgage decisions must not be made on the basis of a person's race or nationality.

purchasers may be able to negotiate discounts in the price on the basis of necessary repair work brought to light by the survey. There are several types of survey; the two most common are the homebuyer's survey and the full structural survey.

The homebuyer's survey is a cost-efficient way of having a building checked if it seems that it is in generally good repair. It should turn up any major problems that may affect the selling price or the subsequent value of the property. Homebuyer's surveys are carried out by qualified surveyors to a standard format, which shows what state of repair each part of the property is in and what the ramifications might be. Information ranges from cracks in window panes to evidence of rising damp in the cellar.

Homebuyer's surveys are hedged about with disclaimers on behalf of the surveyor. The documentation will state what parts of the property the surveyor has not been able to gain access to and what clues to the existence of a possible problem should be followed up. Such disclaimers make it difficult (but not impossible) for the purchaser to claim negligence if a serious defect comes to light after the purchase has been completed. So if a home-buyer's survey turns up a potentially serious fault, the purchaser should have a structural survey carried out.

Structural surveys are far more thorough than home-buyer's surveys, and should bring to light all serious problems. They are generally used where the property is particularly old or clearly in a bad state of repair.

Apart from assessing the state of repair of the property, a surveyor also decides whether the price asked for the property is a reasonable one. Because of this, it is wise to seek out a surveyor with a good knowledge of the local area who will be up-to-the minute on local property values.

Using a conveyancer

Conveyancing is the name given to the several legal actions that must be carried out in order to transfer a property from one party to another. It can be a complex process, particularly if there are irregularities or grey areas to do with such matters as who owns the property, what its boundaries are and where there are unusual covenants on the property (see page 18–19). A few people carry out their own conveyancing, but most seek the help of a person qualified to do so and with the experience to solve problems satisfactorily and quickly. Both the vendor and the purchaser will require the services of a conveyancer, who are generally either solicitors or licensed conveyancers. Both solicitors and licensed conveyancers are covered by professional indemnity insurance and are obliged to abide by their professional association's code of conduct.

As with all services, the purchaser should agree with the conveyancer the probable cost of the service and a time period for it to be carried out. Some of the fees paid to a conveyancer are actually passed to other parties. This includes the deposit for the property, which is passed on to the vendor and Stamp Duty and search fees, which are passed on to the relevant organisations. All these costs should be listed at the outset by the conveyancer, and if at any time those costs change, the client should be informed in advance. Money paid to the conveyancer which is in fact destined for someone else's bank account must be kept in a separate 'client account' by the conveyancer and not used for any other purpose.

Problems with a conveyancer may arise if, for example, his searches failed to uncover important information about the property which results in a loss to the purchaser. In cases where the conveyancing process was not carried out correctly, the client can sue for negligence.

Buying property at auction

Buying at an auction rather than on the common property market can be very economical. However, as when buying any item at auction (see page 43), the buyer needs to be very careful that he knows what he is buying. In general, a prospective buyer will need to have the mortgage loan arranged in advance, and will need to have carried out a survey and other legal searches before the auction takes place. On the day of the auction, the successful bidder is likely to be asked to place the deposit immediately, and will generally need to complete the sale within 28 days. After the hammer has fallen there is no going back, so be very sure that you want this property!

Warning!

While it makes sense to use the same conveyancer to act in your purchase as well as your sale, never use the same conveyancer as your vendor or purchaser!

Key terms

commonhold
A new form of property ownership in which those who own flats in a block may become owners of the freehold of their own flats and join together in the ownership of the common parts. See pages 23–24.

completion
The moment at which a property transaction is completed and ownership passes from one party to another. See page 28.

conveyancing
The process of carrying out the legal work necessary to enable property to be bought and sold. See pages 34–35.

covenant
A promise to carry out a certain action or to refrain from carrying out a certain action. See pages 18–19.

easement
A right which a landowner may have over neighbouring land. See page 19.

encumbrance
Any liability that may have an affect on a property, for example, a negative covenant. See pages 18–19.

enfranchisement
The process by which leaseholders may purchase the freehold to their property. See pages 22–23.

eviction
Action to remove a person who is in residence and does not have the right to be so.

freehold
A form of property ownership in which the freeholder owns the land and any buildings on that land. See pages 18–20.

leasehold
A form of property ownership in which the leaseholder owns a

long tenancy, paying rent to a landlord in the form of the freeholder. See page 20–21.

licence
A form of tenancy agreement, most often used for lodgers. See pages 15–16.

multiple agency
A type of agreement with an estate agent in which the vendor is entitled to instruct more than one agent and pay commission to the one who introduces the eventual purchaser. See page 30.

possession order
A court order that orders a person to leave a property.

registered social landlord (RSL)
Any of a number of kinds of organisations that may be in the business of providing social housing. See page 17.

sole agency
A type of agreement with an estate agent in which the vendor agrees that he will not instruct any other agent, usually for a defined period of time. See page 30.

sole selling rights
A type of agreement with an estate agent in which the vendor agrees that no-one (whether an estate agent or not) is to sell the property but the agent in question. See page 30.

tenancy
The right to make use of a property owned by another person. See pages 10–18.

treasure trove
Treasure discovered on private land that has been deliberately concealed there. See page 25.

vendor
The person who offers his property for sale.

2 Buying and Selling

In a world fuelled by consumption, it is hardly possible to go a day without buying something. This chapter looks at the ways in which the law protects consumers, for example, from being palmed off with defective goods, poor services or pressured into buying something they do not want. It starts by looking at the responsibilities of sellers, both of goods and services, and looks at the differences between buying from a business (perhaps a shop or a mail-order company) and at an auction or from a private individual. It then outlines the steps you should take if you are unhappy with a particular transaction.

The chapter then goes on to look at what special protection there is for people who buy from home, perhaps online, from a television shopping channel, by mail-order from magazines or catalogues, or from doorstep salesmen, and covers the regulations on unsolicited goods. Having dealt with the responsibilities of both buyers and seller, the chapter then looks at the law on guarantees and warranties, who is liable if you are injured or your property is damaged by a product, and, most importantly in this day and age, how the law on consumer credit works.

Goods and services

Consumer law covers two types of things that can be traded: goods and services. Consumer goods are objects, things such as food, clothing, vehicles, furniture and appliances, but also live creatures such as pets. The law makes a very important distinction between goods (or 'personal property') and property (or 'real property'; see page 26–35 for more on buying property). Services are tasks carried out for us, such as painting and decorating, a hair cut, a massage, etc. Objects supplied as part of a service, for example, the bricks used to build a wall, are classified as goods.

Consumer contracts

When we buy goods or services, we are entering into a contract (written or spoken) with the seller. I as the consumer agree to pay the price, and she as the seller agrees to supply the goods (or services). Regardless of whether we are aware of its existence or not, though, this contract is governed by various Acts of Parliament, and these Acts bring to the contract 'implied terms' which, on the whole, protect the consumer.

The statutory rights given to the consumer under these Acts cannot be removed by a contract made between a consumer and a seller. The law on the trading of goods and services also includes a number of criminal offences, and so the seller could be prosecuted in certain situations.

The Acts of Parliament that relate to the buying and selling of goods and services include:

◆ the Sale of Goods Act 1979 (amended with the Sale and Supply of Goods Act 1994)
◆ Consumer Protection Act 1987
◆ Supply of Goods and Services Act 1982 (amended 1994)
◆ Unfair Contract terms Act 1977 and Unfair Contract Terms in Consumer Contracts Regulations 1994 (see pages 50–51).

These Acts cover situations in which a business sells goods and services to a consumer. Slightly different rules apply if you are buying from a private individual who does not make it his business to sell things, and at auctions.

Buying and selling goods

When you buy as a consumer, the seller implicitly promises that the goods are:

◆ of 'satisfactory quality'
◆ fit for the purpose for which they are sold
◆ as described by the seller
◆ the property of the seller
◆ safe to use.

Implied and express terms

For an explanation of implied terms and express terms in contracts, see pages 197 and 198.

If you buy goods and later find that they are not suitable for one of the first three reasons described above, you have every right to return them to the seller and ask for a full refund, but you would be well advised to do so as soon as possible after the purchase. (See pages 41–43 for information on returning goods.)

Satisfactory quality

Goods that you buy should be of a quality that any reasonable person would expect in the circumstances. This does not stop sellers selling you goods that have faults; they simply have to point out the defect, and you have to agree to buy regardless of the defect. If you do have a defect pointed out, or the defect is so obvious that any reasonable person would have seen it, and you buy the goods but later decide that you don't want them because of that very defect, you don't have an automatic right to return the goods. If the seller does not point out a hidden defect at the time of purchase, you have every right to return the goods.

The phrase 'of satisfactory quality' also covers goods that fall apart after only a short time.

Fit for the purpose

Goods must actually do the job they can reasonably be expected to do. Music CDs should play music, food should be edible, washing machines should wash clothes and kettles should boil water. Again, they should also last a reasonable amount of time after the purchase.

If you tell the seller you want the goods to serve a particular purpose, by selling you the goods, he implicitly promises that they are fit for that specific purpose. For example, you may be looking for a radiator to heat a space of 180 square metres, and the radiator you are sold, which is said by the salesman to heat 180 square metres in fact heats only 120 square metres. In this instance, you may return the radiator as soon as you aware that it does not do the job you outlined at the time of the sale, and you are entitled to your money back.

As described

Sellers have a responsibility to describe their goods accurately, and this is, of course, especially important when selling at a distance. A sweater described as being made of 100% wool must be just that – not 50% wool and 50% polyester.

The property of the seller

It is a criminal offence to knowingly sell property that is not yours without the owner's permission. Stolen property belongs either to its original owner or to the insurance company that paid up when the property was stolen. If you unknowingly buy property that is stolen, you are not guilty of receiving stolen property, but you may have to give the property back to the original owner or the insurer.

In some cases, the insurance company will ask you for a small part of the value of the goods to offset the payment it made to the original owner, and then allow you to keep them, but no-one wants to pay for something twice!

Always check the ownership of high-value purchases such as cars (see pages 202) before you buy, and be extra cautious if buying from a private seller and it is not possible to make an official check.

Safe to use

If you are injured or your possessions damaged as a result of using goods that are not safe, you may be able to get redress from two quarters. First, you may be able to claim against the manufacturer for putting unsafe products onto the market, and second, you may be able to bring a claim against the seller for selling you goods that were not fit for their purpose. Get legal guidance from Citizens Advice, your local law centre or a solicitor.

Returns and refunds

Many sellers have a policy of accepting returned goods without question and for any reason, in the interests of good customer relations, but this is not a legal right. Unless the seller has this policy, consumers may only return goods and expect a refund or a replacement if the reason falls into one of the categories listed on page 39.

If, for any of the above reasons you are unhappy with goods you have bought, inform the seller as soon as possible. If you wait too long, the seller may be able to claim that you 'accepted' the goods, and if you do this, your right to return them or get a full refund may disappear.

When you pay the seller and take goods home or you take delivery, you accept them. The law gives you a reasonable amount of time to inspect the goods and satisfy yourself that they are of satisfactory quality, fit for the purpose and as described by the seller. If you do not complain within a reasonable time period, you could be said to have accepted the goods and you lose the right to return the goods and ask for your money back.

If a fault develops in the goods after an amount of time has passed, you may still be able to return the goods for a refund (in this case perhaps only a partial refund, or perhaps a free repair), as long as you inform the seller as soon as the fault appears and return the goods to the shop (with proof of purchase) as soon as you can. The important thing is to stop using the product immediately the fault appears, showing that it has proved unfit for the purpose. However, you would not be entitled to a refund or replacement if the fault appeared because you yourself misused or damaged the goods.

At the point of purchase, a seller may ask you to sign a document stating that you have inspected the goods and accept them. Any document like this, or one in which you waive your right to return the goods if they are found to be unsuitable under the criteria on page 39, is invalid in law, and the seller would not be able to enforce it.

When goods don't come up to scratch from the outset, the law says that you are entitled to receive a full refund. In practice, sellers will often offer a replacement which the buyer is free to accept in place of a refund. Some sellers may ask you to accept a repair to the goods, but you are not under any obligation to have brand new goods repaired if you don't want to. In the same way, some sellers may tell you that they are not responsible for the goods, and that you must contact the manufacturer. This is incorrect. The contract for the sale was made between you and the seller, and not between you and the manufacturer (except in cases where a product is unsafe, see page 41). The seller is responsible under the law.

Many sellers offer a credit note or vouchers rather than a replacement or refund. If you are returning goods for one of the

Receipts

It is important to retain receipts, especially for expensive purchases. If for some reason you have not retained a receipt, you may still be able to prove you made the purchase by showing a bank or credit card statement.

reasons on page 39, you do not have to accept a credit note or voucher (although this may suit you). Your statutory rights entitle you to a full refund or a replacement.

If you fail to get the required response when you return the goods to the seller, the next step would be to put your complaint in writing, either to the shop in question, or to the head office of a chain:

◆ clearly state the problem with the goods
◆ explain the response you received when you went back to the shop
◆ ask for what you want (a refund or a replacement)
◆ give a reasonable time limit for a response (say, 14 days)
◆ enclose a copy of the contract or receipt, but don't send the original.

If you receive no response, or a response that is not helpful, it is time to seek further advice. The best place to go for this is your Citizens Advice Bureau or law centre. You may also wish to approach the appropriate ombudsman (see page 298).

Buying at auction

When you buy goods at an auction you should be more than usually vigilant as regards your legal rights. While auctioneers must describe goods accurately, you will be asked to accept the goods and affirm your acceptance within a very short space of time (often on the day of the auction). This is perfectly legal. In addition, your purchase may be contingent upon you removing the goods from the site of the auction immediately after the sale. These variations to your normal rights as a consumer will be published by the auctioneer, often in the catalogue for the sale. Read them carefully.

Make sure you give yourself enough time to inspect the goods thoroughly before the auction begins. If you are not an expert (perhaps the auction is for wine, cars, art, for example), steer clear or take an expert with you.

Buying from private individuals

The unofficial market is alive and kicking in the UK, enlivened by the arrival of car boot sales, free small ads and internet classifieds. If you buy goods from a private individual you have fewer rights than if you were buying from a shop or other business. It is wise to take someone with you if buying from a private individual in order to have a witness to any statements made. It is also a good idea to make the transaction in the

Faulty goods – action plan

◆ Do not inspect goods in the shop. Wait until you get home and have time to look at them and test them thoroughly, but make sure you inspect the goods as soon as possible after purchase.

◆ If you are not happy with your purchase, decide which category it falls under. Is its quality reasonable for the price you paid? Is it fit for the purpose for which it is intended? Does it fit the description given to you by the seller?

◆ Decide what you want from the seller. Do you want to have the goods replaced, or do you want a full refund?

◆ Inform the seller as soon as you can that you are not accepting the goods. If it is not possible for you to do this in person within a few days, telephone the seller and tell him you do not accept the goods. If necessary, follow this up with a letter outlining your complaint and telling him when you will come to the shop. If the goods have been delivered to your home, ask the seller to pick them up straight away (you should not be asked to pay for this service).

◆ If the seller refuses to give you either a replacement or a full refund, try to resolve your complaint with a more senior person in the organisation.

◆ If you still get no satisfaction, contact your Citizens Advice Bureau or local law centre. You may wish to consider pursuing a claim in the Small Claims Court. If you do so, the best you can expect is your money back and any expenses paid. It is unlikely that you would receive a payment for disappointment or distress unless the seller had specifically claimed that you would not be disappointed.

seller's own home or to get as much information as you can about him or her so that you know where to go if things go awry. And the golden rule in these situations is 'caveat emptor' – buyer beware. In practice it is very difficult to get redress if something goes wrong with a purchase from a private individual, so make sure the goods are working and are suitable before you buy.

It is unlawful for someone whose business is selling goods to pass himself off as a private seller in order to circumvent the law. If you have a suspicion that someone is doing this, do not purchase anything from them; inform your local authority's Trading Standards department, and if they think an offence is being committed, they will investigate.

Buying second-hand goods

When buying second-hand goods (including antiques) from shops, your rights change in only one respect. Second-hand goods may have suffered damage, wear-and-tear - they may even not work at all. Even if the seller does not point out the defects before you buy, you may not be able to return worn or broken second-hand goods for a refund or replacement.

Buying and selling services

Services you commission from someone else are governed by a set of similar rules to the goods you buy. All services must be:

◆ carried out with a level of skill and care that can reasonably be expected
◆ finished within a reasonable time period, or within the time period specifically agreed
◆ at the agreed cost or, if no cost was agreed, at a reasonable cost.

If services do not come up to scratch for one of the reasons defined above, you have the right to cancel the contract or

Buying vehicles

For specific information on buying cars and other vehicles, both new and second-hand, see pages 200–203.

refuse to pay some or all of the contract value. You may also seek compensation through the courts.

Reasonable skill and care

This criterion is similar to that of goods being 'fit for the purpose'. A plumber should be skilled enough to leave you with pipework that doesn't leak, and a conveyancer should carry out the standard Land Registry checks before completing a property deal on your behalf.

Reasonable time period

It is always wise to agree in writing a time period for work to be completed. If you do not do so, the law says that the person providing the service should finish the work within a reasonable amount of time. In order to work out what a reasonable period of time is, you may have to ask other suppliers of the same service how long they would take. If the work is not finished by the date specified in your agreement, or in a reasonable amount of time, you may be within your rights to cancel the rest of the contract and pay for only the work so far completed. But as ever, don't take any steps before taking legal advice.

Reasonable cost

Always, always, agree a cost for services. This applies especially for costly work you want done on your home – a minefield for most householders – and for some professional services where there can be hidden costs.

A reputable service-supplier will give you first an 'estimate' of the cost – an educated guess at the rough cost. When you have made decisions on all the details of the service, ask for a firm 'quotation'. The supplier cannot expect you to pay more than the quotation unless you specifically agree before the extra cost was incurred. The quotation will form part of your contract with the service-supplier.

If you do not have a written agreement on how much you will be charged for the work, the law says you can only be charged a reasonable amount. In order to find out what is a reasonable amount, you will need to seek estimates from other tradesmen who supply the same service in your local area.

Goods offered as part of a service

In some situations a supplier of a service may also source materials or other goods on your behalf, for example, a builder may source bricks and cement, and a plumber may acquire pipework, a boiler and radiators when putting in central heating for you.

As for the purchase of other goods, you can expect the goods offered to you as part of the service to be fit for the purpose, of satisfactory quality, as described and safe to use. Because in this case, your contract is with the supplier of the service, it is this person who is liable if something isn't right, and not the shopkeeper who originally sold the goods.

Problems with services

When entering into a contract with someone to supply a service (for example, a solicitor, an estate agent, a builder, plumber or any other tradesman), choose someone from the outset who has a good reputation. Ask friends and relatives for personal recommendations, and check whether the supplier you choose is a member of a professional organisation.

If a service has been supplied that is not up to scratch, you may ask for compensation from the supplier (perhaps in the form of a reduction in the overall cost), or for the unacceptable parts of the work to be repaired or re-done.

If something goes wrong and you fail to get a sensible response from the person who supplied you with the service, you should seek guidance from the relevant professional organisation. They may have a conciliation service in which you and the supplier in question would try to come to an agreement. If you fail to do so, then you may seek either 'arbitration' or to make a claim in the Small Claims Court (but not both).

Some professional organisations also run schemes to compensate customers if one of their members goes into bankruptcy and cannot honour their contract.

Criminal offences in the sale of goods and services

If you are injured as a result of the purchase of goods or services, or your possessions are damaged, you may be able to claim for compensation against the manufacturer. You may also be able to claim against the seller for selling you goods that are not of 'satisfactory quality'. In addition, the manufacturer or the company who first imported the goods into the European Union could be charged with a criminal offence.

It is also a criminal offence to give consumers misleading information about prices or about statutory rights. Misleading information about prices most often occurs around goods that are in a sale. A shopkeeper cannot, for example, tell you that the original price was £100 if it has never been offered for sale at that price. It is also a criminal offence to tell you that your statutory rights do not apply. So, displaying a sign saying 'no returns for ANY reason' or disclaiming responsibility for the quality of goods, is a criminal offence.

If you think that a shopkeeper is providing misleading information and you would like to see that this is investigated, talk to your local authority's Trading Standards department.

Buying from home

In the last few years, home-shopping has exploded, particularly with the arrival of the internet, but it has brought with it a whole raft of problems. The main problem stems from not really knowing whether the organisation you are dealing with is reputable, or, indeed, where to find someone to answer a complaint, if you have one. Following a few rules when shopping from home, especially on the internet, could reduce problems from the outset:

◆ Only buy from reputable businesses, whose name you know
◆ Never buy from someone who calls you on the telephone unless you have asked them to call you, or you have called them
◆ Check that any home-shopping website includes a physical address in the UK in case you need to return goods or make a complaint; don't expect the business to be UK-based just because its web address contains .uk.

Trading Standards online

If you have reason to believe a UK-based online trader is misrepresenting its goods or services, speak to your local authority's Trading Standards department or the Advertising Standards Authority (see page 307). One of these organisations may investigate the case, and may bring a prosecution if you are right.

Businesses based abroad may not be subject to English law, and you may find that you don't have the same rights as a UK consumer. It may also be harder to enforce those rights abroad

◆ When paying online, check that you have been directed to a secure part of the website. Your screen should display a closed padlock

◆ Make sure you are told: the exact price you will be expected to pay (including postage and packing); how long you have to cancel the contract if you wish to; how to complain and who to; what the goods or services consist of (if this has not already been done, for example, in a catalogue); details of any guarantees; and what the delivery date will be

◆ Avoid any organisation or individual asking you to send cash in the post

◆ Always keep copies of orders and contracts.

Cancelling a home-shopping order

Every shopper has the right to cancel a purchase or contract when shopping from home. If you purchase goods by mail order, over the telephone or via the Internet, you may cancel your order for any reason within seven days of receiving the goods. If you have entered a contract for services, you also have seven days to cancel, but if the contractor has already started work, this right may be lost. You may also lose the right to cancel a contract if you ordered such things as personalised goods, made-to-measure items or perishable goods, etc.

If you do cancel an agreement or order, the supplier must return your payment within 30 days. If you are returning goods, simply because you don't like the colour, for example, and they are not defective, you may have to pay for the cost of returning them. Of course, a supplier can choose not to accept a return of goods if you have damaged them while in your care.

All this aside, any consumer has a right to return goods or

Identity theft

For more on having your financial details 'stolen', see pages 280–282.

refuse to pay for services that are unsatisfactory or otherwise fall below a standard of quality implied by the law, and this applies to goods and services bought from home. If you are returning goods for one of these reasons, the law says that you do not have to pay for the cost of the return. See pages 41–43 for more on this.

Door-to-door selling

If a consumer buys goods or services from a sales representative in his own home, or at least somewhere away from the salesman's office, he is protected from high-pressure selling by a variety of laws and a code of practice. Anyone signing a contract for goods or services anywhere away from the salesman's office has the right to cancel the contract within seven days (the so-called 'cooling-off period'), if the goods or services cost over £35. However, if you invited a salesman into your home and then signed a contract, you may not have the right to cancel. On the other hand, if the contract is for credit over £50, you are entitled to cancel regardless of who instigated the visit, and the selling organisation must always tell you of your legal right to cancel at the time of signing the contract.

Always keep copies of any contract you sign, and if you wish to cancel, do so in writing (sent by recorded delivery if you want proof of posting).

Unfair terms

As we have seen, when you buy goods and services, you as the consumer are entering into a contract with the supplier or retailer. Special laws protect consumers from terms in standard contracts that could be said to be 'unfair', terms that go much further than necessary in protecting the supplier or retailer to

Unsolicited goods

If you receive goods that you have not ordered, write to the sender within 30 days and ask them to arrange to have them collected. The sender then has three months in which to do so. You must not use the goods or allow them to be damaged while they are waiting for collection. If the goods are not collected within this period, they become yours.

the detriment of the consumer. If a term in a contract is found to be unfair, you are not legally bound by it. Under these laws, contracts must be:

◆ reasonable and fair
◆ written in plain English.

If you negotiate special terms with a supplier or retailer, or the terms are required by law, these terms may be exempt under the legislation.

If you think that the terms of a contract you have signed are unfair, contact the Office of Fair Trading (see page 313), which can offer specialist advice.

Guarantees and warranties

Some manufacturers and suppliers offer guarantees or warranties with their goods or services. What is the difference? In general, a guarantee is given to the customer when they buy the goods or service. A warranty is usually a paid-for extra. If you have a guarantee from a manufacturer, you still also have all your usual rights as explained in this chapter, and are still entitled to enforce those rights against the trader who sold you the goods or services and against the manufacturer if the goods turn out to be unsafe.

Pressure selling at home

◆ Never allow a salesperson to come into your home without proper identification, even if they have arrived at your invitation rather than on a 'cold call'
◆ Never sign a blank form or contract, and never sign a contract you haven't read thoroughly
◆ If a salesman is pressurising you or has stayed longer than you wanted, ask him or her to leave
◆ Never be pressured into signing a contract without being given time to consider its terms, and always research alternative suppliers before entering into any agreement
◆ Always ask about your cancellation rights.

Consumer credit

Goods and services may be paid for using cash or credit. Consumer credit is the term given to loans and other types of credit offered to consumers. The law regulates the businesses that offer credit and protects the consumer by making sure that he gets enough information about the agreement into which he is entering.

There are a number of ways in which a consumer might 'borrow' the funds to pay for goods. They include:

- debit cards
- credit cards
- charge cards
- store cards
- hire purchase agreements
- conditional sale agreements
- credit sale agreements
- finance agreements.

Debit cards

Debit cards are usually issued by banks and building societies offering banking services. When a debit card is used, the funds are debited directly from your bank account, much in the same way as writing a cheque. Because the money is debited directly from your bank account, there is no debt to charge interest on (unless, of course, you go overdrawn). If you purchase goods or services using a debit card, the contract of purchase is just the same as if you had used cash or a cheque. If what you paid for turns out to be defective or otherwise unsuitable, you should seek a replacement or a refund from the seller.

Credit cards

Credit cards enable the consumer to buy goods and services and to pay for them either within the time period specified on

Mortgages

For information on how mortgage loans are sold and regulated, see pages 32–33.

the first account statement, making at least a minimum payment every month. If you pay off your outstanding balance by the deadline each month there should be no interest to pay, but some credit cards charge an annual fee. Outstanding balances that are not paid off by the monthly deadline usually attract interest.

When you purchase goods and services by credit card, the goods or services belong to you from the time of purchase.

If you pay for goods or services by credit card and something goes wrong, and the seller refuses to act on your complaint, you may also make a claim against the credit card company (as long as the purchase costed between £100 and £30,000). Some credit card companies also offer insurance so that if you damage goods you may be able to make a claim. This means that in some circumstances (and especially if you pay off your bill every month), using a credit card can be more advantageous than using cash or a cheque.

Charge cards

Debts incurred using charge cards, such as American Express and Diners Club, must be paid in full every month. Generally you do not pay interest on the debt, but there will normally be an annual charge for the service. Again, when you purchase goods and services using a charge card they belong to you from the outset.

Store cards

These cards are usually offered by retailers and work in the same way as credit cards. However, in this case the retailer is also the finance-provider, so you have fewer avenues open to you if things go wrong.

Higher charges for card payments

Some retailers charge a small percentage extra on goods or services paid for by credit card, usually to cover charges made by the card-issuing company. This is perfectly legal, but the retailer must make it clear that the extra charge is being made, and tell you the difference between the cash price and the credit card price.

Hire purchase agreements

When a consumer buys goods on hire purchase, he chooses the goods he wants, and then the seller sells them on to a finance company. In turn, the finance company hires out the goods to the consumer, and in return, the consumer pays for the goods with a specified number of fixed payments. The consumer then has the option to purchase the goods, usually on payment of an agreed nominal sum.

In theory, because you are hiring the goods, it is possible to terminate the agreement and return the goods to the finance company at any time during the agreement. However, you will still have to pay off any overdue instalments and if you have paid less than half the price agreed at the outset you may have to pay it all. Additionally, if you allow your payments to fall into arrears, the finance company purchase may repossess the goods and is not obliged to put the goods up for sale in order to reduce your debt.

If you find yourself falling behind with payments, you are not entitled to sell the goods to pay the debt because you do not own them.

Conditional sale agreements

In a conditional sale agreement, the transaction takes place in a similar way to a hire purchase agreement. The essential difference is that there is no hire element; you are committed to buying the goods from the outset. The finance company pays for the goods on your behalf, and owns the goods right up until the time you make the last payment. So if you pay half the cost and then default, you are likely to lose both the goods and the money you have already paid out.

Advice on debt

If you find yourself with debts that you are unable to pay, seek advice as soon as possible. Defaulting on any debt could lead to damage to your credit status, making it less likely that you will be able to persuade people and organisations to lend you money. A good place to start would be your local Citizens Advice Bureau. See also pages 307–315 for other places you may be able to get help.

Credit sale agreements

In this arrangement, you as the consumer choose the goods you want and the finance company, instead of buying the goods on your behalf, lends you the money to buy the goods from the seller. The goods belong to you from the moment the contract is signed. If you sell the goods on, or they cease to exist in some way, the debt to the finance company still exists until you pay it off.

Selling credit with goods and services

The law regulates those who sell consumer credit agreements very closely. Any business that tries to sell credit to you in your home (e.g. to pay for double glazing or a kitchen) is committing an offence unless they have a licence to do so and you have invited the salesperson to visit. If you do sign an agreement with a business that does not have a licence, or which agrees to provide you with credit at home without being invited by you, that agreement is unenforceable.

Discrimination in the marketplace

When offering goods and services, it is unlawful to discriminate on grounds of sex, race or disability. This means that a provider of goods and services must treat men and women, people of different nationalities and races, and able-bodied and disabled people the same. The law covers goods and services we don't pay for as well as those we do, and covers:

- shops
- other public places such as hotels, restaurants, night clubs, etc. (so it is not legal to offer free entry to women, on a certain night, for example)
- credit agreements such as loans, credit cards, mortgages, etc.
- travel and transport services such as buses, trains, and holidays
- services that are supplied by your local authority, such as sports facilities.

There are some exemptions, and these relate mainly to situations in which having a person of a particular sex present would cause embarrassment or would be considered indecent, including:

- ◆ service such a single-sex health clubs, that are offered only to men or women
- ◆ single-sex private members clubs
- ◆ insurance policies where it can be statistically proven that men are a greater risk than women or vice versa (for example, car insurance)
- ◆ care situations in which a personal care service is offered, for example in care homes and hospices.

If you feel you have suffered discrimination at the hands of someone offering goods or services, the first thing to do is to make a complaint to the establishment. If you feel there is a serious case to answer, and want to either receive an apology that is not forthcoming, claim compensation, or stop others being discriminated against in the same way, contact the Equal Opportunities Commission for further advice, or talk to your local Citizens Advice Bureau or law centre. It may be that you can take your case to the County Court, and you may be awarded compensation for hurt feelings or personal injury.

Key terms

charge card
Similar to a credit card, but must be paid off by the deadline each month. Not governed by the Consumer Credit Act. See page 53.

conditional sale agreement
A form of consumer credit agreement in which the finance company owns the goods up until the moment the consumer makes the last payment. See page 54.

consumer protection
The name given to the legislation that protects consumers from injury or damage to possessions caused by goods that are unsafe.

credit card
A method by which consumers can finance purchases up to a pre-arranged credit limit. See pages 52–53.

credit sale agreement
A form of consumer credit agreement in which the finance

agreement is between the consumer and the finance company.
See page 55.

debit card
A method of paying for goods and services which debits your
current account as soon as the transaction takes place. Only
governed by the Consumer Credit Act where there is an agreed
overdraft facility in place. See page 52.

goods
Objects such as clothes, furniture, food, cars, appliances, animals.

hire purchase agreement
A form of consumer credit agreement in which the finance
company buys the goods from the supplier and hires them to
the consumer for the hire period, at the end of which the
consumer may exercise a right to buy them. See page 54.

services
When a person puts his labour or expertise at your disposal, he
is offering you a service. See page 45–47.

unfair terms
Standard clauses in consumer contracts that are weighted against
the consumer to the unfair advantage of the supplier or retailer.
See page 50–51.

3 Your Relationships

All our lives are filled with relationships with other people: family, friends, neighbours. In some cases the law binds us together with a network of rights and responsibilities, but it also has things to say about how we act towards one another (even complete strangers) and gives us ways of resolving disputes.

This chapter starts by outlining the relationship that, historically, our society has been built on – marriage – giving the rules for marriage and describing some of the legal advantages it brings. It also discusses the mechanics of divorce. Next, it compares the legal situation of people who choose not to marry (or who are not entitled to marry), pointing out some important differences and going on to discuss some offences that may take place within family relationships, including marital rape and domestic violence.

Finally, it looks at our relationships with the community at large, in particular our neighbours and at a few ways in which the law can be used to deal with disputes between neighbours, problems with antisocial behaviour in the community and some other offences such as harassment and stalking.

Marriage

In the UK, any two people may marry as long as they meet the following criteria:

- they are of opposite sexes
- they are free to marry (either they have never been married before or they are divorced or widowed)
- they are over the age of 18
- they are over the age of 16 and have the consent of a parent or some other person with parental responsibility (see page 101)
- they are not closely related to their intended spouse.

Marrying family members
The law stipulates that a person cannot marry one of his or her

close family members. These include:

◆ daughter or son
◆ sister or brother
◆ half-sister or half-brother
◆ niece or nephew
◆ the children of a half-sister or half-brother
◆ aunt or uncle
◆ half-aunt or half-uncle
◆ granddaughter or grandson
◆ step-daughter or step-son
◆ adopted daughter or adopted son.

Adopted children may marry their adoptive siblings or other relations (but not their adoptive parents) as long as there is no blood relation between them. If an adopted child marries his or her birth parent, the marriage is legally void, even if the parties were not aware of the connection.

First cousins (i.e. children whose parents are siblings) may marry.

Conducting a marriage

The marriage of two people, while often considered to be a matter of intense privacy for the individuals concerned, is actually a matter of intense interest to the community. The law is concerned to recognise marriage as a special relationship in terms of the joint ownership and inheritance of goods, property and rights (such as tenancy rights, for example, or the right to reside in the UK). So it lays great emphasis on ensuring that marriages are made according to the law. It does this by giving

---

Engagement

These days, engagements have no legal value, although they can be a suitable way to confirm to one another and the outside world the fact that there is a firm commitment between two people. Breaking off an engagement has no legal ramifications – it is not possible to sue a person who ends an engagement. A woman is by law entitled to retain an engagement ring and other gifts freely given, unless she has agreed to return it should the engagement fail.

---

the community at large the opportunity to object to a marriage (perhaps the intended groom is already married, or the intended bride is unknowingly the groom's sister – who would know but close associates such as those living locally?), and by entering the fact of that marriage into a national register in order to be able to prove the relationship exists, when, for example, registering a child, perhaps for citizenship purposes (see page 262).

All marriages must take place in an authorised place and an authorised person must be present and enter the details into the register. An authorised place in England or Wales could be one of the following:

♦ Registry Office
♦ Church of England, Church in Wales or Catholic Church
♦ Jewish synagogue or private home
♦ a Society of Friends meeting house
♦ a public place with authorisation to accommodate marriages, such as stately homes or hotels
♦ other religious buildings.

Private places (such as hospitals, prisons, private homes other than above) may be authorised for special reasons.

All marriages must be registered by the person who conducts the ceremony, and if that person is not authorised to register the marriage, it must take place in an authorised person's presence and then that person must sign the register. All Church of England vicars and Catholic priests are authorised to register marriages, and, of course, at a Registry Office, the Registrar conducts the ceremony and the legal business afterwards.

Couples intending to marry must give public notice of their intention. If they intend a Church of England ceremony, this is

Objections to marriages

Objecting to a marriage is a serious business, and should not be taken lightly. However, any member of the public may make an objection if they have evidence that the marriage may not be legal. Making false statements when objecting to a marriage is a criminal offence.

done by publishing 'banns', which are read three times in the parishes of both bride and groom in the weeks preceding the marriage. For other ceremonies, the couple needs to attend the Registry Office for the locality in which they are resident (regardless of where they are planning to actually conduct the marriage ceremony) and give the Registrar notice that the marriage is to take place. The details are entered into the marriage notice book, and any member of the public is entitled to inspect them. If anyone has an objection to the marriage, they should approach the Registrar.

The couple is entitled to be married 15 days after the notice is entered. If, however, the marriage is delayed for more than a year, a new notice must be entered into the marriage notice book.

At the marriage (or before in some cases), the couple will need to prove who they are and that they are free to be married. This is done in several different ways depending on who is to conduct the marriage, but at a Registry Office marriage, the couple will be asked to give:

- name and address
- birth certificate if under 23
- father's name (although this can be omitted if not known)
- passport if not from the UK
- proof of the ending of any previous marriage, e.g. the decree absolute if either of the couple is divorced.

Marriages that take place in Registry Offices – civil ceremonies – may not make any religious references, although the couple will be consulted as to music, readings and any other

---

Variations in marriage requirements

Some of the regulations governing marriage vary, and there is space here only to give a broad outline and the general rules. If you are considering a ceremony that is not to take place at a Registry Office, your minister of religion or local Registrar will be able to advise on the various requirements, including pre-nuptial marriage counselling and special permission to marry from the religious community.

discretionary matters. All marriages must be attended by two independent witnesses. Registry Office staff are not qualified to act as witnesses.

Bigamy and polygamy

It is unlawful in the UK to be married to more than one person. Bigamy is the offence of unlawfully contracting to marry a person when a previous marriage has not legally ended. In such cases, it is the second marriage that is considered void in law, rather than the first. Whether or not the bigamous partner is prosecuted depends on the circumstances of the case, but if the purpose of the marriage was to commit fraud then it is likely that a prosecution will take place.

Polygamy is the practice by which a man is entitled to have more than one wife. This is standard practice in some countries, but is unlawful in the UK. If intending to marry people from such countries, UK citizens are warned to ensure that their intended partner is free to marry, or their marriage would be void in the UK.

Marriage by proxy and under duress

For any marriage to be confirmed, both parties must be willing and present. It is not possible to contract a marriage in the absence of one of the partners. Each partner must answer for him- or herself and no other person is entitled to 'stand in' for them.

In some cultures, arranged marriages are very much the norm, and many are the beginning of a strong, respectful and successful relationship. Arranged marriages are not unlawful in the UK, but marriages made under duress are, and if the duress can be proved, the marriage can be made void. If a person suspects that a partner in a marriage has been forced against his or her will to marry, or indeed, if your marriage is being arranged and you do not consent, you should seek advice from someone in authority – the police or a school teacher, or the local Citizens Advice Bureau or law centre. It is possible to annul such marriages after the event, but the longer the non-consenting partner remains in the marriage, the harder it is to prove duress.

If you suspect that a person has been taken abroad in order to be married against her will, the police should be informed.

Marriage abroad

Many people these days are opting to carry out their marriage abroad – either because their partner is a citizen of another country or because a Caribbean beach is so much more picturesque than the local Registry Office.

If both partners are UK citizens and simply want a romantic setting for their marriage, or if one of them is a foreign national, it is important to be sure that the marriage contracted would be lawful in the UK. A marriage contracted in a foreign country that does not qualify in the UK as a marriage (perhaps one partner is too young, for instance, or one partner is legally already married) would be considered void, even if you were only there for a few days. Equally, you will probably be bound by the laws of the country in which you married, and there may be significant legal differences affecting your marital rights.

If in doubt, talk to the operator who is planning your marriage trip, or to the British consular post in the country of choice. Citizens Advice may also be able to put you in touch with specialist advisors. It may be that you will need to repeat your marriage vows in the UK.

Marriage – rights and obligations

Marriage is a contract between two people, and it brings with it certain rights and obligations. Briefly, they are:

- a married woman is entitled to take the surname of her husband if she so wishes. She can also join her name with his to make a double barrel. For more on changing a name, see pages 278–280
- a married couple is expected to live together
- married couples are expected to maintain one another financially – the breadwinner is expected to cover the debts of the dependent partner if the marriage is structured in this way. Even when a couple is separated or divorced, this right to maintenance continues
- married couples are expected to have sex. Failure to

Marriage and citizenship

For more information on the rights of spouses and family members as regards nationality, residency and citizenship, see pages 258–273.

consummate a marriage can be grounds for an annulment, by which, legally, the marriage is considered never to have taken place. The marriage is expected to be an exclusive relationship, and adultery is a ground for divorce

♦ a married person will have entitlements to residency in the country of his or her spouse. A foreign citizen who marries a British citizen is entitled to take up residency in the UK, and may in due course take on the British citizenship. See pages 258–273 for more on this

♦ if one spouse dies without making a will, the surviving spouse has some automatic rights as to inheriting property

♦ married couples are entitled to claim a share of their joint property and financial resources

♦ married couples are entitled to claim a share of their spouse's pension rights, including death-in-service payments

♦ married couples are entitled to make certain financially valuable gifts to each other without attracting taxes

♦ married couples are expected to tell each other secrets ('marital confidences') that they would never tell other people. This being the case, a court could not call a spouse as a witness for the prosecution of a partner in a criminal case (except in certain circumstances), and may also be excused from speaking for the defence. Equally, it may be possible to get a court to stop a spouse spilling the beans about the couple's private life on the same basis

♦ married couples take automatic joint parental responsibility for the children they have together unless this is overridden by order of a court.

Married couples and wills

A will that has been made before marriage is automatically revoked by the marriage unless it has been made in anticipation of that marriage (and says so). People who are getting married should always try to review their wills and make new ones on the occasion of their marriage. See pages 135–143.

Some couples seek to restrict the automatic rights of their partner by drawing up a 'pre-nuptial agreement' in which they record, for example, pre-existing property that is to remain the sole property of one partner. Such agreements may be overruled by the courts in divorce disputes but will normally be taken into consideration.

Marital rape

Before 1991, rape in marriage was considered not to be possible according to the law. However, since that time it has been a criminal offence for a man to force himself on his wife without her consent, although sentences for marital rape seem to be more lenient than rape that takes place outside of marriage.

Ending a marriage

Just as entering a marriage is an intensely legal matter, so is ending one. Marriages may be annulled, couples may separate permanently, but in the vast majority of cases, the final step is divorce.

Annulment

Annulments may be possible in certain cases, either because the marriage was not legal in the first place, or because one of the criteria by which a marriage is defined has been violated. Annulments may take place in one of the following circumstances:

- one of the partners was under age at the time of the marriage
- the marriage was contracted under duress or when one partner lacked the mental capacity to fully understand what was happening
- the couple are too closely related in blood
- the marriage ceremony itself was not properly conducted
- the marriage is polygamous
- non-consummation
- refusal to consummate
- the woman was carrying the child of another man at the time of the marriage
- one party was suffering from venereal disease at the time of the marriage.

Separation

As the word indicates, separation is where a married couple ceases to live together as man and wife, either by one partner moving out of the marital home, or by separating their lives into different rooms and living them as if they were not married. Some separations are only temporary, while the couple take the heat out of some dispute and rethink their relationship, but others may in the end lead to divorce.

There are several ways in which a married couple may agree to separate:

- informal agreement, in which the couple simply agree verbally or exchange letters constituting a written agreement to separate
- deed of separation: the couple ask a solicitor to draw up a legal document in which their agreements are recorded. This may cover maintenance payments, agreements on the ownership and use of property, and understandings relating to parental responsibility for children
- occupation order (see page 72)
- judicial separation.

Each method has its own formalities, limitations and pitfalls, and couples contemplating separation should ideally consult an advisor such as a Citizens Advice Bureau or law centre. None of them is a legal ending of the marriage, and the rights and obligations of each partner still persist. However, having a written agreement of separation may go towards showing the divorce courts that the couple has agreed on certain points.

Divorce

Some divorces are simple and reasonably amicable. Others, especially those involving children, financial hardship, the denial of one party that the marriage has failed or in some cases the pure acrimony between the partners, offer a much more bumpy ride. In divorce cases, the person asking the court for a divorce is called the 'plaintiff' and the other partner is known as the 'respondent'.

In order to divorce, a couple must have been married for at least a year. One party must show that the marriage has broken down irretrievably, using one of the following reasons (called 'grounds'):

◆ the respondent's adultery
◆ the respondent's unreasonable behaviour
◆ the respondent's desertion amounting to two years or more
◆ the consent of the respondent to the divorce and a separation of at least two years
◆ separation of at least five years.

If there are no children, and both partners agree to the divorce, this can be a simple form-filling exercise. Legal stationers offer DIY divorce packs containing all the relevant forms and instructions on what to do with them. The forms can also be downloaded from the internet or obtained from the nearest county divorce court. A straight-forward divorce in which the respondent simply signs on the dotted line and walks away should take less than six months. In simplified form (and where there are no children involved), the process is as follows:

◆ the plaintiff files with the court the following papers: the marriage certificate and the divorce petition; the respondent may already have agreed and signed the papers prior to filing
◆ the court officially receipts the papers and sends to the respondent the divorce petition and a notice of proceedings
◆ the respondent signs and returns the appropriate documents, including one in which she acknowledges that the documents have been received by her, and that she consents to the divorce
◆ the court sends to the plaintiff more documents,

Agreements between married couples

The law does not have to abide by any contractual agreement made between married partners. It may certainly take agreements into consideration when deliberating on, for example, child custody or the distribution of property, but may also overrule contracts that it considers unfair or made without adequate legal advice.

including an affidavit, which must be signed and sworn at a solicitor's office or at the court. The affidavit is a sworn statement of the facts of the case, to be used in court as evidence of irretrievable breakdown

♦ the District Judge hears the case, and, if satisfied, will set a date for the decree nisi. This is simply the first decision in the case, and neither party will be asked to attend, although they will be sent a copy of the decree

♦ six weeks and one day after the decree nisi, the plaintiff is able to ask the court to declare decree absolute, and again this is done by filling in a form and sending it to the court

♦ when the decree absolute is issued, the marriage is considered legally to have ended.

Arrangements for maintenance

The obligation to maintain one's spouse continues beyond marriage, and applies both to men and women. This means that the less well-off partner can demand a financial settlement from the other. This settlement can be in the form of an immediate payment of capital or the transfer of property such as the marital home (particularly if there are children) in what is known as a 'clean break' settlement. Otherwise, it may come in the form of periodic maintenance payments.

It is rare for a court to order maintenance to a partner who has a similar earning capacity to the other or where the marriage was short, there are no children and both partners are still young. On the other hand, older women who have never worked and who have spent the best part of their lives maintaining the family home may be entitled to significant benefits, including the 'earmarking' of some of their husband's pension rights on his retirement.

In general, the courts use a simple calculation as a starting point for working out what financial assistance a less well-off spouse should receive from the breadwinner. It adds together the income of both individuals and then divides by three. This third is the starting point for considerations. However, all sorts of matters may be taken into consideration. The husband (for it is still usually husbands who have the greater earning capacity) may lose his job, or he may start a new family. Equally, the wife may be eligible for benefit payments that mean she does not need so much from her husband.

If a spouse remarries, he or she is no longer eligible for maintenance by a previous partner.

Arrangements for children

A second area in which divorcing couples may come into conflict is the children. The obligation to maintain a spouse can be overruled with a clean break settlement or may cease on remarriage of the maintained spouse, but both parents are legally responsible for the maintenance of their children at least until the age of 16, and beyond if they remain in full-time education.

If there are children in a marriage that has broken down, the court will not issue a decree absolute until it is satisfied that what has been agreed is best for the children. At the outset, the plaintiff will need to send the court a Statement of Arrangements detailing the agreements that the couple have come to over their children's living arrangements, care and financial maintenance. If the District Judge is not satisfied with this statement, he may set a date for a court hearing at which the couple must attend, and afterwards issue a court order detailing further arrangements with which the couple must comply. The spouse responsible for the children may later ask the court to use its powers to enforce the order if her partner does not comply with its requirements.

Disputes in divorce

It goes without saying that marital disputes that reach the courts can be very expensive in legal costs. Therefore, it is best to come to court with an agreement which both partners are prepared to abide by. The first step is always to discuss the matter with separate solicitors (choose one who specialises in family law), but then a cost-effective way of resolving a dispute and coming to an agreement likely to satisfy the courts is through mediation. Various bodies offer this service, which provides an arena in which both parties are able to air their fears and grievances in an effort to reach agreement. These include Relate (see page 314 for contact details). Other suggestions can be made by a solicitor, Citizens Advice Bureau or local law centre. You may be eligible for help with the cost of mediation.

Both partners are well-advised to finalise any agreement made through a mediator with the independent advice of a solicitor.

Cohabitation

Only 30 years ago, couples who lived together without the formalities of marriage were said to be 'living in sin' by the scandalised family and neighbours. Now, many people choose to do so, creating sometimes long, stable and fulfilling family relationships. The term cohabitation can be used to refer to heterosexual couples or to lesbian and gay couples.

Cohabiting couples are not bound by the same rights and obligations as married couples, and even though they may have a relationship that is to all intents and purposes identical to a married relationship, the law still maintains a sharp differentiation in some areas. The following list is just a few examples of the differences:

- married partners may inherit automatically from a partner who dies intestate; cohabitees are well advised to make wills in each other's favour, although in some cases cohabiting partners may be able to claim part of an intestate partner's estate as a dependant (see page 143)
- in the break-up of a relationship between cohabitees, partners are not entitled to claim for maintenance, but property may be divided if there is a joint tenancy or tenancy-in-common (see pages 24–25). But cohabiting partners may be able to claim rights to a protected, secure or assured tenancy (see pages 13–14 and 16–17)
- cohabiting men are not automatically entitled to take their partner's child as their own. They cannot claim parental responsibility unless they have the agreement of the child's mother or a court order. However, a cohabiting father can be made guardian of his children by their mother and on her death would take parental responsibility. Married and cohabiting partners are treated the same by the courts when it comes to the responsibility to maintain children after the relationship has ended
- if cohabiting partners have separate bank accounts, they remain separate, even on the death of one partner (the cash in the account becomes part of the estate). However, if they have a joint account, both partners are entitled to make use of the money in the account and

on the death of one partner, the funds in the account pass to the other

◆ unlike married partners, co-habiting partners can be called to give evidence for or against their partner in criminal cases

◆ cohabiting partners are not eligible for widow's pension. Other pension rights linked to the earnings of one's partner depend to a large extent on the individual pension scheme. Typically, some payments for death-in-service may be signed over to a cohabitee

◆ women who are cohabiting are not automatically entitled to take the name of their partner as are married women. However, some choose to take their partner's name, changing it by deed poll. See pages 278–279

◆ mixed-sex couples are assessed in the same way as married couples when it comes to state benefits. However, lesbian and gay couples are assessed as if they were single people. If you are applying for a student grant, any cohabitation (heterosexual, lesbian or gay) is ignored for the purposes of assessment, and this is not the case for couples who are married

As can be seen from the above, many of the differences between cohabiting and getting married come down to losing the automatic rights to property and financial support that marriage brings. Cohabitees should do their best, therefore, to formalise any arrangements they may make, particularly over issues of parental responsibility for children and joint shares in property. Above all, they should make a will if they wish their partner to inherit anything at all from their estate.

Domestic violence

Domestic violence is an umbrella term that covers a wide range of abusive behaviours among people who are in close relationships with each other. They can include members of the same family living together, or members of former families who may be living separately. Domestic violence can appear in the form of threatening or abusive language, emotional abuse, physical attacks, offences of a sexual nature, such as indecent assault or rape, and in the most extreme cases it may even include murder. The victims of domestic violence are generally women and children (although this is not necessarily always the case), and it can leave a person psychologically, if not physically, shattered.

The courts now have a range of powers aimed at putting a stop to domestic violence, either in marriage or in cohabitation. They include:

◆   occupation orders, in which the court decides who is entitled to occupy the marital or family home. It is not necessarily the case that the owner of the property is awarded occupation rights. Police have the power to arrest individuals who ignore occupation orders.

◆   possession orders, in which public landlords such as councils and housing associations can start proceedings to evict a person whose spouse, co-habiting partner or other family-member has been forced to leave the home because of the violent behaviour of the tenant.

◆   non-molestation orders, in which the courts can order individuals to cease a certain behaviour and excludes them from certain places. Police can arrest individuals who ignore non-molestation orders.

◆   exclusion orders, in which the courts can exclude a person from his or her home if that person presents a risk to a child.

Help for victims of domestic violence

There are a number of nationwide organisations that are able to help those who are being subjected to domestic violence, including finding a place of safety, a refuge, for the victims and their children if necessary. They include such organisations as Victim Support, Women's Aid, and the Samaritans. See pages 307–315 for contact details.

Neighbourly relations

Many of the millions of people living in the UK do so cheek-by-jowl with others in towns and cities. Just as we can't choose our relatives, so, too, it's unusual to be in a position to choose our neighbours. The best most of us hope for is that the neighbours are 'all right', and it's a blessing indeed if our neighbours become firm friends.

Our relationships with our neighbours are governed in a patchwork manner by all sorts of different laws, and it's probably best to look at several areas in which neighbours most often seem to clash: noise, encroaching trees, the actions of children and antisocial behaviour.

Noise

While we would all like to occupy our property with 'quiet enjoyment', there is actually no absolute right to peace and quiet. However, excessive noise, whether it be from factories, a booming stereo or a rowing couple can be controlled.

Excessive noise is considered by the law to be a 'nuisance', one of a number of statutory nuisances, which include noise, air pollution such as bonfires, smells, poor hygiene, dilapidated buildings, etc.

Local authorities are under a legal obligation to ensure that such nuisances do not continue, and noise is the domain of the Environmental Health Officer. The local authority has a range of powers in these cases. It will normally start by measuring the noise to see if it is, indeed, excessive. If so, it may issue an abatement order, which instructs the person in question to reduce the volume. It can also confiscate sound system equipment in certain cases. If an abatement order is ignored, the local authority may go to court for a 'nuisance order', and if this is similarly ignored, a fine may be imposed. Local authorities have the right to enter a vehicle or building if the alarm is sounding and is causing a nuisance.

It is possible to take your neighbour to court, bypassing the local authority altogether, but this could be costly. In cases of nuisance such as excessive noise, the law would take into consideration two questions: how unreasonable is the behaviour complained of, and how long it has gone on for. It tries to take an objective view of the situation, and does not usually rule in favour of people who find themselves more sensitive to certain nuisances because their own situation is unusual. For example, a man who works a nightshift, and finds his neighbour's daytime DIY activities wake him is less likely to find favour in the courts than a man who works days and objects to his neighbour drilling holes in walls at two o'clock in the morning.

Trees

If a tree growing on someone else's property overhangs your

boundary, you are within your rights to prune away the branches if you wish. However, the tree belongs to your neighbour, and so you should give the pruned branches back to him. Fruit that is growing on a tree overhanging your garden belongs to the owner of the property on which the tree is growing, and you should give him access to your property so that he can pick it and collect windfalls.

If a tree looks likely to fall down and damage your property, contact your local authority, which has the power to require a tree-owner to make the tree safe. If the tree causes damage to your property (either by a branch falling, for example, or by its roots undermining buildings) you may be able to seek compensation from your neighbour. Your first port of call should be your local Citizens Advice Bureau or law centre.

Unruly children

Boisterous behaviour by children can cause damage to neighbouring property and upset to neighbours looking for some quiet time. The archetypal situation is the football sent flying over the fence into the prize begonias by a budding David Beckham. In this situation you are not entitled to keep the ball, and should simply return it. If, however, damage is done to your property, you may ask the child's parent to pay for the damage, and pursue this in court if you so wish.

Dangerous dogs

The law on dangerous dogs extends across gardens. If a neighbour's dog is threatening people occupying a neighbouring garden, it could become subject to the Dangerous Dogs Act. See page 253.

Parties – avoiding upsets

If you are planning to have a party that may disturb your neighbours, inform them first of your intentions, and give them as much notice as you can. Inviting them along means that they are not sitting at home fuming because of the noise or they may opt to go out for the evening or away for the weekend. If your neighbour asks you to reduce the noise after midnight, try to make sure that you do.

Resolving neighbourhood disputes

Taking your neighbour to court should be the last in a long list of actions you may be able to take to resolve a dispute with your neighbour.

The first is, of course, to talk. Try not to do this when you are angry or upset. Sleep on it and then approach your neighbour in a reasonable way when you have cooled down. It sometimes helps to write down your concerns before tackling your neighbour and ensure that they are objective. Ask your neighbour to put himself in your shoes. Be polite and explain the reasons why his behaviour upsets you so much. Try to be conciliatory rather than confrontational.

If the neighbour is a tenant, get in touch with his landlord. It may be that under pressure from neighbours the landlord chooses to ask the tenant to leave.

If you are not happy with the response you receive when you have spoken to your neighbour, and the offensive or nuisance behaviour continues over a period of time, and is one of the statutory nuisances dealt with by local authorities, contact their Environmental Health Department. If the neighbour is a council tenant or living in another form of social housing, contact the public landlord in question to make a complaint.

For other kinds of dispute, you may both wish to try mediation. Mediators can provide a forum in which to have the complaint raised and discussed in a conciliatory manner, possibly leading to a written agreement. Your Citizens' Advice Bureau should be able to give you a list of mediators in your area, or see page 312 for details of Mediation UK.

If all else fails and you are considering asking the court for an injunction and/or compensation, try sending a solicitor's letter first. But if this fails, take good legal advice before embarking on expensive legal action.

Antisocial behaviour

Antisocial behaviour is a term that covers many different types of behaviour that are threatening, or cause distress to neighbours and other people who come into the area. For a behaviour to be called antisocial, it must above all be persistent over time. Antisocial behaviour can include such behaviours as:

◆   threatening and abusive behaviour; bullying
◆   racial harassment or homophobic behaviour

- excessive noise
- rubbish dumping
- keeping pets in such a way as to cause a nuisance
- vandalism and similar damage to property in the area
- activities surrounding and including drug dealing.

Antisocial behaviour can be countered from several angles:

- in public housing, the public landlord may evict or rehouse the offender
- in private housing, the behaviour may break the tenancy agreement and the landlord may be able to ask the tenant to leave
- the local authority may be able to take action on the grounds of nuisance
- the police may be able to act if the behaviour includes actions that are criminal offences, such as physical attacks, racial abuse, drug-dealing, harassment, etc.

One of the main problems with antisocial behaviour is that many of its victims are too intimidated to act as witnesses or bring charges. In such cases, local authorities may employ

Neighbourhood disputes – action plan

- Talk to your neighbour and explain your concerns; do so when you are calm, not in the midst of an angry outburst. Ask politely that the behaviour that is bothering you be stopped
- Contact your neighbour's landlord and complain, asking him to pass on your complaints to your neighbours
- Contact the local authority or public housing landlord
- Ask your neighbour to attend mediation with you to put both sides of the case and come to an agreement without going to court
- Send a solicitor's letter, outlining your complaint and threatening legal action
- As a last resort, take your neighbour to court seeking an injunction and/or damages.

'expert witnesses' to gather evidence against the perpetrator and stand up in court when he is prosecuted. If you are the victim of antisocial behaviour, contact your landlord, local authority or the police. If you are unsure which body to call, visit your local Citizens Advice Bureau, who should be able to advise.

Stalking

Stalking is the popular term given to a set of behaviours that threaten or harass an individual. The Protection from Harassment Act 1997 was intended to prevent behaviours on the part of non-family members that can be termed harassment, and which cause the victim to feel threatened or distressed. Under the act, a victim of a stalker may ask the court to make a non-molestation order, which makes the stalker liable for arrest if he or she does not cease the behaviour complained of or enters the vicinity.

Key terms

abatement notice
Court order requiring that a nuisance is stopped. See page 73.

annulment
A court order instructing that a marriage should be considered either at an end or never to have taken place. See page 65.

antisocial behaviour
One of any number of behaviours (or a combination), which leaves a neighbour feeling threatened, but also including actual abuse both physical and verbal. See pages 75–77.

banns
Announcement of a forthcoming marriage in a church. See page 61.

bigamy
The criminal offence of knowingly entering into a marriage while a previous marriage is still in existence. See page 62.

co-respondent
In divorce proceedings, a third party, for example, the person with whom the respondent committed adultery.

decree absolute

The final decision in a divorce proceeding, used as proof that a marriage has ended in legal terms. See page 68.

decree nisi

The first of two decisions in divorce proceedings. See page 68.

divorce

The legal ending of a marriage. See pages 66–69.

engagement

Agreement between two people that they intend to marry. See page 59.

exclusion order

Court order excluding a person from a particular area. See page 72.

marital rape

The criminal offence of forcing one's wife to have sex against her wishes. See page 65.

marriage by proxy

Contracting a marriage in place of another person. See page 62.

non-molestation order

Court order instructing an individual to stay away from another, particularly used in cases of child abuse or domestic violence. See page 72.

nuisance

Wrongfully interfering with another person's use and enjoyment of his property. See page 73.

occupation order

Court order giving a certain individual or family rights to occupy a property. See page 72

plaintiff

In the case of divorce proceedings, the person who starts legal proceedings for divorce.

polygamy
The practice of marrying more than one wife. See page 62.

possession order
Court order instructing a tenant to leave a property. See page 72.

respondent
In the case of divorce proceedings, the person against whom legal proceedings are carried out. See page 68.

separation
When a married couple splits up. See page 66.

void
Any contract that is not enforceable in law is said to be void; e.g. a marriage that is not legal.

4 The Law and Young People

This chapter takes a look at how the law views children and young people. In very general terms, the law as regards these members of our community is geared towards protection and care, although there are ways in which young offenders may be punished in an effort to balance justice for the victims of criminal acts and re-education for the offenders themselves.

The chapter starts by setting down a useful list of some of the things children and young people are legally allowed to do as they grow to adulthood. It then covers matters relating to the relationship between parents and their offspring, including issues of parental responsibility, adoption and child abuse and protection. Next it goes on to explain the legal aspects of this country's compulsory education system, a young person's entitlement to take paid work, and how the courts deal with young people who commit offences. Finally, it takes a brief look at the bones of the law as regards young people, sex and contraception.

Growing up

The following list shows some of the restrictions on children and young people as they pass from childhood to adulthood.

From the date of birth
- you must have your own passport if you wish to travel
- you are entitled to sue someone else, but for now, you will have to do this through the agency of a 'next friend', an adult
- you are entitled to hold premium bonds and a National Savings account (with your parents' help).

5 years old
- you may go to the cinema; you may watch any movie rated U, but you must be accompanied by an adult if the film is rated PG

◆   you may go into a bar or public house, but only if you use the garden or the restaurant rather than the bar

◆   you must enter the full-time education system or begin your education at home (see page 92).

10 years old

◆   the law considers you to be capable of committing a criminal offence, and so you can be prosecuted (see pages 94–97), although the prosecution must be able to show that you understood the nature of your actions

◆   if convicted of a criminal offence, you may be fined up to £250

◆   you can open your own bank or building society account if the manager agrees.

12 years old

◆   you are entitled to buy a pet (see page 250)

◆   you can start training to take part in dangerous performances (see pages 90–91), but you will need a permit from the local authority

◆   you are entitled to go to the cinema unaccompanied by an adult to watch any film rated 12; you may also buy or rent videos and DVDs with this rating.

13 years old

◆   you are entitled to take certain kinds of part-time paid work.

14 years old

◆   you are now officially no longer termed a 'child' but a 'young person'

◆   you are entitled to enter a bar or pub accompanied by an adult (and with the consent of the manager), but you may not buy or consume alcohol

◆   you may drive a small mowing machine, small tractor, small pedestrian-controlled vehicle, electrically assisted pedal cycle, moped, invalid car

◆   you may be convicted of a criminal offence without the need for the prosecution to show that you understood the nature of your actions

◆   if convicted of a criminal offence, you may be fined up to £1,000

♦ you become responsible for buckling your own seatbelt in a car

♦ you are allowed to go to court as a spectator.

15 years old

♦ on conviction for a criminal offence you may be sent to a young offender's institution

♦ you are entitled to work up to 30 hours a week during the school holidays (see page 90)

♦ you may go to the cinema to watch a film rated 15, and you may rent or buy videos or DVDs with this rating.

16 years old

♦ you may leave school on the school leaving date (see page 89) for your year and take full time employment

♦ you are entitled to join a trade union

♦ you can get married with the consent of your parents (see page 58)

♦ girls may give their consent for sexual intercourse, be advised on contraception and given supplies by a doctor without parental knowledge or permission, and have an abortion without the knowledge or consent of their parents

♦ you may buy cigarettes or other tobacco products and paraphernalia

♦ you can change your name by deed poll; your parents are no longer entitled to change your name by deed poll without your consent

♦ you may leave home without the permission of your parents; although you may be prevented if your parents obtain a court order

♦ a restaurant may serve you beer or cider with a meal

♦ you can buy fireworks

♦ boys can join the armed forces if they have their parents' permission.

17 years old

♦ you may hold a driver's licence for: a motor cycle up to 125cc, a motor tricycle, a car with up to 8 passenger seats, a lorry or van up to 3,500kg laden, a large tractor or small road roller.

♦ you may enter a betting shop, but as a spectator only

◆ you may be arrested and held by the police without the need for them to inform your parents.

18 years old

◆ you may vote in general, local and European elections
◆ you may get married and/or leave home without the consent of your parents
◆ men may consent to homosexual sex in a private place
◆ you may make a will
◆ you may buy and consume alcohol in a bar, pub or from an off-licence; some bar owners and managers, however, limit entrance to people over the age of 21
◆ you may own property and enter into contracts
◆ you are entitled to see copies of your adoption papers and make use of the Adoption Contact Register (see page 86)
◆ you may be the direct beneficiary of a will without the need for a trust
◆ you may join the armed forces without the permission of your parents
◆ you are entitled to consumer credit (with the agreement of the finance company), including holding a cheque guarantee card and having an overdraft
◆ you may enter into a mortgage agreement
◆ you may be asked to serve on a jury
◆ you may go into a betting shop or casino (subject to the manager's agreement), and gamble
◆ in criminal cases, you will be taken to the adult court and receive your sentence as an adult
◆ you may drive a lorry or van up to 7,500kg laden
◆ you are entitled to sue somebody in your own right without using a 'next friend' to act on your behalf
◆ you are entitled to watch films rated 18 at the cinema and to purchase or rent videos and DVDs in this category

Registering a child's birth

For information on registering the birth of a child, see pages 276–277.

- ◆ you are entitled to enter a sex shop and purchase video material rated R18; you are also now allowed to buy pornographic magazines and other printed material
- ◆ best of all, you are now entitled to get a tattoo and be hypnotised in a public performance.

21 years old

- ◆ you may stand as a Member of Parliament
- ◆ you may hold a driver's licence for all types of vehicles, including buses and large heavy goods vehicles
- ◆ you may adopt a child
- ◆ you may apply for a licence to sell alcohol.

Parental responsibility

The concept of parental responsibility is enshrined in the Children Act 1989. It is in general terms defined as the sum of the rights, duties and obligations that fall upon those caring for children. If they are married when a child is born, both parents have joint parental responsibility. This means that they can act together or separately in any matter concerning their child. If the parents are not married when the child is born, only the mother automatically has parental responsibility. Even if he is cohabiting with the mother of his child, the father has no formal rights to make decisions on his child's behalf unless the mother gives him those rights.

In certain cases, parental responsibility can be passed over to someone else (a grandparent or other relation, perhaps) if the parent is not coping with the child in some way or other. It is also passed over to someone else in cases of adoption.

Parental responsibility ceases at the age of 18.

Parents' authority over their children

Parental responsibility means that the parent or carer has the right to make a number of decisions on behalf of the child, including:

The rights of married people

See pages 70–71 for more on the rights of married people as opposed to those who are cohabiting.

- ◆ her name – until a certain age, parent may change a child's name without her consent
- ◆ her religion
- ◆ where she goes to school
- ◆ where she lives
- ◆ whether she receives medical treatment
- ◆ whether she is allowed to leave home or, if she is under 18, whether she is allowed to get married.

All this aside, it is possible for a young person or child to ask the courts for a ruling in serious situations where she is being forced to do something against her will.

Children and divorce

The Children Act 1989 also tells the courts how to deal with children in cases where their parents are no longer living together: either they are separated or divorced. In many cases of marriage breakdown, the couple resolve their differences between them, or with the help of a solicitor or mediator (see page 69), and come to a workable solution as to where the children should live, and how to manage visits to their other parent. In some cases, an agreement cannot be reached, and then the courts may need to get involved. Under the Children Act 1989, the courts may be able to hand out one of four different types of order in an effort to find a workable solution, always with the needs, welfare and desires of the children in mind:

- ◆ **residence orders** are instructions as to where a child should live. It could be made in favour of the mother, or the father, or the two of them jointly, in which the child would divide her time between two homes. In some cases, residence orders can be made in favour of people other than parents (for example, grandparents), and if this is the case, that person takes on parental responsibility while the residence order is in operation.
- ◆ **contact orders** enable children to stay in touch with the parent they don't live with. They include not only visits and stays, but also telephone calls, e-mails and any kind of communication between parent and child.
- ◆ **prohibited steps orders** prevent a parent taking a significant step without obtaining permission from the

other parent. This may include such actions as moving abroad with the children.

◆ **specific issue orders** make rulings on certain points of the child's upbringing on which the parents cannot agree.

Court orders are expensive, and any separated parent would be better advised to settle such questions through talking and through mediation if at all possible.

Adoption

Any adult over the age of 21 may adopt a child, and any adult over the age of 18 may adopt his own child. Married couples can adopt jointly, but where a couple is cohabiting, one of the partners must adopt as a single person.

The adoption process is generally lengthy, but culminates in an adoption order being issued by the court, removing parental responsibility (and rights) from the natural parents and their family, and transferring it to the adoptive parent or parents. Once the adoption order is signed and sealed, the adoptive parents take up full parental responsibility for the child, with the power to make whatever decisions his natural parents would have made. The biological family agree to remove themselves from the child's life altogether.

Adoption orders are not normally made without the consent of the child involved, or if that child is not of an age to understand the proceedings, at least with the best interests of that child to the forefront. So, if an older child or young person is to be adopted, his feelings and thoughts would most certainly be taken into account.

At the age of 18, adopted people are entitled to see copies of their adoption papers. They are also entitled to make use of the Adoption Contact Register (see page 307). This is a list of names from both sides of the adoption process – biological mother and adopted child – who have decided that they wish to get back in touch with their child or parent.

Protecting children from abuse

Children are the most vulnerable members of our community, and sadly, they can suffer abuse of all kinds from members of their own family – those very people charged in law with their welfare. Abuse can include any of the following:

- physical abuse, including physical attacks that go beyond reasonable discipline
- sexual abuse, including vaginal or anal intercourse, but also unwanted sexual touching or invitations
- emotional abuse, including bullying, belittling and verbal threats
- neglect or abandonment.

A range of actions is available to local authorities, which are charged with looking after child welfare if abuse is discovered or a parent is shown to be not coping with the care of his or her children:

- **child assessment order**: this court order enables the local authority social workers to assess the child's health and circumstances. It is taken out when parents refuse to allow social workers access to children they consider to be at risk
- **child protection**: if the assessment considers that a child is at risk from abuse or has been abused or neglected, they may be put on the Child Protection Register, and a social worker will be assigned to visit the child at regular intervals
- **police protection**: used when a social worker considers a child to be in immediate danger. Children may be held in police protection for up to 72 hours
- **emergency protection order**: if the risk of harm persists beyond the initial 72 hours, the local authority may apply

---

Help

If you are suffering abuse or feel threatened in any way, talk to someone outside the family. See page 309 for information on Childline (0800 1111), or talk to a teacher, doctor or social worker. All these adults will keep what you tell them confidential, and they will be able to take steps to stop the abuse and place you out of harm's way.

---

for an emergency protection order to keep the child in local authority accommodation for a further seven days, and the order may be extended, but only once.

♦ **care orders**: these court orders may enable the local authority to remove a child from his parents home to a children's home or foster care. A care order may be temporary or may last until the child is 17. A care order may be discharged if the parent's circumstances change and they become able to look after the child again. When a child is placed in local authority care, the authority shares parental responsibility with his parents.

A number of other actions may be taken in cases of abuse. An injunction may be sought in the courts ordering the abuser to cease his or her behaviours and exempting him or her from certain places. People living in public housing may find themselves evicted if any member of their family has left the household permanently because of domestic violence (see pages 71–72). In addition, the police may seek to prosecute the abuser if a criminal offence can be proved against him or her. If the prosecution is successful, a victim of abuse may be able to seek financial compensation.

Young people at work

The law seeks to protect young people from exploitation in trade and industry by setting age limits and the types of work in which teenagers can engage. In addition, regulations restrict working times and hours, and give rules for rest breaks and holidays. The exact regulations vary from area to area and depend on byelaws imposed by the local authority.

Registration of young workers

All employees under the school leaving age must have a permit issued by the local authority. It is the employer's responsibility to apply for the permit, and employers may be fined if they do not do so. This system seeks to protect young people from overwork, work in unsuitable jobs and dangerous jobs.

Under the age of 13

Children under the age of 13 are not allowed to do paid work, except in certain circumstances. These include doing so-called 'light work' in the family business, such as in agriculture.

Aged 13

Children aged 13 may do light work in one of a number of categories laid down by the local authority. These categories will usually include:

- delivering newspapers
- working in a hotel
- working in riding stables
- car washing
- agricultural work
- work in a shop, café, beauty salon or office.

Aged 14

For young people who are aged 14 and over, horizons widen. Instead of specifying a list of categories in which children may work, local authority regulations now give a list of work that people of this age cannot do, including:

- door-to-door selling, canvassing, collecting money or telesales
- work in industry, such as mining and construction
- work that can be considered dangerous, including handling toxic materials and working at heights of more than 3m (15ft).
- work in night clubs, on licensed premises, in commercial kitchens, in fairgrounds or amusement arcades, in betting shops, or in places likely to lead to exposure to pornographic material
- delivering milk, or other substances
- rubbish collection
- street trading (with some exceptions)
- some sorts of work in residential care homes.

Leaving school

The official school leaving age is roughly 16. After the third Friday in June in year 11 of secondary school, a young person may leave school and take up any kind of paid work. However, young people at work after this age are subject to specific rules as regards the minimum wage (see pages 173–174) and employers must apply special Health and Safety regulations (see page 183).

Hours of work

Again, the hours a young person is allowed to work depend on their age and whether he or she is also expected to go to school on that particular day.

No person under school leaving age should work before 7 am or after 7 pm. In some cases you may work for an hour before the start of school on a school day, but should not be working during school hours. On school days, work is limited to two hours per day. On Saturdays, young people over 15 may do eight hours work, but if you are under 15, you are limited to 5 hours work. On Sundays, young people may not do more than two hours work.

In school holidays, if you are over 15, you may work up to eight hours per day, to a maximum of 35 hours per week. If you are under 15 you may only work five hours per day and with a maximum of 25 hours per week. In any event, you must take at least two weeks holiday per year during which you do not go to school or to work.

Young people under 16 should not work more than four hours at a time without taking a rest break of at least one hour.

Public performances

There are specific rules regarding young people taking part in public performances. Young people under the age of 16 may take part in public performances that take up no more than three days in any six-month period. If you are under the age of 13, it must be shown that your part cannot be taken by someone older.

Babysitting

A child or young person is entitled to babysit for another child and to receive payment for this service regardless of age. The only requirement is that the babysitter is considered mature enough to carry out the task responsibly.

If performances are to take up more than this time (even if you don't have to take time off school, you will need a licence from the local authority if:

◆ people are paying to see the performance
◆ it is being recorded for broadcast, or
◆ it is to take place in licensed premises.

In granting the licence, the local authority will ensure that your education is not likely to suffer as a result of these activities. If your performance takes you out of the UK, you will have to get a licence from a Magistrates' Court.

You will not need a licence for school performances and plays.

It is illegal for young people under 16 to take part in dangerous performances, and if you are under 12, you cannot even be trained for such performances. These include such performances as high-wire acts.

Discipline at home

Discipline in the home is considered a family affair, and parents are not bound by the same rules as teachers (see page 93). However, there is a fine line between fair and reasonable discipline and abuse.

The punishment a child receives should be proportionate to the wrong committed. It should be reasonable and fair. Corporal punishment, such as slapping or smacking is permitted, but punching and beating a child, especially about the head, would normally be considered abuse or assault.

Parents and others who assault children in their care are committing a criminal offence, and may risk a prison sentence. In addition, a child who is injured by a parent may be able to sue them under civil law and claim compensation.

Childminders are also legally able to discipline children with a slap or a smack, but rarely and only with parental consent.

Children and education

By law, all children must have full-time education from the first day of the term that comes after their fifth birthday to the third Friday of the June in which they are 16. This legal obligation falls upon the child's parents – it is a parental responsibility to ensure their children take part in education. In return, the local authority has an obligation to find a school for each child that is within walking distance from their home (two miles for children under the age of eight and three miles for children over eight).

Non-attendance at school

Any parent is responsible for their child's attendance at school. If a child is not attending school (or getting an education elsewhere), the ultimate maximum penalty is a fine of £2,500 or a prison sentence of up to three months. If you can show the courts that you have done everything in your power to insist that your child goes to school (as might be the case for teenage truants, for example), the penalty may be reduced to £1,000, payable by each parent.

However, before this stage, the local authority would ask the courts to issue an education supervision order (ESO). This order means that you must follow instructions as to the education of your child, and can include guidance and advice on how to get your child back into school.

Education at home

Parents are entitled to educate their children outside the mainstream education system, for example, at home. The teacher does not need to be qualified, and the schooling is not required to follow the national curriculum, but you must be able to show that the child is receiving a suitable education. If the local authority feels that the child is not being educated properly, an ESO will be issued, and you may be forced to send your child to school.

Choice of lessons

In state schools in the UK, teachers must teach the national curriculum. However, as a parent, you have a right to remove your child from the following lessons and activities:

◆ lessons involving sex education which is not part of the national curriculum
◆ religious education, activities and/or worship.

You may also be able to have your child excused school at certain times to attend independent religious education or worship.

School discipline and sanctions

Teachers may use detention to punish poor behaviour, but they must give parents 24 hours notice in writing if the detention is to take place after school hours. Following the principle that the punishment should fit the crime, teachers must be able to show that the detention is a suitable and proportionate response to the behaviour in question.

It is illegal in England and Wales to punish a child physically. This includes smacking, caning and shaking. But teachers may restrain a child in certain circumstances:

◆   if they are about to damage property
◆   if they are hurting someone else, including a teacher
◆   if they are committing an criminal offence.

Schools may also deal with persistently unruly children by excluding them from the school altogether. This is a serious step to take, and regulations exist to ensure that the child gets a fair hearing. In addition, the steps in the exclusion process, including exclusion hearings, must take place within certain time limits. If your child's school is contemplating exclusion, you should seek legal advice, although unless you are receiving state benefits you will not be able to get community funding.

Discrimination at school and college

It is illegal to discriminate against you on grounds of your race, sex or disability. This applies to situations in school or college as much as it does to situations at work, for example, or when renting a room or flat. So, for example:

◆   it is illegal to suspend or exclude a child of African origin in circumstances where a child from another ethnic group would be treated differently
◆   in a mixed-sex school, careers advice must be offered equally to both boys and girls
◆   the range of subjects taught in a single-sex school must not be influenced by the absence of pupils of the other sex.

This law also extends to parents of schoolchildren or college students. If you feel that you or a child of yours is facing discrimination of any kind at school or in college, the first thing to do is to try to discuss it with your child's teacher, head teacher or college principal. If you feel this has not resolved the problem, you may wish to make a complaint to the school governors or local education authority. Seek advice from your local Citizens Advice Bureau, or contact the Equal Opportunities Commission (see page 310), or the Advisory Centre for Education (see page 307). For more on the discrimination laws see pages 192–196.

Young people and the legal system

The British legal system sets a minimum age for what it calls 'criminal responsibility'. This is the age at which the courts consider a child can take responsibility for his or her actions, and can therefore be required to answer for them in a court of law. The age of criminal responsibility is 10. This means that no child under the age of 10 may be prosecuted for a criminal offence. However, if a child under this age is a persistent offender, the courts may issue a care order or a supervision order (see page 97). Children between the ages of 10 and 14 can only be prosecuted if the prosecution can show that he or she knows the difference between right and wrong. Young people over the age of 14 are considered capable of taking full responsibility for their actions, and so can be convicted of the same criminal offences in the same way as adults.

The legal system endeavours in many ways to curb criminal behaviour in young people without the use of prison sentences. The courts that deal specifically with young people are especially designed to be less daunting than the courts that try adult cases, and there is a range of penalties available to the courts aimed at giving the young person every opportunity to mend his or her ways but at the same time seeking justice for the victims of crime.

Cautions

Cautions are used by the police to warn children and young people that their behaviour is not acceptable. They are used for minor offences, and are, in the least serious cases, handed out by police officers on the spot.

If a child is involved in a more serious offence, then he or she may be called to the police station for a formal caution. This might be the case if this is the child's first offence. The parents and the child are requested to attend the police station, where the child is addressed by a senior police officer. To be given a caution the child must admit the offence and the parents must agree that the child may be cautioned. The caution is recorded, but does not form part of the child's criminal record. It is used, however, if the child gets in trouble with the police at a later date.

If the child does not admit the offence, or the parents refuse to allow him or her to be cautioned, the police may decide to prosecute.

Prosecution

If a child has committed an offence, and a caution is not a suitable response (perhaps the child is a persistent offender, or the offence has caused damage to property) the police have two avenues open to them.

For minor offences such as minor motoring offences (see pages 208–214), they would usually refer to their own Juvenile Bureau, which would decide whether to prosecute. If the Juvenile Bureau decides to do this, the young person is summonsed – sent an order to attend court on a certain date.

If the offence is a more serious one, the police station's custody officer may decide to press charges immediately, and the child will be bailed to attend a court hearing. He and his parents agree that the child will attend the hearing, and if he does not do so, the police may arrest him.

In certain circumstances, the child will not be bailed, but held in custody. Any child or young person under 17 who has been refused bail must be held (usually) in local authority accommodation, rather than in cells.

The court system for young people

Young people under the age of 18 are usually referred to the Youth Courts unless their case is one of murder or manslaughter, in which case, the case is heard in the Crown Court regardless of the age of the accused. The Youth Court is less formal than other courts, having done away with the trappings of legal authority such as wigs and gowns, and having changed the very formal language in which legal proceedings are normally carried out.

Young people tried in the Youth Courts must be accompanied by a parent or guardian. The hearing is heard by magistrates rather than a judge and jury, and they are private proceedings. This means that while a case can be reported, the child cannot usually be named, or his photograph published and no information can be given that could identify the child.

Non-custodial penalties for young offenders

If the young person is found guilty of a criminal offence in a Youth Court, the magistrates have a range of options open to them. These options are aimed mostly at setting a suitable punishment for the offence short of a custodial sentence, because it has been found that young people who have served custodial sentences are more rather than less likely to re-offend. Options include:

- **discharge**, either conditional or absolute: the court will not impose a penalty for very minor offences, or where the offender was found to be guilty only on a technicality. A conditional discharge means that the offender must not commit another offence within a given time period (up to three years), but if there is another offence in that time, the offender will be dealt with over both the new and the original offence. An absolute discharge means that there is no penalty at all.
- **binding over to keep the peace**: the court will order that the offender promises to be on good behaviour for a fixed period of time. Fines for breaking this promise differ depending on the age of the offender. Parents may also be bound over to guarantee the behaviour of their child.
- **a fine**: the court will order the offender to pay a fixed fine either immediately or in instalments. The level of the fine depends on the age of the offender.
- **a compensation order**: the offender is ordered to pay compensation, either as a fixed sum or in instalments.
- **an attendance centre order**: the court orders that the child shall attend an attendance sentence (usually on Sundays) organised by the police. The number of hours for which the child must attend varies according to her age.
- **a probation order**: a child may be placed under the supervision of a probation officer for a set period of up to three years. He must agree to the probation, and there may be restrictions on his activities, including

residence in a probation hostel, and undergoing a drug or alcohol rehabilitation centre. Only those over the age of 16 are given probation orders.

◆ **a supervision order**: the court may order that the child is placed under the supervision of a local authority worker for a set period of time. It may also include restrictions on the child's activities and a curfew. If the child is under 14, the parents must agree to the order. If the child is over 14, he must agree.

◆ **a community service order**: those aged over 16 may be ordered to work unpaid in the community for a fixed number of hours.

◆ **a combination order**: this combines both probation and community service orders.

Custodial penalties for young offenders

Despite the wide range of options open to the Youth Courts, it is sometimes necessary to impose custodial sentences on persistent offenders or those who have been found guilty of serious criminal offences.

In considering a custodial sentence, the court must be satisfied that the offence is of a very serious nature or that if the young person were allowed to walk free into the community, someone would be in danger.

Young people under the age of 21 may not be sent to prison, but those aged 15 or over may be sent to a young offender's institution. The Youth Court can impose a maximum sentence of one year for a first offence and a maximum sentence of two years for the second and later offences.

If the offence is very grave indeed, it will be tried in the Crown Court rather than in the Youth Court, and this court has the power to detain the offender for an indefinite period of time.

Contracts

If you are under the age of 18, the law considers that you are not bound by a contract. You cannot be sued if you fail to abide by the terms of a contract, and your parents can only be sued regarding a contract you made if they have agreed to act as guarantors (i.e. to make payments on your behalf if you do not do so).

There are two exception to this: employment contracts and contracts for necessary items such as food, clothing or a place to live.

If you are under 18 and you make a contract with a person over 18, that person is bound by the terms of the contract while you are not.

Sex and pregnancy

The law sets limits on the sexual activity on young people, usually geared at protecting them from perceived harm.

The age of consent

In England and Wales, the age of consent for girls is 16. This means that it is unlawful for a man or boy to have sex with a girl under 16 (with or without her agreement). If this does happen, it is the male who can be prosecuted but not the girl. Boys, on the other hand, are legally entitled to engage in sexual intercourse at any age, unless the relationship is homosexual, in which case, the age of consent is 18.

Men who have sexual intercourse with girls under the age of 13 are committing the offence of 'unlawful sexual intercourse' and in court, there can be no defence. This means that if the act is proven to have taken place, the man will automatically be convicted. Men who have sexual intercourse with girls between the ages of 13 may have one of two defences. If they are under 24, they may be found not guilty if they can show that they thought the girl consented and was over 16. An alternative defence is that the man believed he was legally married to the girl at the time intercourse took place.

There is no law on age limits for lesbian sex, although there may in some circumstances be a case for indecent assault if one partner does not consent.

Contraception

It is every woman's right to receive contraception advice and contraception (in the form of the Pill, perhaps) from her doctor. If a young woman is over 16 she does not need to seek her parents' permission before getting contraception and advice from her doctor. If she is under 16, she should still be able to get advice and supplies from her doctor if he believes that she is at risk of pregnancy and that she understands the advice he is giving her. In this case, a doctor will usually urge the young woman to seek her parents' permission, but parents who find a doctor has given their under-16 contraception cannot do anything about it in legal terms.

Boys of any age may receive a doctor's contraceptive advice without the permission of their parents, and both boys and girls of any age are permitted to buy over-the-counter contraceptives in a chemist or from a vending machine.

Abortion

Any young woman over the age of 16 is entitled to make her own decision as to whether to end an unwanted pregnancy in abortion, and if she meets the criteria for abortion set down by law (see pages 107–108), most doctors would consent. It is not necessary for a young woman over 16 to seek her parents' consent.

Few doctors, however, would give the necessary consent for a girl under 16 to have an abortion without the knowledge or consent of her parents.

Having said that, it is possible in certain circumstances for parents to seek an injunction in the High Court to force a young woman under the age of 18 to either undergo an abortion or to have the baby.

Harassment of young people

Children and young people may find themselves subjected to harassment in the same way as people at work. Harassment is usually dealt with under the Sex Discrimination laws, because the victim is being treated differently to the way the harasser would treat a member of the opposite sex. Harassment includes:

- unwelcome comments about the way you look
- indecent remarks which you find offensive
- outright requests for sex or sexual favours (sometimes

Indecent photographs and films

It is an offence for anyone to take indecent photographs or make films or videos of children under the age of 16. It is also an offence to trade in such items.

              in return for favours such as better grades)

◆   any other behaviour that makes you feel intimidated or humiliated.

If you feel you are being harassed by a member of staff at your school or college, or by a fellow pupil or student, the first step is to make it clear that their behaviour is offensive to you and ask them to stop. If the behaviour continues, tell your teacher, head teacher, or other member of staff. If the school or college authorities fail to stop the offensive behaviour, take advice at your local Citizens Advice Bureau or the Advisory Centre for Education (see page 307).

To help your case, record all incidents, including where and when it incident took place, who else was there, what the incident consisted of, how you responded and how it made you feel. A record like this could be useful evidence in court.

Key terms

adolescent
A person aged between 16 and 18.

age of consent
The age at which girls may lawfully give their consent to sexual intercourse, and boys to homosexual sex. See page 98.

care order
Court order which removes a child from a potentially harmful situation to a place of safety. See page 88.

caution
A kind of warning, often used by police to deter children and young people from criminal or anti-social behaviour. See pages 94–95.

child assessment order
A court order that allows local authority workers to make an assessment of a child's welfare. See page 87.

criminal responsibility
Being capable of understanding the nature of one's actions in terms of crime and the law.

emergency protection order
Court order by which a local authority may take a child to secure accommodation for his or her own safety. See pages 87–88.

parental responsibility
All the rights and duties a parent or carer has for a child. See pages 84–85.

residence order
Court order determining where a child is to live. See page 85.

minor
A person under the age of 18.

supervision order
Court order that allows for supervision of a child by a local authority social worker. See page 97.

unlawful sexual intercourse
Sex with a person who is below the age of consent. See page 98.

Youth Court
Formerly known as a juvenile court, the Youth Courts hear criminal prosecutions against young people and children under the age of 17. See pages 95–96.

5 Your Health

Britain's healthcare legislation gives individuals, whether in the NHS or in private healthcare, a battery of rights to treatment and medical advice. This chapter looks at a few ways in which the law affects us when we fall ill. It covers the issue of 'informed consent' – that is, the patient's agreement to be examined, treated and to undergo surgical procedures. On the other side of the coin is the question of refusing treatment, living wills, and most controversially at the time this book was being written, the question of voluntary euthanasia, or the 'right' to die.

The chapter then looks at the law as regards organ or whole-body donation. It also sets out the requirements that must be met before a woman can terminate her pregnancy.

Later, the chapter deals with the powers given to various healthcare professionals under the Mental Health Act 1983, and what can be done under the law when an individual becomes incapable of looking after their own affairs.

Informed consent

In general, the law indicates that every patient treated by a healthcare professional, whether on the NHS or privately, whether by an orthodox medical practitioner or by an alternative therapist, should be treated with their agreement (consent). It goes further, in that it requires the patient to be informed about the treatment, and he must, as far as possible, understand what is happening so that he can make a decision on whether to give his agreement or not. In some circumstances, however, doctors may be able to impose treatment without the patient's consent.

Being informed
No-one can make a decision or a choice without knowing the full story. The law requires that doctors give the patient enough information on which to base decisions that could affect his entire life and the lives of those around him.

- the patient must be told the diagnosis (what is wrong) and the prognosis (the course the medical condition is likely to take unless the doctors intervene)
- the doctor must explain the treatment she recommends, and the possible results of the treatment, including side-effects and risks. She must be satisfied that the patient understands enough of the information to make an informed decision
- the doctor must also explain any alternative treatments, giving possible results, and the risks and side-effects of each one
- the doctor must not keep information from the patient in an effort to sway his judgement, but it is her choice how much information is necessary for the patient to be sufficiently informed to make the decision
- the doctor must tell the patient that he has the right to ask for a 'second opinion' – that is, to be examined by another practitioner and to hear her diagnosis and recommendations for treatment

Giving consent

For any treatments carried out in a hospital, patients should be asked to sign a 'consent form', indicating that they have received all the information required to make a decision and agree to the procedure in question.

In other situations, however, the moment of consent may be a little harder to define. The law allows for 'implied consent' – a patient gives consent without saying or signing anything, simply by doing what was asked by the doctor, perhaps during a routine examination. A patient gives his implied consent to the treatment if he takes the prescription offered, goes to the chemist, and takes the medication, for example.

If you do not wish to be examined, or don't understand why an examination is necessary, stop the consultation and make your wishes known or ask for more information.

Medical accidents

For information on what to do if you or someone close to you has suffered during treatment, see pages 125–127.

Treatment without consent

In some circumstances, it is not possible to get the consent of a patient before treatment, or a patient's condition threatens the health of the general public. So the law lays down certain exceptions – circumstances in which a person can be given medical treatment without their consent, or even against their will. This list of exceptions includes, but is not limited to, the following:

- people covered under the Mental Health Act 1983; see page 108–110
- people with certain very serious diseases that can be spread easily (called notifiable diseases)
- people who are unconscious and who cannot therefore give their consent, and whose life would be in danger if the treatment is not administered straight away
- a parent (or someone with parental responsibility, for example a court) needs to give their consent to treatment for a child under the age of 16, although if a child is considered mature enough to understand the choices, his wishes should be taken into consideration. If a parent refuses treatment, however, a doctor may in some cases be able to override this decision.

Refusing treatment

For all modern medicine has done to improve the lives of most people, it has also brought us to a difficult dilemma. In some circumstances, it is possible to prolong the life of someone (perhaps by mechanical means, or using drugs) when that person would normally have died. Saving life is, of course, worthwhile, but in some cases, prolonging life is to prolong suffering, and some people would prefer not to receive treatment in these circumstances. Refusing treatment is not to be confused with voluntary euthanasia – the active taking of a person's life, in accordance with their wishes (see page 106).

Taking care of dependants

For information on your legal right to time off work to take care of dependants, see pages 187–188.

We all have the right to simply walk away from a doctor if the treatment suggested is not acceptable, even if it means we might die if we do not receive treatment. If a doctor forces treatment on a patient, she may be guilty of assault (see pages 151–152). However, some conditions can eventually lead to a state where the patient is no longer capable of making this decision. Perhaps he has lost the ability to communicate because he is in a coma or has some other condition with this effect. In such circumstances, somebody else has to make the decision, and in this case, it is the next-of-kin or doctors who do so.

Living wills

Some people feel strongly that if something should happen to them that leaves them in a state offering a very poor quality of life, they would prefer to be allowed to die. It is possible to make an advance statement to this effect, making your wishes known before you lose the ability to communicate your wishes. This can be done in two ways.

A patient who is facing a long illness which leads to severe long-term disability may discuss with his doctor at what point he would like treatment to stop. Doctors should record the patient's wishes in his medical records and act on them when the time comes.

Alternatively, a person can draw up a document called a 'living will' or 'advance directive' setting down the values that he holds, and requesting that at a certain point in certain very specific circumstances, treatment to prolong his life is discontinued, and that only palliative care (see page 113) is given. A document such as this should be drawn up while the person is thinking clearly ('of sound mind'), and witnessed much in the same way as a will is witnessed (see page 141). It is usually kept with the person's medical records, and it is wise to give the next-of-kin a copy.

Sterilisation

Legally, a wife or husband does not need to seek permission of their opposite number before they can undergo sterilisation, but, in many cases, clinics will insist on getting that permission before they carry out the procedure.

There is no legislation specifically governing living wills, but they do work as an advance indication of your wishes in certain very well-defined circumstances.

Living wills do not ask doctors to perform any illegal act, but some doctors may decide on ethical grounds that they cannot continue to treat someone who has made one.

Anyone considering drawing up a living will is advised to take legal advice, because there are certain circumstances in which the document may turn out to be invalid.

Voluntary euthanasia

The act of taking one's own life is no longer against the law in the UK. However, taking another person's life, regardless of the circumstances, is a criminal offence, even if you are acting in accordance with the wishes of the person in question. At the present time, the law regarding voluntary euthanasia is very cloudy, and in some countries in the European Union, helping a person who is terminally ill to die is not against the law. It is probable that anyone found to have taken a person's life in this way, by administering a fatal dose of a drug, for instance, or even taking a person to another country to die, would be liable to arrest if not prosecution.

Organ donation

Medical science has advanced by light years in the past few decades, enabling people with previously untreatable conditions to be given a whole new lease of life through organ transplantation. Agreeing to donate our organs (or indeed our whole body) after we have died is a very personal choice, but, legally, other people have a greater say in this than we may think.

Medical records

Every patient in general has the right to see his medical records, and the NHS should supply them within 40 days of the request being made. This right only applies to a patient's own records, and not normally to other people's, such as a spouse or child. However, doctors may agree to your seeing someone else's records if it is in the interests of the patient.

A person may indicate her willingness to donate her organs or her whole body after she has died, by signing and carrying a donor card and registering with the national organ donors registry. However, after death, her body becomes the responsibility of her personal representative (see page 150), and he can choose whether to give permission for the donation to take place. This is why it is so important not only to carry a donor card but also to discuss your wishes with your personal representative and other members of your family and get their agreement to carry them out should you die.

Sometimes, doctors ask to use the organs of people who have not expressly given their consent by registering or carrying a card, and again, it is up to the personal representative to decide whether to give that permission.

Abortion

Terminating an unwanted pregnancy is not against the law in the UK, but the process is heavily regulated under the Abortion Act 1967 to ensure that women's health is protected.

The decision to have an abortion ultimately rests with the mother, and she does not legally require the permission of the father of the child, even if that man is her husband.

The woman must be less than 24 weeks pregnant at the time of the abortion. The only exception to this is if the foetus is discovered to be abnormal, and those abnormalities threaten the mother's life. In this case an abortion can be carried out later in the pregnancy. She must have the agreement of two doctors, and they will only give their permission if they believe one or more of the following statements to be true:

◆ there is a serious risk that the child will be born with abnormalities

Teenage contraception and pregnancy

See page 99 for specific information on parental permission for terminating a pregnancy in a woman under the age of 18, and on prescribing contraception to young people.

- continuing the pregnancy would bring greater risks to the mother's mental or physical health than terminating the pregnancy
- having the child would risk suffering to other children in the family.

Doctors may also consider arguments the mother may have concerning her social or financial situation.

Abortions may only be carried out in licensed establishments, such as NHS hospitals and private clinics.

The law and mental health

Among its many benefits, the Victorian era brought us a new branch of medicine, aimed at studying and treating disorders of the mind. In its early decades, this new branch brought with it many horrors: the asylum; unregulated experimentation in the treatment of mental disorders; the abuse of many patients. Today, thankfully, the treatment of mental disorders is far better regulated, giving the patient many rights while ensuring that the community is as far as possible protected from those whose illness may make them a risk.

The Mental Health Act 1983 lays down regulations relating to people with a serious mental disorder or mental impairment. It says under what circumstances such a person can be forced to stay in a hospital, in what situations he can be treated without his consent, and in what circumstances he can be released. The legislation gives wide powers to doctors, but it is also intended to ensure that the patient is not detained or treated with no good reason.

Being 'sectioned'

Many people suffering from a mental disorder are only too happy to undergo hospital care and treatment. However, in some cases, it is necessary to force a person to stay in hospital. This is done under Section 2, Section 3 or Section 4 of the Mental Health Act, and is popularly known as being 'sectioned'.

Section 2 of the Act is entitled 'Admission for assessment'. It enables doctors to detain a patient in hospital in order to assess his condition. The following restrictions apply:

- three people must agree that the detention is necessary:

two doctors (preferably including the patient's personal GP or someone who has treated him before) and a social worker (usually known as the approved social worker, or ASW)

◆ the patient may only be detained if the patient can only be properly assessed in hospital; or if his illness is of a type that makes the patient a danger to himself or to other people if he remains at large in the community

◆ the detention can last a maximum of 28 days, but at the end of that time, the doctors may detain the patient for a further period under Section 3.

Section 3 of the Act is far more wide-ranging than this, enabling doctors to detain a patient for treatment over long periods of time (years in some cases), subject to the following restrictions:

◆ again, three professionals must give their agreement to the detention, as above

◆ the patient may only be detained if they suffer from one of a number of specific forms of mental disorder laid down by the Act

◆ the treatment must be likely to improve the patient's condition, and that treatment must be of a type that can only be given in hospital

◆ the treatment is necessary to prevent harm to the patient or to members of the public.

Section 4 of the Act covers emergency situations. Only one doctor is required to have the patient detained, but the maximum period of detention is 72 hours. A person detained under Section 4 may only be assessed and not treated. However, doctors may in that time decide to detain the patient further, under Section 3.

Nearest relative

The Mental Health Act allows for a patient to be represented by someone outside the healthcare profession. This person is known as the patient's 'nearest relative', and may be a spouse, parent or child. The nearest relative may be able to have a person admitted to a hospital, but this is increasingly rare. The main role of the nearest relative is to look after the patient's interests. She must be kept informed by the social worker leading the patient's case, and can object to the patient's detention (although this may be overruled in court), and ask that the patient is discharged (although this may be overruled by a doctor). If the social worker believes that the nearest relative is being unreasonable, he may ask the court to nominate another person to act in this capacity.

Other powers

The Mental Health Act is a quite complex piece of legislation, and the above is just a sample of some of the powers and rights it confers. It also covers the circumstances under which a patient may discharge himself, who can prevent a discharge, types of treatment that can be carried out without the patient's permission, receiving visitors, and the role of the Mental Health Act Commission in protecting the rights of patients.

Anyone involved with a person who has a mental disorder that is likely to see them hospitalised should seek further information, for example, from a Citizens Advice Bureau.

Taking over legal responsibility

With an ever-ageing population, more and more people are finding themselves less able to run their own affairs than they used to be. Having someone else help with the shopping is a very different matter to having them operate a bank account, draw a pension or dispose of our property. The law allows a person who is experiencing periods of disability or is anticipating an illness in which her mental capacity is weakened to hand over legal responsibility for her affairs to a trusted friend or relative. There are four ways of doing this.

Agency

A person may ask someone else to take care of specific tasks, such as drawing a pension or picking up benefits from time to time, simply by filling in the form supplied by the benefits agency.

Authorisation

If such an arrangement becomes necessary on a regular basis, the person should contact the Benefits Agency and ask that their nominee is made an 'authorised agent'. This will enable that person to collect benefits regularly.

Ordinary power of attorney

An ordinary power of attorney is a legal agreement in which a person (called the 'donor') gives another person (the 'attorney') the legal power to act on her behalf. This may be used, for example, to enable another person to conclude a property deal while the donor is abroad or to carry out other specific types of actions such as buying and selling shares on the donor's behalf. A power of attorney can cover a certain time period or certain specific actions. However, if the donor becomes incapable, perhaps through illness, an ordinary power of attorney would cease.

Enduring power of attorney

Similar to an ordinary power of attorney, this legal agreement enables the donor to pass over legal responsibility for her affairs to another person. It is different in that it does not cease when the donor loses her capacity to make legal decisions and agreements. So an enduring power of attorney is useful if the donor is faced with a physical or mental condition that is likely to render her incapable in the future. If there is no enduring power of attorney in place when a person becomes incapacitated, her relatives may have to apply to the courts for permission to take responsibility for her legal affairs, and this is a process that can take time and can be expensive.

Legal requirements for powers of attorney

The following are some of the rules governing powers of attorney, whether they are ordinary or enduring:

- a donor may only give her attorney powers that she herself holds. So if she is a child or young person under the age of 18, she can only convey the rights that someone of her age has in law.
- the donor must be mentally capable when she makes the power of attorney, just as she must be 'of sound mind' when she makes a will.
- anyone over the age of 18 can act as attorney, but a person who has been made bankrupt may not hold an enduring power of attorney, and if the attorney becomes bankrupt while holding an enduring power of attorney, that agreement ceases.
- the donor may decide to appoint more than one

♦ attorney, making the possibility of fraudulent activity less likely.

♦ an enduring power of attorney allows the attorney to sell property, but he cannot make the donor live somewhere else against her will.

♦ the attorney must always act in the best interests of the donor, and must keep accounts of all transactions carried out on her behalf. The duties of attorney cannot be left to someone else.

Anyone considering granting power of attorney to someone else should take advice from a solicitor.

Key terms

active euthanasia
An act, normally carried out by a doctor, that ends a patient's life (for example, turning off a life-support machine).

appropriate adult
Under the Mental Health Act, a person who is responsible for protecting the rights of someone with a mental disorder who has been detained by the police.

approved social worker (ASW)
Social worker assigned to the case of someone detained under the Mental Health Act. This person should have experience in mental health cases.

assisted suicide
Alternative term for voluntary euthanasia (see below).

attorney
When talking about powers of attorney, the law calls the person authorised to act on behalf of someone else the attorney. See pages 111–112.

donor
When talking about powers of attorney, the law calls the person handing over responsibility for her affairs the donor. See pages 111–112.

enduring power of attorney
Legal agreement whereby a person can hand over her legal power to another, enabling that person to act on her behalf, even when she has lost the mental capacity to act herself. See page 111.

informed consent
Agreement to medical examination or treatment made on the basis of information given by healthcare workers. See page 102.

Mental Health Act Commission
Organisation that monitors the rights of people who are detained in hospital under the Mental Health Act.

mental illness
Under the Mental Health Act, mental illness is defined as a mental disorder, for example schizophrenia.

mental impairment
Under the Mental Health Act, a condition that leaves a person with a mental capacity that is not completely developed. A mental impairment may affect that person's ability to function in society, or his intelligence, and may make him aggressive or not capable of taking responsibility for his actions. The Mental Health Act distinguishes between mental impairment and severe mental impairment.

nearest relative
Under the Mental Health Act, a person, usually a spouse, adult child or parent, to whom information must be given about the legal reasons for that person's detention, and who is entitled to request a detainee's discharge from hospital. See page 109.

ordinary power of attorney
Legal agreement by which a person can nominate someone else to act on her behalf. See page 111.

palliative care
Health care that is aimed at making a person feel comfortable, rather than treating a disorder. Palliative care would include administering painkillers, but not, for example, drip-feeding a patient who can no longer digest food.

physician-assisted suicide
Form of euthanasia in which a doctor prescribes the fatal drug but does not administer it.

psychopathic disorder
Under the Mental Health Act, a mental disorder that makes a person dangerously aggressive or irresponsible.

right to die
Popular term for being entitled to make a decision (for example, to refuse treatment) that effectively ends one's own life.

voluntary euthanasia
Bringing about the death of a person in accordance with his wishes.

6 Accidents and Injuries

Accidents happen. Minor accidents can leave the victim both injured and angry. And major accidents can lead to irrevocable losses, pain and suffering, sometimes changing the victim's life for good. This chapter looks at the range of actions a person can take if she has been injured in an accident that could have been someone else's fault, or indeed, through a criminal act.

It starts by looking at three key concepts in the law concerning personal injury: negligence, causation and contributory negligence. It goes on to list the main kinds of recompense an accident victim might wish to claim, from getting a simple apology through to claiming financial compensation. It looks at ways in which financial compensation can be claimed, how to pay for a court action, the different kinds of damages and time-limits for bringing a claim. Then it looks at three specific circumstances: clinical injuries, work-related injuries and criminal injuries.

Defining terms

There are three concepts in the law that come up time and time again in relation to injuries and accidents: negligence, causation and contributory negligence. In order to bring a court case against someone, the claimant (the victim, or the victim's representative) must prove both negligence and causation. Financial compensation may be reduced if it can be proved that the victim herself was also negligent.

Negligence

Some accidents are caused by our own actions: tripping over an object we left on the stairs, having a traffic accident for which we were to blame. However, other accidents and injuries may have been caused by an action (or lack of action) on the part of someone else: a local authority, the owner of shop, residential or office premises, another road-user, even a passer-by. In order to lay blame for his injury, an accident victim must be able to show that the person he is blaming was negligent. Negligence is defined in law as doing something that a reasonable person would not have done, or failing to do something that a reasonable person would have done. If the person blamed for the accident is a professional, then the victim must show that this person did not bring to bear a reasonable level of professional skill.

Causation

A victim of an accident needs to be able to prove not only negligence on the part of the responsible person or organisation, but also that this negligence led directly to the injury

---

Accident action plan

♦ As soon as possible after the accident, visit your doctor and ensure that he examines you thoroughly, taking note of all injuries

♦ Contact your insurer and/or report the accident to the police if this is necessary

♦ Take photographs or make sketches of the place where the accident took place as soon as possible

♦ Write down your account of the accident step-by-step while it is still fresh in your mind

♦ If there were people nearby when you had your accident, get their names and addresses and ask them whether they would be prepared to act as witnesses

♦ Take photographs of any injuries as soon as possible

♦ Take advice from a Citizens Advice Bureau or other legal advisor as soon as possible to find out what kinds of action you may be able to take against the person or organisation you feel to be responsible

♦ Take advice from the Benefits Agency as soon as possible if you think you may wish to claim benefits because of your injuries

♦ If you are not in a position to do any of these things, have a friend or relative do them for you.

For things to do after a traffic accident, see page 207. For things to do after an accident at work, see pages 127–128.

---

experienced. This direct connection between the injury and the act that caused it is known as 'causation'.

Contributory negligence

Anyone defending himself against a claim may be able to show that the victim herself did something (or failed to do something) which contributed to the accident taking place or made the resulting injury worse. Proving contributory negligence does not necessarily mean that the defendant is off the hook, but it may mean that any financial compensation may be reduced.

Arguing the case

In a personal injury case, the claimant (the victim) must show that the defendant was negligent, and that this negligence led directly to the injury sustained. The defendant in turn may be able to argue against the claim in one or more of three circumstances:

◆ unavoidable accident: the accident happened because of something that was completely unforeseeable or could not have been avoided (for example, a person has a heart attack while driving and the car crashes into a cyclist)
◆ assumption of risk: the victim knew the risks involved with a particular course of action and went through with the action regardless
◆ contributory negligence: the victim acted in a way that increased the risk of the accident taking place or the resulting injuries (see above).

Courses of action

Just as injuries range from the minor to the fatal, so too, the courses of action an accident victim can take vary widely. It all depends on what redress the victim feels she wants. It may include:

Time limits

See pages 124–125 for information on time limits for bringing a claim.

ACCIDENTS AND INJURIES

◆ an apology
◆ an assurance that the organisation will change its policy or train its employees better in order to ensure that the accident does not happen again
◆ disciplinary action against the individual involved
◆ financial compensation for pain and suffering, damage to goods or loss of income.

Gaining an apology

Many victims of minor accidents simply want to have an apology from the responsible person and perhaps an assurance that steps will be taken to ensure that the same thing does not happen to someone else. This is particularly the case if the accident has not led to a permanent injury or to loss or damage of some kind. An apology may be forthcoming if you make a complaint to the organisation concerned.

The first approach should be to the person the victim holds responsible directly, in writing. The letter should outline the circumstances of the accident, the injuries or other damage sustained, and it should outline, politely, the ways in which the responsible person could have acted to avoid the accident. It should also ask for the response the victim is hoping for. If this approach gets no satisfactory reply it may be necessary to repeat the same procedure with the company's head office, or the body governing the responsible person's profession.

Always keep a copy of letters you write and retain any replies. If the matter is discussed on the telephone, make notes (including the date and name of the person you spoke to) and then send a letter giving your understanding of the conversation.

ADR

ADR is short for 'alternative dispute resolution', and refers to the many ways in which people can reach an agreement without resorting to using the courts. It includes mediation, arbitration and conciliation, among other processes. In general, any form of alternative dispute resolution is cheaper than going to court and in some cases leads to a far more satisfactory solution because all parties have voluntarily entered into an agreement.

Mediation

If an organisation or individual does not accept responsibility for an accident, or the victim wishes to ask for more than just an apology, it may be possible to do so without going to court. In recent years, mediation – using a professional mediator to help two parties resolve a dispute and reach an agreement – has become a viable alternative to court. It is cheaper, usually quicker, and often leads to an agreement that both sides are happy with. One drawback, however, is that the other party cannot be forced to agree to enter into mediation.

Mediation can be used to reach all sorts of resolutions, but in the case of a personal injury, it may be used to gain:

◆ an apology and an admission of responsibility
◆ an explanation of how the accident happened
◆ an agreement to implement a policy change to ensure the same thing doesn't happen again
◆ financial compensation for the victim.

Mediation is not free, but the cost should be shared between the two parties, and it is generally significantly cheaper than taking a personal injury case to court. Your Citizens Advice Bureau may be able to put you in touch with a local mediator who is experienced in personal injury cases. Alternatively, contact Mediation UK (see page 312).

Mediators are generally not in a position to give legal advice. They are merely there to help two parties reach an agreement. If you come to a resolution while in mediation, always seek a solicitor's advice on the agreement you have reached before signing on the dotted line. You may find that you change your mind after you have received legal advice.

Going to court

If a victim is looking for compensation, and is unlikely to get this through mediation, she should consider very carefully going to court to sue for financial compensation, called 'damages'. Any personal injury case will require the service of a solicitor specialising in such cases. For a list of such solicitors, contact the Association of Personal Injury Lawyers (see page 308). Alternatively, the victim may wish to make use of a 'claims assessor' or a 'claims management company.

If the victim wishes to sue for damages, she will have to show that the defendant was negligent and that this negligence led to the injury sustained. This will require the collecting of evidence. This includes:

- the notes and photographs made at the time of (or immediately after) the injury
- evidence from a doctor and other expert witnesses on the injury sustained, and how it could affect the victim's health in the future
- evidence of expenses that the victim has had to pay out because of the injury (including receipts)
- estimates of future financial losses, such as loss of income, if the injury means that the victim cannot work as before the injury.

Clearly, pulling all this evidence together can incur large costs, both on the part of the claimant and on the part of the solicitor. So, when deciding whether to bring a case to court, the victim should try to weigh up the possible cost of the action against the possible return in the form of damages.

Normally, only the victim herself can go to court to sue for damages in a personal injury case. However, if a person has died in an accident, her relatives and dependants may be able to claim compensation. If a child is involved, then her parents or guardian would have to bring the action. If the victim cannot bring a claim for some other reason (perhaps she is incapacitated by a condition affecting her mind, or is in a coma), then a relative, guardian or other responsible person may be able to bring the action on her behalf.

Claims management companies

Claims management companies help victims of accidents bring a

---

Warning!

If you are considering taking legal action in a personal injury case, do not contact the person or organisation you thinks is responsible, and do not respond to any communication before taking legal advice.

claim for damages. They do this by assessing the case and then employing a specialist solicitor to carry through the legal work. Claims management companies are unregulated, which means there are no standards they have to meet in dealing with the case. However, any solicitor acting for the victim will be bound by the rules of his own professional body.

Claims management companies usually work on a 'no-win no-fee' basis (see pages 122–123).

Claims assessors

Like claims management companies, claims assessors help victims of accidents bring their case to court. However, they dispense with the services of a solicitor. Again, these companies are not regulated, and so there are no rules about how much they can charge, or how they should behave. They also generally work on a no-win-no-fee basis.

Paying for legal action

Legal action is almost always more expensive than we imagine. Before embarking on a court action, claimants should weigh up the likely costs against the damages that may be awarded, and taking the risk that they may lose into account. There are several ways a claimant may be able to find the money to pay for legal action in personal injury cases (assuming she is not going to pay for the action out of her savings): public funding (previously called legal aid); personal insurance; and entering into a no-win no-fee agreement.

Legal services

As for all services, those wishing to engage the services of a solicitor, a claims manager company or assessor should get an estimate in writing of the cost of the action. This should be accompanied by an explanation of the service, and the basis on which the fee will charged. Because claims assessors and claims management companies are not regulated in the same way as solicitors are, it is wise to get a statement at the outset of what you can do if you are not happy with the service provided.

ACCIDENTS AND INJURIES

Public funding

Public funds (previously known as legal aid) are only available to people on low incomes and for certain types of personal injury case:

- clinical accidents
- injuries caused by the police
- some circumstances in which the injury was caused deliberately.

Ask at your Citizens Advice Bureau or local law centre for further information on whether you may be able to get public funding in your particular case.

Personal insurance

Some personal insurance policies (including car, contents and travel insurance) cover legal situations, although they may set down limits on the amounts payable. Check your policy, and then with the insurance company itself.

No-win no-fee agreements

Many solicitors, claims managers companies and claims assessors will act for the claimant on a no-win no-fee basis. In general, this means that if the case is won, the cost of bringing the action is paid by the defendant. If the case is lost, the person acting on the claimant's behalf will not charge a fee.

This is all well and good, until the claimant loses. Then, she would be liable for:

- all the legal costs incurred by the defendant
- the fees payable to her own expert witnesses
- expenses the solicitor has incurred in gathering other

Help from a trade union

A trade union might be willing to help an accident victim with the cost of legal action, particularly if the case can be used as a test case. If you are a member of a trade union, it is always worth asking if help is available in any legal situation, even if it doesn't relate directly to your work.

---

       evidence on the claimant's behalf
◆   the claimant's own expenses.

When entering a no-win no-fee agreement, therefore, the claimant is usually asked to take out insurance against losing, which would cover the costs in the event of losing the case. Even so, the claimant would still have to pay the cost of the insurance, and this type of insurance is not cheap. The Law Society has endorsed an insurance scheme called Accident Line for this purpose (see page 307).

Damages

'Damages' is the term used by lawyers to mean financial compensation awarded by a court. In personal injury cases, damages are divided into 'general damages' and 'special damages'. Damages may be reduced if the court upholds a claim on behalf of the defendant that the claimant was partly to blame for the accident (contributory negligence, see page 117).

General damages

This term relates to compensation awarded simply because the accident took place, and for the pain and suffering the injury has caused the victim, and is likely to cause in the future.

Special damages

This term relates to specific amounts paid out to cover specific costs incurred as a direct result of the injury. For example, the cost of treatment, loss of earnings, travel expenses, etc. Special damages would also include compensation to help pay for future expenses, such as ongoing therapy, re-fitting a home to account for a disability, paying for drugs and medical equipment such as a wheelchair, etc.

    The court may reduce the damages if it can be shown that the claimant did nothing to reduce ('mitigate') the costs she incurred. It is also possible that the Benefits Agency will seek to claw back part of an award of special damages to cover benefits paid to the victim because of the injury. It does this through a body known as the Compensation Recovery Unit (CRU).

Settling out of court

The two parties in a personal injury case may come to an

agreement before the case reaches the courts. This is termed an 'out-of-court settlement'. The legal advisors on both sides will have agreed on the rights and wrongs of the case, and one party has usually admitted responsibility. Out-of-court settlements are advisable because they limit the costs of the court action and resolve the case more quickly than a court would. In addition, it may be desirable to keep the case out of the media spotlight.

The victim's solicitor will be able to advise on whether to accept such a settlement.

Time limits

By law, a victim of an accident needs to bring a case to court within a certain time period. The time limits vary depending on the details of the case.

If the accident came about because someone else was negligent, then the time limit is three years. This is counted from the time the accident took place, or the point at which the victim knew she had an injury or medical condition as a result of the accident. For example, exposure to coal dust may lead to emphysema (a condition of the lung), in which case, the victim may be able to sue within three years of having the condition diagnosed.

If the accident led to the victim's death, a parent, other relation or personal representative (see page 150) also has three years in which to bring an action.

If the accident was down to the negligence of an airline or a shipping company, the victim may have only two years to sue.

If a child is involved, the time limit begins on the child's 18th

---

Warning!

All personal injury cases are different, and all this book can do is outline the general terms of the law. Anyone involved in an accident that has left them injured and facing losses should seek specialist legal advice as soon as possible. Many solicitors will carry out a short initial interview, without charging a fee, in order to assess a victim's entitlement to make a personal injury claim, and it is worthwhile getting this preliminary legal advice.

birthday, although a claim can be brought before then by the child's parents or guardian.

If the injury was the result of a physical attack, the victim may have six years in which to sue.

In all cases, it is vital to seek advice as soon as the accident takes place or the injury or illness is diagnosed, and to aim to bring an action (if that is what is required) at least six months before the time limit expires.

Clinical Injuries

A clinical injury is defined in law as an injury that is inflicted as a result of the professional negligence of the practitioner involved. So, for instance, it might cover a case in which a child died of an illness that was misdiagnosed because a GP did not examine her properly. It might also cover a brain injury suffered because a nurse administered the wrong drug. It does not cover injuries and deaths that take place as a result of medical treatments or surgical procedures without the practitioner being negligent. So, for example, the family of an elderly person who dies under anaesthetic during a hip-replacement operation would probably not be able to make a claim because it is widely accepted that the older a patient is, the greater the risk involved in having an anaesthetic. However, if this risk was not explained, or informed consent (see pages 102–103) was not obtained prior to the procedure, there may perhaps be a case.

Clinical injuries may be claimed against any type of medical practitioner (including members of the ambulance service), both private and NHS.

Clinical injuries cases are notoriously complex, involving discussions of the original illness as well as the injury. It is essential to seek out a solicitor who specialises in such cases. The Law Society will be able to recommend individuals, and you may be able to get recommendations and advice from a charity called Action for Victims of Medical Accidents (see page 307 for contact details). Solicitors' firms must have been awarded the Legal Aid Board Clinical Negligence Franchise in order to pursue clinical injuries claims with the support of public funding.

If an injury has been sustained, it may be possible to get one of the following, either through the courts, through the hospital, clinic or National Health Trust involved, or through a professional body such as the General Medical Council:

◆ an apology and an explanation of how the injury came about

◆ financial compensation (damages) to cover the cost of treatment, medical equipment and drugs; any other expenses

◆ disciplinary action against the practitioner, instigated by the practitioner's professional body, sometimes (but rarely) leading to the practitioner being suspended or struck off.

It would be ill-advised to take any action regarding a clinical accident case without legal advice. Any claim would normally start with the practitioner himself, or the hospital he works at, and if there is no satisfactory response, the NHS complaints procedure may be brought into play. If you feel a particular health practitioner has acted unprofessionally, you may wish to contact his professional association to make a complaint.

Accidents at work – action plan

◆ Inform your employer or a 'responsible person' (e.g. your supervisor) immediately.

◆ Ensure that your employer lists the accident and its circumstances accurately in the company's accident book; this is a legal requirement under Health and Safety legislation (see pages 182–184).

◆ Ensure that your employer registers the accident with the Incident Contact Centre if necessary; this is also a legal requirement.

◆ Make sure that the appropriate steps are taken to get treatment for your injury, including a visit to your family GP.

◆ If you feel someone has been negligent, and your injury is serious, take the steps in the action plan on page 116.

◆ Take advice from your union if you have one or from your local law centre, Citizens Advice Bureau or a specialist solicitor.

In some cases, victims of clinical accidents may be offered a kind of settlement called an *ex gratia* payment, but this should not be accepted unless it is completely satisfactory, and the victim does not intend to go to court. Take specialist legal advice before accepting any payments.

Work-related injuries

Almost 50% of all accidents that happen in this country take place at work. If a person is involved in an accident at work, the employer may be liable both under the common law duty to take care of people around him (i.e. the victim may be able to show the employer was negligent – see pages 115–116), but also under the Health and Safety at Work Act (1974). Under this legislation, employers who have more than a certain number of staff are obliged (among other things) to:

◆ assess the risks involved in each task an employee is asked to carry out
◆ ensure that employees are competent and that they are trained and supervised properly
◆ ensure that employees are given suitable tools, equipment and materials, and that they are trained to handle them
◆ ensure that premises are suitable for the tasks being carried out and that they do not present risks to employees
◆ record accidents that take place at work
◆ take out Employer's Liability Insurance
◆ have a policy on health and safety.

In addition, if an employee takes her employer to court because

Faulty goods

If you are injured by a product that turned out to be faulty (or food that was not fit for consumption), you may be able to bring a claim against the company that produced the product or the company that was responsible for importing it into the European Union. See page 47.

of an injury sustained at work and the employer treats her badly afterwards (for example, dismisses her, unreasonably refuses her promotion, etc.), the employee may be able take legal action (see page 165).

If you are considering taking your employer to court, a good place to start would be your trade union, if you are a member of one, or a specialist solicitor.

Illnesses contracted at work

It is now known that working in certain conditions may lead to a worker contracting a certain disease in later life. These include such diseases as asbestosis and emphysema. Because such illnesses generally occur a long time after the victim's exposure to their causes it has in the past been difficult to show causation (see pages 116–117). However, as the general evidence that connects working environments to certain diseases increases, and the number of successful claims on similar grounds rises, claims against employers are becoming more frequent. Such claims may include compensation for such illnesses as:

- repetitive strain injury (RSI)
- hearing loss due to work with noisy machinery
- work-related stress
- various respiratory disorders
- various skin disorders.

Criminal Injuries

Some injuries are caused by a criminal act. Compensation in such circumstances can be divided into two groups.

Compensation from the offender

In circumstances where a crime has been committed and the victim has sustained injuries or losses, a successful prosecution may include a claim for compensation for the victim. Such

---

Injuries caused by the police

For information on how to complain about injuries sustained while in police custody, see pages 289–290.

---

compensation is paid by the offender to the court (and the court pays it to the victim). There is (or should be) no contact between the offender and the victim during this process. Inevitably, compensation is limited to the amount the offender can reasonably afford and is very often ordered to be paid in instalments.

Compensation may be paid to cover a range of losses (not just personal injuries), including:

◆ loss of or damage to property
◆ losses due to fraud
◆ travelling expenses incurred by the victim because of the offence
◆ fees to medical practitioners
◆ damage caused by a stolen vehicle while in the hands of the offender
◆ damage to property while in the hands of the offender
◆ pain and suffering on the part of the victim.

Criminal Injuries Compensation Authority

This body assesses cases of victims injured in the course of a crime of violence, such as an assault or a rape, or similar. It also covers injuries incurred by a person helping the police to apprehend an offender. The crime must have taken place in Great Britain, and there is a time limit for applications.

The compensation is paid by the government rather than by the offender, and may be as much as £250,000 (although awards are frequently closer to the minimum tariff of £1,000).

To claim compensation in this way, the victim must report the incident to the police immediately, and should then apply to the Criminal Injuries Compensation Authority (see page 309). This can be done direct to the Authority or via a support group such as Victim Support (see page 315).

Key terms

after-the-event insurance
Insurance taken out after an injury has been sustained to cover the costs of a court case should the claimant lose. See page 122.

before-the-event insurance
Insurance taken out before an injury is sustained, perhaps as part of motor insurance or a house contents policy.

ACCIDENTS AND INJURIES

causation
Proving causation means proving that a person's actions (or non-actions) led to a specific outcome (in this case, to an injury). See pages 116–117.

claims assessor
A business that can help an accident victim bring a case to court. See page 121.

claims management company
A business that manages a claim for compensation, usually employing a solicitor to do the legal work. See pages 120–121.

clinical injury
An injury sustained during the course of a medical examination or treatment, and caused by the negligence of a medical practitioner. See pages 125–126.

compensation
Financial award made to a victim of an accident to cover losses and damage.

compensation recovery
If a victim has claimed social security benefits because of an injury and later receives compensation, the Benefits Agency may claim back the benefits already paid out before the compensation is paid over to the victim.

conditional fee agreement
Alternative term for a no-win no-fee agreement. See page 122.

contributory negligence
Negligence on the part of the victim of an accident which contributed to the likelihood of the accident happening or added to the injury sustained as a result of the accident. See page 117.

criminal injury
An injury sustained during a criminal offence, or while helping the police to deal with an offence as it takes place. See page 129.

damages
An amount of money, usually awarded as a fixed sum by a court

to a claimant who has sustained a loss because of someone else's unlawful action. See page 123.

duty of care
In very general terms, the duty an individual owes to another to take care that his actions (or non-actions) do not lead to injury to the other's person or belongings.

ex gratia **payment**
Form of compensation, paid before a personal injury case comes to court, and usually without the responsible person or organisation accepting responsibility.

medical injury
Alternative term for a clinical injury. See pages 125–127.

mitigate
Acting in such a way as to reduce the effects of something. In personal injury cases, the victim should act to mitigate the costs incurred because of an injury. That is, she should keep her outgoings as low as possible. See page 123.

negligence
Acting in such a way as to be in breach of the duty we all have not to injure other people or damage their property. Negligence also includes failures to act. See pages 115–116.

no-win no-fee agreement
Agreement with a solicitor or other provider of legal services by which the claimant only pays the practitioner's fee if the case is won. See pages 122–123.

occupier's liability
If an accident takes place on property that is not the victim's own, the 'occupier' of that property could be held liable to pay compensation. The occupier could include the owner of a residential house, an office, a shop or other business premises.

out-of-court settlement
Agreement made between two parties in a personal injury case before the case comes to court. See pages 123–124.

7 When Someone Dies

This chapter deals with one of the most unpleasant facts of life – that of our death. It covers how we can make sure our last wishes are executed, and what the law says about dividing our property if we die without making those wishes known. It also looks at the legal steps we need to take when a person dies.

The vast majority of people try not to think about dying, and as a consequence, only a small minority have thought to make plans for this eventuality. A will is a legal document with which you are able to state what you want to happen after you die. It covers the disposal of your property, the kind of 'send-off' you would like, the appointment of personal representatives and plans made for the care of dependants such as children.

If you fail to make a will, your property will be distributed according to the law, and this may mean that it is distributed in a way that you would not want.

Dying intestate

If a person dies without having made a will, he or she is said to have died 'intestate'. If this is the case, the property of that person is distributed according to rules of succession, starting with the dead person's spouse, then his children, his parents and then his other relatives in a certain order. The law on who inherits what is quite complex, and much depends on whether you leave a spouse behind. If you do leave a husband or wife behind, the following rules come into play:

- if the estate is worth less than £125,000, the spouse inherits everything.
- if the estate is worth more than £125,000 and there are children or grandchildren, the spouse inherits the 'personal chattels' (broadly, the household and personal effects), £125,000, plus a life interest in one half of the rest of the estate (that half is invested and the spouse receives the income produced by the investments. The children share the rest of the estate equally if they reach

the age of 18 or get married before they are 18, with provision for the children of any child who dies before the intestate person to take their parent's share.

◆ If no children or granchildren reach the age of 18 or marry under the age of 18, but there are parents or siblings, the spouse inherits all personal chattels, £200,000 plus one half of the rest of the estate outright. The parents and/or siblings share the rest of the estate equally.

Of course, the definitions of the word 'spouse' and of the word 'child' are very important here. A spouse is defined as someone who is legally married to the deceased, even if they are separated. But it does not include a person who has been living with the deceased (a 'cohabitee' or 'partner'), nor does it include a divorced husband or wife. (However, it is possible that a cohabiting partner, and, indeed, a divorced spouse, may inherit under the rules of dependency, see page 143.)

A 'child' is defined as a legitimate or illegitimate child and also an adopted child. But, significantly, it does not include a stepchild. Again, though, a stepchild may be able to claim some part of the estate under the rules for dependants (see page 143).

If there is no spouse (or your spouse does not live more than 28 days after your death), your property will be distributed to your relatives in the following order:

◆ your children (or their children if any child has died)
◆ your parents
◆ your brothers and sisters (or their children if your brothers and sisters have died)
◆ your half-brothers and half-sisters (or their children if your half-brothers and half-sisters have died)
◆ your grandparents
◆ your uncles and aunts
◆ your half-uncles and half-aunts.

As with the children, all the classes of relatives other than parents and grandparents take on the 'statutory trusts', which means that each individual needs to attain the age of 18 or marry under 18 to become entitled to inherit, and the children of any individual who dies before the intestate person takes the share of their parent.

Living people in higher categories take priority over people in categories below, and so do their children. For example, Andy has no wife, but leaves behind his grandfather, Arthur, and one sister, Rita. His other sister, Gina, is already dead, but she has a daughter, Maddy. In this case, Rita would inherit half the estate and Maddy would inherit the other half in place of her mother, Gina. Arthur inherits nothing because his category is excluded by the presence of living people in a higher-priority category. If Rita also had been dead, Maddy would have inherited everything.

If you die leaving no living relatives at all, your property goes to the Crown, and the personal representative should contact the Treasury Solicitor's Department (see pages 314–315).

Intestacy and property

If you own or are a protected tenant in property, things can become even more complicated.

If you own your home jointly with your deceased spouse in a joint tenancy (see page 24), the property would automatically become yours quite apart from any other entitlement you may have. If your home is owned by your deceased spouse alone, and is less than the statutory entitlement given above (see pages 132–133), you can insist that the property passes to you as part of this entitlement. If your home is worth more than your entitlement as spouse, you can insist on taking the house, but you would need to pay the difference to the estate.

If you are not married to your partner at the time of their death, you are not automatically entitled to any share in the home unless you can claim that you made significant contribution towards it, such as contribution towards the purchase price, deposit or mortgage payments.

If you are a protected tenant and you die intestate, the

Intestacy and dependants

The intestacy rules name categories of people automatically entitled to receive a share of an estate, and these are the spouse and then relatives. However, a small number of people may also be able to make a claim as dependants. See page 143.

following people are entitled to succeed to the tenancy in the following order:

- the spouse
- a cohabiting partner who was living with the tenant as husband or wife
- any member of the tenant's family who had been living with him for more than two years when he died.

Partial intestacy

It is possible to draw up a will and still die intestate. Perhaps your will is not drawn up correctly, or can be shown to be illegal in some way. Also, if one part of your will 'fails', the property with which that part of the will deals could become subject to the laws of intestacy.

Drawing up a will

The law on intestacy assumes that your nearest are your dearest, but the way the law works may not reflect what you would want to happen to your property, but more significantly, to the people you care most for, after you die. It is most important to make a will if:

- you have a significant relationship with someone to whom you are not married and you want that person to be a beneficiary of your estate
- you have a child or children for whom you want to make provision
- you want to determine who deals with your property after you die.

As long as it is prepared and witnessed correctly, a will remains valid until it is revoked. A will is invalidated in the following circumstances:

Administrating an intestacy

For information on dealing with a deceased person's estate when they do not have a will, see pages 143–144.

◆　　 if you destroy it, and clearly intend to destroy it.
◆　　 if you make a new will that clearly and expressly revokes the old will.
◆　　 if you get married (unless you say in your will that you are making it with your forthcoming marriage in mind).

If you are separated from your spouse, your will remains valid. If you are divorced, the will remains valid but the sections leaving gifts or legacies to your spouse become invalid.

It is possible to make a will simply by writing it on a piece of paper and having it properly witnessed (see page 141), but it is best to take advice, especially if you have valuable property or complex personal relationships.

Who is able to make a will?

Anyone over the age of 18 is entitled to make a will. In order to do make a legally valid will, you need to be 'of sound mind', that is, your judgement should not be clouded or impaired significantly in any way. If you suffer from any illness that makes you less capable than you would normally be, the best thing to do is to visit a doctor shortly before making your will so that he or she can attest to your soundness of mind at the time should someone decide to contest your will's validity on these grounds.

Reasons to review a will

If you wish to add new clauses to your will, it is often simply a matter of making an addition to it (called a 'codicil', see pages 141–142). However, there are certain circumstances in which you should review your will, and perhaps draw up a new one. These circumstances include:

◆　　 changes in your family, such as a birth or a death, or the occasion of a child's coming of age (in legal terms, at the age of 18)
◆　　 financial changes, including acquiring property that you would like to include specifically in your will, or having your assets rise above the threshold for tax
◆　　 your marriage. Marriage automatically makes a previous will invalid, unless that will says you are making it with your forthcoming marriage in mind
◆　　 your separation. Separation has no effect on a will, so if

your separation from your spouse or partner means you feel differently about the provision you have made for that person in your will, you should review it immediately

◆ your divorce. If you divorce your spouse, any legacy or gift to them in your will is made invalid, unless you expressly say in your will that your spouse should receive this gift or legacy regardless of whether you remain married or get divorced. If you have named your spouse as your executor, and you subsequently divorce, that person is excluded from acting in this capacity.

◆ going to live abroad. If you decide that you intend to live permanently abroad, it would probably be less complex if you make a will according to the laws of the country in which you intend to live. You are advised to seek advice from a legal practitioner in your new home country.

What does a will cover?

A will usually covers the following points:

◆ your last requests as to disposal of your body (including how it will be paid for) and perhaps organ or whole-body donation (see page 106); however, given that the will may not be read until some time after your death,

---

A soldier's will

You cannot generally make a will without writing it down. However, there is one exception to this. A member of the armed forces or a sailor at sea can, when on active duty, make an informal will, that is, a spoken will or a written will that is not witnessed. The theory behind this is that a soldier or other combatant faces death on the battlefield (however that may be defined), and so he or she may not have time to make a written will prior to facing that situation. The law covers those on their way to a war zone and those actively engaged in combat, but not those in administrative or non-combatant roles. Clearly, so-called soldier's wills are very difficult to prove.

it's important that your relatives know what your wishes are
- names of the guardians of your children, if you have any
- names of the executors of your will, that is, those people whom you trust to enact your wishes according to your will
- any specific gifts or legacies, that is, the giving of particular objects to named individuals
- your plans for the residue of your estate, that is, what remains after your legacies and gifts have been dealt with, and all other debts (such as taxes) have been paid.

Guardians for your children

If you have children under the age of 18, it is very important that you name a guardian who will look after them should you die. Obviously, you will need to discuss this very carefully with the proposed guardian - suddenly gaining a family is not to be taken lightly, and you need to be sure that your chosen guardian or guardians are happy to take on this responsibility. Often, guardians are close relatives, such as grandparents or siblings.

You may appoint a guardian to act only if both parents die, or in place of one parent, working together with the surviving parent. In the case of single mothers, the father has the right to appoint a guardian for his child only if he was married to the mother at the time of the child's birth or if he was given parental responsibility by a court of law.

There is a popular myth that godparents automatically become guardians of their godchildren should something happen to both parents. Being a godparent imposes a number of social obligations, but certainly no legal responsibility.

Appointing guardians is not to be taken lightly, especially if the potential guardian is the child's estranged parent. Seek advice from a solicitor in all cases where you wish to secure care for children after your death.

Executors

An executor is the person whose responsibility it is to see that your last wishes are carried out. It is normally best to appoint two executors, and often, this would include a close friend or member of the family (someone easy to find when you die) and a legal expert, such as a solicitor. Many people choose the solicitor who drew up their will in the first place. If you do include a solicitor as an executor, remember that this person will charge for their professional services, and that this fee will come out of your estate.

Some people appoint a third executor as a substitute should one of the first two be unable or unwilling to act for you.

Obviously, it is important to ask your chosen executor or executors if they are willing to act for you before you name them in your will. At the same time, if you are named executor to a person's will and do not wish to act on their behalf, you are not legally obliged to do so.

If you do not name an executor in your will, then the the residuary beneficiaries are normally the people who are given the authority to wind up your estate and ensure that your wishes are carried out. See pages 143–145 for more on executors and personal representatives.

Legacies

After naming guardians for children and executors, and dealing with your wishes as to burial and the donation of organs, a will would normally go on to deal with the distribution of your property - your possessions, money and other assets.

It is best to start by dealing with specific legacies - named items that are to be given to specific individuals: items of jewellery, perhaps, or other special possessions that are of more sentimental than monetary value. It is important to be as specific as possible when naming and describing each item, especially if you own more than one: 'my gold locket' is better than 'my necklace'; 'my Mini Cooper' is better than 'my car'. Equally, it is advisable to give a person's full name and relationship to you in order to be absolutely sure specific gifts go to the right person: 'my son, Andrew Martin Smith', for example.

Some lawyers advise that it is better to be more general in the naming of specific legacies ('my car' or 'all my jewellery', for example) to cover the eventuality that the specific object mentioned is no longer in your possession at the time of your death.

The remaining property, possessions and money that you have not specifically bequeathed is called the 'residue', and your will would normally go on to say who should receive what proportion of the residue after all debts and taxes have been paid. The residue is not defined as a specific sum - just everything that is left over at the end of the day. This amount may be left to just one person, or divided between two or more people. Again, make sure that the people you mention in this respect are identified clearly. If some beneficiaries are under age, a trust needs to cbe created.

Substitute beneficiaries

It may be that at the time of your death, one or more of the people named in your will have already died. A beneficiary's death is a good reason to review your will, but it is also a good idea to name 'substitute beneficiaries' if your property is particularly valuable, or you care a great deal about who should benefit from it.

If you do not name a substitute beneficiary, the legacy intended for someone who has died will become part of the residue and will therefore fall to the person you name as the beneficiary of the residue.

Leaving joint property

If you own property jointly with another person, you will need to find out whether it is owned as a 'tenancy in common' or a 'joint tenancy'. A tenancy in common means that you own a share of the property and the other person owns the other share. If this is the case, you are entitled to bequeath your half of the property in your will. If the property is held as a joint tenancy, the property will automatically pass to the person you share it with on your death, and you are not entitled to leave it to someone else.

Help with writing a will

If your assets and your family circumstances are straightforward, with no beneficiaries under 18, it may be a very simple matter to draw up your own will. However, it may still be worthwhile spending a small amount of money to have a solicitor do this work for you. At least then you will have the peace of mind that comes from knowing that your will is an accurate reflection of your wishes, and there will be as few as possible legal problems when it comes time to act on them.

Pension and insurance policy benefits

Often, pension rights and the benefits of insurance policies are ascribed to a named person (your spouse or your children), and these rights cannot be bequeathed in your will. However, it is always advisable to check with your pension or insurance provider that this is the case.

Leaving gifts and legacies to children

While it is legally possible to leave objects to children under the age of 18, minors are not allowed to inherit property, cash or other assets of this kind. If you wish to make a bequest to a child, you will need to leave it 'in trust' and appoint trustees to look after it until the child comes of age, or until the child reaches the age you stipulate. If you wish to set up a trust, it is best to talk to a solicitor when making your will.

Witnessing a will

A written will needs to be signed by you and by two independent witnesses. Witnesses to a will cannot be beneficiaries of the will, and neither can their spouses. It is wise to chose witnesses who are known to your executors so that in the event of a dispute as to the validity of the will, they can be found.

Changing your will

Throughout life, our circumstances are constantly changing, and it may be that you want to change some detail of your will without going to the trouble of writing a whole new one. It is possible to make an addition to your existing will, or expressly change a particular part of it. An addition or amendment of this kind is called a 'codicil'. The codicil should be dated and witnessed in the same way as an ordinary will. It should state very clearly that it adds to or changes a particular part of your

---

Tax thresholds and rates

Obviously, the rate of taxation and tax thresholds change from year to year, so check the current thresholds when you draw up your will, and keep an eye on them as your estate changes in value.

existing will, but that it does not take its place, and all other clauses remain the same.

You should never make changes to an existing will after it has been signed and witnessed except by codicil.

Inheritance tax

At the time of writing, the threshold for inheritance tax was £250,000. If your estate is worth less than this (after any bequests to your spouse), there will be no tax to pay on your death assuming that no substantial lifetime gifts have been made. However, if your estate is worth more than this, there will be some tax to pay, and you should consider seeking advice from a solicitor. There are some categories of gift that do not attract inheritance tax:

◆ legacies to your spouse
◆ legacies to UK charities
◆ gifts made more than seven years before the date of your death
◆ gifts worth no more than £3,000 in any one tax year
◆ gifts of business property.

Challenging a will

If you feel you do not benefit sufficiently from a will, or that

Will-writing: check points

◆ Have you stated that you intend to revoke all other past wills?
◆ Have you dated your will?
◆ Have you signed your will?
◆ Is your will signed by two independent witnesses, neither of whom are beneficiaries under the will?
◆ Have you named trustworthy executors who have told you they are willing to act on your behalf?
◆ Have you thought about specific gifts and legacies?
◆ Have you considered a beneficiary and a substitute beneficiary for the residue of your estate?
◆ Have you told people where they can find your will in the event of your death?

you don't benefit at all, and should, you may be able to challenge the will in a court of law.

A will can generally be challenged on the following grounds:

◆ that the deceased was not of sound mind when the will was made
◆ that the deceased was coerced into making the will by force, fraud or undue influence
◆ that there are suspicious circumtances surrounding the execution of the will, for example, the will benefits greatly the person who drafted it, or a close member of that person's family
◆ that the will has not taken into account the needs of the person's dependants (see below).

If you intend to challenge a will, talk to a solicitor as soon as possible after probate has been gained (see page 150) – in some cases, time limits apply.

Providing for dependants

The law allows people who consider themselves to be dependants of the deceased to claim part of the estate, even if they are not mentioned in the will, or are not entitled to a share according to the rules of intestacy. In simple terms, the court may uphold claims for 'reasonable maintenance' from the following groups of people:

◆ a spouse, ex-spouse who hasn't remarried or cohabitee
◆ a child
◆ any other person who was supported by the deceased.

If you think you may have a claim as a dependant, you must generally make your claim within six months of probate being gained or the letters of administration being issued, so contact a solicitor or Citizens Advice Bureau as soon as possible.

Your personal representative

When a person dies, someone has to take care of his or her affairs. If the deceased has made a will, this person is known as the 'executor'. If the deceased has not made a will, or the will fails to name an executor, or the executor is not willing or unable to act, then this person is known as the 'administrator'.

Of course, in life there are many things that only we can deal with - withdrawing money from a bank account, for instance, or cancelling a credit card. The first step a personal representative needs to take is to gain the authority to speak and act for the deceased person. If there is a will, the validity of the will has to be proved and the executor empowered. This is called 'gaining probate'. If there is no will, this is called 'gaining letters of administration'.

For further information on applying for probate or letters of administration, contact your local probate registry (listed in the telephone directory). Once you have this authority, you will have the power to un-freeze bank accounts and use the funds to pay all remaining bills and to act in any other way on behalf of the deceased person's estate.

Entire books have been written about how to gain probate or letters of administration and administer an estate, and the details are not within the scope of this book. However, these are some of the responsibilities you may face should you take on the task:

- ensuring that the death is suitably advertised so that creditors, especially unknown creditors, can be said to have been given notice of the winding up of the estate
- ensuring that everyone who owes money to the estate pays up, and this includes state benefits and tax rebates owed to the deceased
- checking that the assets are properly insured
- finding all those who are beneficiaries under a will, or under the rules of intestacy, and making sure that they receive their legacies and gifts
- ensuring that all taxes are paid
- notifying the relevant authorities of the death, including the Benefits Agency, the tax authorities, and relevant pension funds and insurance companies
- clearing property of possessions; ensuring pets go to suitable homes
- overseeing the sale of property, if necessary
- closing accounts, including for utilities, credit cards, bank accounts, etc.
- cancelling memberships, including clubs, societies and libraries
- arranging and paying for (from the estate) disposal of

the body according to the wishes of the deceased
◆ dealing with any claims against the estate, for example, from dependants not mentioned in a will or entitled to a legacy under the rules of intestacy, or from individuals who wish to challenge the contents of a will.

It may well be worth asking a solicitor to help with some of these tasks, particularly if the estate is large, or if there is no will. When discussing this with a solicitor, don't forget to ask for an estimate of the cost, in writing before you start. While solicitors' costs will be paid from the estate, it is up to the personal representative to ensure that as much as possible of the estate is preserved for the beneficiaries.

If you are uncertain about how to act, make your Citizens Advice Bureau your first port of call, or look at the Court Service website (see page 309).

What to do when someone dies

If someone close to you dies, your main legal duty is to ensure that the authorities have the opportunity to satisfy themselves that the death was not unlawful and that the relevant bodies are notified. As a next of kin or close friend, you will need to collect a number of forms, depending on the circumstances of the death.

If the death was expected

In the event of an expected death, you should contact the medical practitioner who attended the deceased. If she is satisfied that the causes of the death were natural, then she will issue two documents:

◆ the Medical Certificate, which will be given to you in a sealed envelope addressed to the Registrar of Births, Marriages and Deaths

---

Organ donation

If the deceased has made it known that he or she wishes to donate part of all of his or her body, the next of kin should be consulted. See page 106.

♦ the Formal Notice, which tells you that the doctor has signed the Medical Certificate and advice on how to go about getting the death registered.

If the death was unexpected

If the death was sudden, or you discover a death, you should contact the police immediately. Avoid touching anything in the immediate vicinity of the body until the police arrive.

The other people who will need to be contacted are: the deceased's medical practitioner, their next of kin and their minister of religion.

When the medical practitioner arrives, she will try to determine the cause of death. If this is straightforward, and considered to be from natural causes, she may issue the medical Certificate and Formal notice on the spot. However, she may wish to order a post-mortem examination of the body to be absolutely certain of the cause of death. In this case, she must ask permission of the next of kin.

The role of the coroner

In some cases, the medical practitioner will report the death to the coroner. These cases include:

♦ uncertain cause of death
♦ death from an industrial disease
♦ the deceased was not attended by the medical practitioner within 14 days of the death
♦ the death was violent, or not natural, or occurred under suspicious circumstances
♦ the death occurred during surgery or under anaesthetic
♦ the death occurred in prison or in police custody.

The coroner may order a post-mortem (for which he does not need the permission of the next of kin), and the relatives are entitled to have a doctor represent them at the examination.

If the coroner's post-mortem shows that the death was due to natural causes, the coroner will issue a form called the Pink Form B, with which the death can be registered. This may be sent directly to the Registrar or it may be given to the next of kin to register. If you intend to have the body cremated, you will receive a Certificate of Cremation.

However, if there is any doubt as to the cause of death, the coroner may order an inquest in order to enquire into the causes and circumstances surrounding the death. The next of kin are entitled to examine witnesses at an inquest. There will definitely be an inquest in the following circumstances:

◆ the death was violent, or not natural
◆ the death was caused by an industrial disease
◆ the cause of death is still uncertain after the post-mortem examination.

After the inquest, you may receive one of the following forms:

◆ Order for Burial, which will enable you to start funeral preparations
◆ Certificate for Cremation, which will entitle you to cremate the body
◆ Certificate after Inquest, which is sent directly to the Registry, enabling the death to be registered.

Registering a death

Every death must be registered with the Registry of Birth, Marriages and Deaths for the district in which the death took place. You can register a death in a different district and the information will be sent on to the correct place.

Every death must be registered within 5 days, although there are some exceptions.

When registering a death you will need the Medical Certificate stating the cause of death, or the coroner's Pink Form B, or the coroner's Certificate after Inquest. The last two of these may already have been sent directly to the Registry by the coroner. You should also take with you the deceased

---

Claims for compensation

If the deceased dies in an accident or in some other circumstance for which you could claim compensation, you should contact a solicitor immediately. It is important for you to be represented at the inquest if you intend to make such a claim.

person's birth and marriage certificates, if you can find them. You will be asked the following questions, and it helps if you have made a note of the answers beforehand:

- ◆ the full name (including maiden name if relevant) and usual address of the deceased
- ◆ the date the death took place, and where
- ◆ the deceased's date of birth and place of birth
- ◆ the full name of the deceased's spouse, and their date and place of birth
- ◆ the occupations of both the deceased and their spouse
- ◆ whether the deceased was receiving state benefits or state pension.

You will receive two certificates: the Certificate of Registration of Death and the Certificate for Burial or Cremation (unless you have already received one from the coroner).

You will not normally be issued with a Death Certificate (a copy of the entry of death made in the Registry), but you will find it very useful when it comes to winding up the deceased's estate, so remember to ask for it. There is a small fee to pay, and it's best to order multiple copies.

Registering a stillbirth

If your baby is stillborn, you will receive a Medical Certificate of Stillbirth from your midwife or doctor. You must take this to the registrar as for any death within 5 days. You may enter a name for the child in the registry, and the registrar will give you

---

Moving a body from England or Wales

You may wish to move a body to another country for burial or cremation. In order to do this you will need permission from the coroner (regardless of the circumstances of the death). You must have obtained the permission at least four days before you need to move the body, and it comes in the form of a Removal Notice. You will also require permission to take it into your country of choice. Enquire at the embassy or consulate of the country in question.

---

two certificates: the Certificate for Burial or Cremation and the Certificate of Registration of Stillbirth.

Funerals and cremations

There are three options when it comes to laying a loved-one to rest. You may choose burial, cremation or burial at sea. However, there are no laws governing the form of funeral service. You do not need to have a ceremony, you do not need a religious minister or use a funeral director, and there are no rules governing the place where the service (if you choose to have one) may take place.

Burial at sea

Burial at sea is regulated as to location, and you will need special permission for this kind of send-off. Ask a funeral director for advice or contact the Marine Environmental Protection Agency (see page 312).

Key terms

administrator
A person who ensures that the estate of someone who dies intestate is wound up according to the law. Essentially the same as an executor.

beneficiary
A person who benefits from a gift or legacy under the terms of a will.

bequest
A gift given to someone in a will.

codicil
A written addition or change to a will. See page 141.

estate
The possessions, assets, property and cash left by a person at their death.

executor
A person who ensures that the terms of a will are acted upon. See pages 138–139.

intestate
Dying without having made a will. See pages 132–135.

legatee
A person who receives a legacy, that is, a gift in a will.

living will
A document in which a person records his or her wishes in the event that he or she becomes incapacitated by illness. See page 105.

personal representative
Anyone who acts on behalf of a deceased person to wind up their affairs. The phrase includes both administrators who act for people who die intestate and executors, who execute the terms of a person's will. See pages 143–145.

probate
The process of proving that a will is valid.

residue
The balance of any possessions, assets, property or cash after any specific gifts or legacies have been distributed and any taxes and debts have been paid. See pages 139–140.

testator
The legal term for the person who writes a will.

will
A properly signed and witnessed legal document in which a person records his or her wishes for the distribution of property and for burial or cremation after death. See pages 135–143.

8 Offences Against Property and the Person

This chapter takes a look at some very serious offences. For ease of use, it is divided into two sections: a list of some of the offences that may affect ordinary people; and a section on how to stay within the law if you find yourself confronted with someone who is seemingly intent on doing harm either to your person or to your property, and what support you may be able to find as a victim of a crime.

SOME OFFENCES

The offences described below are listed alphabetically for ease of reference.

Actual bodily harm (ABH)

Causing injury to someone, with a resulting relatively minor injury. The offence's full title is 'assault occasioning actual bodily harm', and it falls under the Offences Against the Person Act (1861). ABH can be tried either in a Magistrates' Court or in the Crown Court. In the Crown Court, the maximum penalty is five years' imprisonment. Compare this with assault (see below) and with grievous bodily harm (see page 153).

Arson

Under the Criminal Damage Act (1971), arson is the destruction or damage of property by fire. Tried in the Crown Court, the maximum penalty for arson is life imprisonment.

Assault

Sometimes known as 'common assault', assault is the least serious of three similar offences, which include actual bodily harm (see above) and grievous bodily harm (see 153). An assault can range from verbal abuse and physically threatening behaviour through unwanted physical contact to actual physical assault. Making someone fear that they will be hurt by the offender may also be classed as an assault, depending on the circumstances. Common assault is generally tried in a Magistrates' Court and the maximum penalty is six months' imprisonment and/or a fine of £5,000.

Burglary

Burglary is defined as entering a building as a trespasser and:

◆ doing unlawful damage, or
◆ stealing property, or
◆ assaulting (including raping) someone inside.

Burglary is an offence under the Theft Act (1968), and under this Act, the burglar may be committing this offence even if he is not successful – the intention or the attempt is enough. Burglary is tried either in a Magistrates' Court or in the Crown Court. In the Crown Court, and the maximum sentence is 10 years' imprisonment if the target building is a commercial or industrial space and 14 years if it is a private residence.

Aggravated burglary is the offence of burglary committed with the addition that the offender was at the time carrying either: explosives, an offensive weapon, a firearm or an imitation firearm.

For information on what to do if there has been a burglary, see page 154.

Conspiracy

Under the Criminal Law Act (1977), amended by the Criminal Attempts Act (1981), conspiracy is the discussion among two or more people in which they agree that one or all of them will commit an offence. Conspiracy is applicable whether or not the offence is actually carried out. Trials for conspiracy take place in the Crown Court and sentences are the same as for the offence that was the subject of the conspiracy.

Criminal damage

Under the Criminal Damage Act (1971), criminal damage is the unlawful destruction or damage of property or the threatened destruction or damage of property. Criminal damage can include disfiguring property with graffiti. Lawful damage of property may take place if the damage takes place in order to protect neighbouring property in an emergency, e.g. a fire that threatens to spread.

OFFENCES AGAINST PROPERTY AND THE PERSON

A Magistrates' Court hears cases of criminal damage in which the damage amounts to sums below £5,000. Here, the maximum sentence is three months' imprisonment and/or a fine of up to £2,500. Magistrates also have the power to order payment of compensation up to a maximum of £5,000.

If the damage amounts to more than this, the case will be heard in either a Magistrates' Court or in the Crown Court. In this case, the maximum sentence is 10 years' imprisonment and/or an unlimited fine. The Court may also order payment of compensation to cover the damage.

Going equipped

This offence under the Theft Act (1968) refers to offenders who are found carrying tools that they intend to use to commit an act of theft, such as burglary. The tools would need to have been adapted for the purpose, and if they were not adapted, the prosecution would have to show that, in all probability, there is an intention to commit the offence. This offence is tried in the Crown Court, and the maximum penalty is three years' imprisonment.

Grievous bodily harm (GBH)

Causing a major injury to someone. This is an offence under the Offences Against the Person Act (1861). The courts make a distinction between GBH with intent and GBH without intent, which basically means either that the offender meant to cause a serious injury or that he did not. GBH with intent can only be tried in the Crown Court, and it attracts a maximum sentence of life imprisonment. GBH can be tried either in a Magistrates' Court or in the Crown Court. In the Crown Court, it attracts a maximum sentence of five years' imprisonment. Compare this offence with actual bodily harm (see page 151) and with assault (see pages 152–153).

Harassment

Under the Protection from Harassment Act (1997), harassment is defined as a set of behaviours that threaten or harass an individual. There are actually two offences here. One is simply behaviour that amounts to harassment. The second, more serious, offence includes behaviour that causes another person to become fearful that there may be a violent outcome. The key difference is that the offender knew or ought to have known that his actions would bring about this fear.

Burglary Action Plan

The police advise on the following course of action:

◆ If you find that the burglar is still on the premises, leave the building and dial 999 immediately. If you don't have a mobile phone, go to a neighbour's house and ask to use their phone. Request the police and explain that there seems to be a burglary in progress.

◆ Do not tackle an intruder, but if you have an opportunity to observe him, make a mental note of height, hair colour, clothing and any features that might identify him later.

◆ If the burglar has already left the premises, do not touch anything. Call the local police station and wait for investigating officers to arrive. They should give you a crime reference number for use in any insurance claim.

◆ Check whether credit cards or cheque books have been stolen. Contact the issuers immediately to cancel them. The same applies to mobile phones.

◆ Check whether your passport or other primary identification documents (see page 277) have been stolen. If so, report them to the issuing authority immediately. For advice on avoiding identity theft, see pages 280–282.

◆ Make a note of any items that have been stolen. If you have details of serial numbers, models and makes, note these down as well.

◆ Make a note of any damage to your home. Have any damage to access points repaired immediately. At the same time, review security and, if possible, improve it. Many burglars return to the same premises more than once in a short space of time. The Home Office publishes a booklet with good advice on securing your home against burglars (see page 311), and the Crime Prevention unit at your local police station will also be able to advise.

◆ Contact your insurance company, explain what has happened, and start the claim process moving.

OFFENCES AGAINST PROPERTY AND THE PERSON

The simple form of harassment is tried in a Magistrates' Court, where it attracts a maximum sentence of six months imprisonment and/or a fine of up to £5,000. Where the victim is led to fear for her safety, the offence may be tried either in a Magistrates' Court or in the Crown Court. In the Crown Court, the maximum penalty is five years' imprisonment.

Incitement

Incitement is essentially persuading or encouraging another person to commit an offence, whether or not that offence is in the event committed. Incitement cases are tried in the court in which the offence itself would be tried. In a Magistrates' Court, the maximum sentence is the same as for the offence itself. In the Crown Court, the sentence is at the court's discretion.

Indecent assault

Under the Sexual Offences Act (1956), it is an offence to assault either a man or a woman with the intention that the assault is indecent. What is indecency? Anything a court believes a reasonable person would consider indecent. Under the Children Act (1960), it is an offence to commit an act of gross indecency towards or with a child under 16, or to incite a child to commit an act of gross indecency.

Manslaughter

Killing another person either with or without intending to. There are several types of manslaughter, grouped as 'voluntary manslaughter' and 'involuntary manslaughter'. For either, the maximum sentence is life imprisonment.

In a murder trial, a person may be found not guilty of murder, but guilty of voluntary manslaughter for one of three reasons:

- the killing came about because the offender was provoked to the point where he suddenly and temporarily lost control of himself, and provocation was enough to make any reasonable person lose control
- the killing was part of a suicide pact and was acted out with the full intention that the killer himself would also die in the process
- the killer could not be held responsible for his act because of an abnormality of mind; this is not the same as being found not guilty of murder because of insanity.

Involuntary manslaughter comes in three different shapes:

♦ constructive manslaughter is causing the death of a person by an unlawful act. The act need not be against the person, but could, for example, be against a building; and the risk of injury needs to be one that would be apparent to any reasonable person, whether it was apparent to the defendant or not

♦ gross negligence manslaughter is causing the death of a person for whom the accused has a duty of care (e.g. a doctor to his patient) by an act or a failure to act

♦ reckless manslaughter is causing the death of a person by an act of recklessness; the offender sees the risk associated with what he is doing and carries on regardless.

Murder

Killing another person, with, in that immortal and well-known phrase, 'malice aforethought'. For a killing to be considered murder, the killer must intend either to cause the victim's death or to commit grievous bodily harm (which then brought about the victim's death). Murder may be committed either through a positive act of killing, or through an act of omission.

British citizens who commit murder in foreign countries are guilty of an offence under UK law, and may be tried in this country. Those in the armed forces who kill an enemy in time of war are generally not considered to be committing murder, although the story would be different if the victim were a prisoner of war.

A conviction for murder carries with it a mandatory life sentence.

Knives and other offensive weapons

Under the Prevention of Crime Act (1953), an offensive weapon is defined as any object that is a weapon or has been adapted for use as a weapon (e.g. a household tool that has been sharpened to a point) or is intended for use as a weapon. So, a flick knife can only be an offensive weapon, and the same can be said for a handgun. But a hammer only becomes an offensive weapon if it is the person's intention to use it as such. Under this law, it is an offence to carry an offensive weapon in a public place without 'lawful authority' (e.g. an armed serviceman) or without a good excuse. It is up to the person carrying the object to prove that they had a good excuse. (Note that carrying a weapon for the purposes of self-defence is not considered a reasonable excuse.) There are some exceptions to the general principle. It is not an offence to carry a weapon if:

◆   it is a tool of a person's trade
◆   it is worn as part of a national costume
◆   it is carried for religious reasons.

This offence is tried either in a Magistrates' Court or in the Crown Court. In a Magistrates' Court, the maximum sentence would be a maximum £5,000 fine and/or a six-month prison sentence. In the Crown Court, the maximum sentences rises to two years' imprisonment.

The Criminal Justice Act (1988) made it an offence to carry any article with a sharp point or a blade in a public place. The exceptions are as above, and again, the burden or proof lies with the person carrying the object. This offence is tried either in a Magistrates' Court or in the Crown Court. In the Crown Court, the maximum is two years' imprisonment.

Under the Knives Act (1997), it is an offence to carry a knife with a blade that is more than 3in (7.6cm) long in public without having a good reason. Smaller knives, such as pocket knives are exempt, but carrying a smaller knife in a public place may lead to prosecution under the Prevention of Crime Act or the Criminal Justice Act (see above).

Under the Offensive Weapons Act (1996) it is an offence to sell or advertise for sale any weapon that is designed to cause injury or that is adapted for causing injury. It is also an offence to sell any of the following to young people under the age of 16:

Warning!

Every case, whether criminal or civil, is different. The information given in this book is not intended to be a substitute for 'live' legal advice which takes specific circumstances and details into account. Do not attempt to take any legal action without consulting a qualified lawyer or advisor.

♦ any highly pointed object, or any object that has been adapted for causing injury
♦ any knife with a blade of more than 3in (7.6cm) or a blade (including some razor blades)
♦ an axe.

Racially aggravated offences

It is a criminal offence to attack or abuse a person because of their race or religious beliefs or to incite racial hatred. Such attacks and abuse include: attacking a person or their family, attacking or damaging their property, threatening or abusing them verbally, or publishing abusive material.

Rape

Under the Sexual Offences Act (1956), rape is an act of forcible sexual intercourse with either a man or a woman, without the consent of the victim. It is an offence for a man to rape either a man or a woman, but under the law, a woman is not capable of committing rape. The offence of rape covers forcible sexual intercourse within marriage. Tried in the Crown Court, a rape conviction carries a maximum sentence of life imprisonment.

Robbery

Robbery is defined as taking property from a person accompanied with threats of violence or actual violence to the victim. It is an offence under the Theft Act (1968), and the maximum sentence if convicted is seven years' imprisonment.

Theft

Under the Theft Act (1968), theft is an act of taking another person's property dishonestly and without the intention of returning it. This offence is tried in the Crown Court and the maximum sentence is seven years' imprisonment. Compare this with the offence or robbery (see above) and the offence of burglary (see page 152).

Car-related offences

For information on offences related to motoring, such as aggravated vehicle-taking, see pages 208–214.

OFFENCES AGAINST PROPERTY AND THE PERSON

Trespass

Trespass is roughly defined as entering the property of someone else without permission and without a lawful reason. This is a civil wrong and not a criminal offence. In some instances, trespass is a criminal offence, but this rarely relates to private residences.

Owners of private property may ask those who have unlawfully come onto that property to leave, and use reasonable force to make them leave. (See page 160 for a discussion of 'reasonable force'.) The landowner can sue for compensation if any damage is caused, and against persistent trespassers, the landowner may be able to get a court injunction to put an end to the trespass. See page 236 for more on property rights.

Under the Criminal Justice and Public Order Act (1994), there is a related offence of aggravated trespass, in which the offender enters private land ('in the open air') with the intention of threatening people who are going about their lawful business on that land or trying to prevent them doing so. This offence generally comes up in relation to the activities of protesters.

DEFENDING YOURSELF OR YOUR PROPERTY

In general, everyone wants to be safe in their own home and when out and about. But occasionally, we are confronted with a person who wants to do us or our property harm. The law on self-defence and defence of one's property and family are not as straightforward as one might imagine, given this fundamental need of all of us to want to protect ourselves and our nearest and dearest.

Rape Crisis

For support, information and advice if you have been the victim of rape or sexual abuse of any kind, contact the Rape Crisis Federation, which can put you in touch with a local centre for support and advice. See page 314 for contact details.

OFFENCES AGAINST PROPERTY AND THE PERSON

Reasonable force

In very general terms, the basic principle of the common law of self-defence is the use of 'reasonable force'. This means that a person may lawfully fight back when confronted with an assailant or someone intent on doing harm, but he must use no more force than he considers necessary to defend himself, his property or other people. A person therefore has a defence for assaulting an attacker if he had a genuine belief that his actions were a reasonable response to the attack at the time the attack took place.

Of course, the moot point is what is to be considered 'reasonable'. And, as with each and every case, whether criminal or civil, circumstances differ and so may the outcome of any court case.

In a case in which a person prosecuted for assaulting an intruder (for instance) pleads self-defence, it is left to a jury to decide whether the action taken was reasonable in the circumstances. Unlike other 'reasonableness' tests, the jury would have to be convinced that the defendant thought his actions reasonable at the time, in the heat of the moment, and not necessarily that a reasonable person (not in that situation) would consider his actions reasonable. It is clear that a householder who knocked an intruder down and then proceeded to kick him while was on the floor out of anger or the desire, in the heat of the moment, to punish him, would be unlikely to find his actions considered 'reasonable force' in court.

Reasonable force may also be used by police officers and the public in the prevention of crime, the apprehension of a person committing a criminal act or a prisoner on the run. It may even extend to the use of a guard dog in some circumstances (but see the section on occupier's liability, below).

Citizen's arrest

Ordinary members of the public are generally considered to have the power to arrest another member of the public if a serious criminal offence has been committed or there is an immediate danger of someone being hurt. In making a citizen's arrest, only reasonable force should be used, and in general, it seems, the police prefer to advise members of the public to exercise caution rather than trying on the mantle of the 'have-a-go hero'.

OFFENCES AGAINST PROPERTY AND THE PERSON

Occupier's liability

Under the rules of occupier's liability, owners of property, including ordinary householders, have a duty of care to ensure the safety of people on their property, and occupiers may be liable to pay compensation if anyone is injured while on their property.

This duty of care even extends to people who are trespassing, including burglars or those intent on doing harm. However, categories of unwanted visitors such as burglars usually get short shrift in the courts unless there is a strong case that the occupier set out on a course of action that would inevitably lead to injuring someone. Equally, a person who keeps a vicious dog to deter intruders and does not advertise this fact at every opportunity may also be liable for injuries the dog actually caused to an intruder, depending on the circumstances.

Victim support

Many people take legal situations in their stride, but some, especially those who have been involved with serious offences against the person, such as rape, assault and burglary, can be left feeling violated, vulnerable and confused. All these are understandable and common responses to what are, essentially (if not legally) crimes of violence. Various organisations can help victims of crime (even, in some cases, if that crime has not been reported or an offender apprehended). They include the legal system's Victim Support organisation.

Victim Support is a national charitable organisation dedicated to offering support, advice and practical help to those affected by crime. See page 315 for contact details.

Victim Support works closely with the police and the Home Office. They run a helpline for a first contact, and can offer a range of local services, free of charge, including:

Criminal Injuries Compensation

For information on how a victim of a criminal offence can gain financial compensation for their injuries, through the Criminal Injuries Compensation system, see pages 128–129.

◆   a Witness Service, which supports those asked to give evidence in court, including giving information on what will happen in court, arranging visits to the courtroom in advance of the hearing to make witnesses less uneasy about appearing, ensuring that witnesses have a private place to wait before giving evidence (going some way towards ensuring that they do not come face-to-face with, for example, an attacker, in the court building)

◆   a counselling service, which offers the victim a person to talk to about the offence and the concerns, fears and feelings that have arisen from it, and a debriefing session after the victim has given evidence.

Key terms

balance of probabilities

In some court cases, the prosecution merely has to show that the offence was, in all probability, committed. This can be contrasted with the standard of proof in which the prosecution must be sure that there is no reasonable doubt that the crime was committed by the defendant.

beyond a reasonable doubt

When weighing up a case, a jury must, in some circumstances, decide whether it has been proved to a standard that leaves no room for a reasonable doubt to creep into their minds. If there is a reasonable doubt that the defendant committed the crime, the jury must acquit the accused.

breaking and entering

Alternative term for burglary. See page 152.

Help in a crisis

For information on other organisations that may be able to help during a crisis see the list of useful addresses on pages 307–315.

OFFENCES AGAINST PROPERTY AND THE PERSON

burden of proof

The need to prove a case in court. In some cases it is up to the prosecution to prove that someone committed a certain offence, in other cases it is up to the defence to prove that there was no offence committed. Some cases have to be proved 'beyond a reasonable doubt' (see page 162) whereas others need to be proved only on the 'balance of probabilities' (see page 162).

express malice aforethought

The legal term given, in murder cases, to the intention to kill someone. See page 156.

homicide

Umbrella term that covers any of a number of offences that involve the unlawful killing of another person, such as murder, manslaughter and infanticide (the killing of an infant).

implied malice aforethought

The legal term given, in murder cases, to the intention to commit grievous bodily harm. See page 156.

indictable offence

Offence that is tried in the Crown Court, on indictment, rather than on a summons. The majority of serious criminal offences (such as murder, manslaughter and rape) are indictable offences.

malice aforethought

An action taken with the intention to do harm: either to kill someone, or to commit grievous bodily harm. This is different from the concept of 'premeditation', which is found in US law, but not in the law of England and Wales. See page 156.

offence triable either way

Offence that may be tried either in the Crown Court or in a Magistrates' Court (the accused may make this decision). Offences such as carrying an offensive weapon are triable either way.

reasonable force

The amount of force necessary, but no more. See page 160.

summary offence

Offence that is tried not in the Crown Court, but in a Magistrates' Court, on a summons, rather than an indictment. Many motoring offences, for example, are summary offences.

9 At Work

Employment legislation in England and Wales has come a long way since the days of Charles Dickens, when children worked long shifts, industrial accidents were commonplace, summary dismissal at the whim of the employer was a constant threat, and having your wages stopped to pay for candles and firewood was normal. Today's employment law lays down the rights of the employee in most areas of working life, reducing opportunities for exploitation, improving the working environment and working practices, and ensuring that employees and employers have avenues through which to pursue claims for all sorts of disagreements and injustices.

Victimisation and dismissal

Two terms appear constantly throughout any discussion of employment law. The first is the concept of 'victimisation'. Very broadly, any employee has the right to exercise his or her employment rights without being victimised for doing so. Exercising your rights includes complaining to your employer if you feel you are being treated badly, and bringing an action against your employer.

Victimisation covers a multitude of actions and events, including: passing you over for promotion, not including you on training schemes offered to others, not giving you a pay rise. If you feel you have been victimised because you have exercised your rights, you may be able to make a claim at an employment tribunal, and you should seek advice immediately because time limits apply.

Just as you are entitled to exercise your employment rights without being victimised for doing so, you are also entitled to

---

Warning!

Claims must be made within three months of dismissal or redundancy. So seek advice immediately.

---

do this without fear that you will be dismissed. Three terms arise when thinking about dismissal: unfair dismissal, wrongful dismissal and constructive dismissal.

If you have been unfairly dismissed you may be able to make a claim to an employment tribunal. You can ask to have your old job back (reinstatement), to be re-employed but in a different job (re-engagement) or for compensation. You must make your claim within three months of the dismissal taking place. Normally you must have worked for your employer for at least a year in order to bring a claim for unfair dismissal, and some workers are not entitled to bring a claim of this sort at all. If you feel you have been unfairly treated, seek advice immediately.

Wrongful dismissal relates only to rights given to you in your contract of employment. So, for example, your contract may guarantee you a certain notice period, and if your employer dismisses you without notice you may be entitled to make a claim for wrongful dismissal. Again, time limits apply, so seek advice immediately.

It may be that you are forced to resign from your job because of something that has happened, because your employer has essentially shown that he does not intend to stand by the contract he has made with you. If this happens, you may be able to make a claim for unfair dismissal at an employment tribunal A situation like this is known as 'constructive dismissal'.

Before you take action of any sort, always seek advice. Good sources of advice are: your union representative if you have one, your Citizens Advice Bureau, a local law centre or a solicitor. If you have a situation that you think can be resolved amicably, talk to your company's personnel manager first – he or she should act as an arbitrator in any minor dispute. But always remember that personnel staff act ultimately in the interests of the company and these interests and yours may not always coincide.

Employee status

To be part of the legal network of rights and responsibilities, you need to be a bona fide employee, as opposed to someone who is self-employed. Some employers try to insist that people working for them are self-employed, thus avoiding the need to pay National Insurance contributions and denying the employee other benefits of employment, such as notice periods and redundancy pay.

How do you know whether you are an employee? In general, the law considers you to be an employee if you:

◆ are paid a regular amount of money at regular intervals, rather than being paid by the job or task
◆ are given work to do by the employer rather than having to find work for yourself
◆ use tools and equipment supplied by the employer, rather than bringing or using your own
◆ do not have the responsibility of finding someone else to do the work if you can't.

Even if you are a trainee or are on probation, you are probably still an employee if you have answered yes to the questions above. By contrast, self-employed people usually:

◆ have to find their own work, often from several different employers, customers or clients
◆ are paid when they complete a particular job, and often have to send an invoice or bill before they get paid
◆ have to supply their own tools and equipment
◆ can use other people to do the work, for example, if they do not have the required skills, are too busy, or fall ill.

If you are unclear what your employment status is, you should seek advice at your local Citizens Advice Bureau or law centre.

If you are not an employee, you may be self-employed or perhaps an agency worker (such as a temporary office worker, for example). If you are an agency worker, you may still be considered an employee, not of the company or companies you actually work in, but of the agency that sent you. However, this may not always be the case, and agency workers are advised to be certain of their employment status from day one.

Changing your status to self-employed

If you are employed and your employer asks you to change your status to self-employed, seek advice immediately. Your employer may effectively be making you redundant, and you may be entitled to redundancy pay. If your contract changes but not your relationship with your employer, you may still be considered to be employed and therefore eligible for all the rights, benefits and legal protection that the 'employed' label brings.

Part-time workers

If you do not work full-time, you are still entitled to be treated in the same way as a full-time worker unless your employer has a justification for treating you differently. So you are entitled to the same rates of pay, the same access to promotion and training, the same benefits when you are sick or on maternity leave, the same access to company pensions and other occupational benefits such as parental leave. Do remember, though, that pay, holiday and other benefits will be offered in proportion to the amount of time you work. So, if you work half time, you will only be entitled to 50% of the holiday entitlement of a full-time worker.

If you are considering making a claim against an employer whom you feel has treated you differently to someone working full-time and doing a similar job, you will need to be able to compare the treatment you have received with someone else. Before you take any steps, take advice from your union, CAB or law centre.

Employers' and employees rights

When you become an employee, you agree to work for the employer in return for certain benefits. In general, the employer should be able to expect the following from you:

- personal service (i.e. you cannot send someone else to do the job if you can't or won't);
- a reasonable degree of loyalty
- honesty in your dealings with the company and your colleagues
- confidentiality (i.e. keeping confidential the details of the business in which you are working).

In return, the employee has many rights under the law. These are called statutory rights and include:

- the right to a statement of the terms of employment,
- the right to work in a safe and healthy environment,
- the right not to be discriminated against,
- or to be unlawfully dismissed from the job.

Employees also have a duty not to breach the trust and confidence of their employers.

Your contract of employment

Your employer must by law give you a written statement of the terms under which you are employed within two months of your first day, regardless of whether you work full or part-time. The statement should cover at least the following basic points:

- your employer's full name and address
- your place of work
- the date the job began, and whether the time you did in any previous job (perhaps with a subsidiary company or in an overseas branch) counts towards your length of service with the company
- your job title or a job description
- your hours of work
- how much you will be paid, how often you will be paid and whether and when your pay will be reviewed
- if the employment is for a fixed period, the statement must give the date it will end
- your holidays
- what pay you will be entitled to if you fall sick
- details of any pension scheme
- notice periods
- disciplinary and grievance procedures
- whether you are expected to work outside the UK, and if so, in what currency you will be paid.

A full contract of employment may in addition include:

- maternity and paternity arrangements
- a code of conduct, perhaps as regards dealing with customers
- equal opportunities statement and practice

Employment agency commissions

It is illegal for a recruitment consultant or employment agency to charge you, the employee, a commission when finding you a job. Seek legal advice if any agency tries to charge you in this way.

- ◆ compassionate leave arrangements
- ◆ benefits such as loans, cars, etc.
- ◆ policy on use of communications equipment, such as telephones and e-mail
- ◆ restrictive clauses (e.g. restricting your activities should you leave the company).

If you do not receive a statement or contract within two months, you have a right to request one without fear of being dismissed. If you do not receive a statement, an employment tribunal could be asked to determine what particulars would have been included on it.

Statutory rights

No employer is allowed to contract with you to waive your statutory employment rights - those given to you by the law. So, for instance, every full-time employee is entitled to four weeks paid holiday including bank holidays. If your contract states two weeks, it doesn't make the contract illegal, it simply makes that part of the contract null and void. Other examples: you cannot contract to be paid less than the minimum wage, or to waive your rights under the Health and Safety at Work legislation (see pages 182–184). Whatever your contract says on these points, in most cases the law overrules it. Of course, an employer can always offer you better terms than the basic minimum requirement, but rarely the other way around.

The terms of your contract – express and implied

Even though the law places great emphasis on the written statement of terms, this is not the only way in which you may be said to have an agreement with your employer. Your statement of contract gives what are known as the 'express

---

Work and children

For information about the legalities of employing school children and on the responsibilities of employers of children, see pages 88–91. This section also includes information on regulations to do with children taking part in public performances.

terms' of your agreement – the terms that are written out and specifically agreed on at the time your employment begins. But other express terms may be agreed verbally in negotiations, found in letters you receive from your employer, or perhaps in a company handbook or announcement pinned to a company noticeboard. Always keep safe any correspondence or paperwork you receive from your employer, even if you have a written contract or statement.

The law also recognises other terms of your employment not explicitly stated anywhere. These are called implied terms and include the duty of trust (an employee should not sell commercial secrets to competing companies, for example), and the duty to obey reasonable instructions from the employer. Such terms also include any agreements made between the employer and a trade union or employees' forum or association, and any agreements made by 'custom and practice'. Custom and practice refers to terms that have arisen through simply happening again and again, to the point of becoming a tradition, rather than being expressly agreed. For example, the employer has given employees a Christmas bonus every year for the last so many years. It could be argued, therefore, that this bonus is so regular as to have become part of the standard remuneration package, and it is conceivable that employees could mount a claim if the bonus were suddenly revoked.

Illegal contracts

A contract of employment is illegal if you:

Verbal contracts

In any employment situation, there will always be a contract, even if there is no written agreement. A verbal contract includes what the employee and employer have said to each other, and the substance of the contract can be inferred from a number of other documents. Always make a note (with the date) of any verbal agreement you make with your employer. Keep the original job advertisement, if there was one. Keep all correspondence you have with your employer. These can all show the various things you have agreed with the employer.

- are being contracted to do something illegal or immoral; or
- agree to have some or all of your wages paid cash-in-hand without tax or National Insurance being deducted.

Changing the terms of a contract

Your employer may wish to change the terms of your contract - perhaps to reduce your pay or increase your working hours. Obviously, an employer generally cannot change the terms of your contract without your agreement, but he could dismiss you (terminating the contract) and then take you on immediately under the new contract. To be inside the law, the employer would have to observe all the rules regarding such things as notice periods.

You may also be able to bring a claim of unfair or wrongful dismissal if your employer has acted against your statutory or contractual rights. Seek advice as soon as you can.

The national minimum wage

Almost every employee over the age of 18 has the right to be paid the national minimum wage from day one of their employment.

Those not entitled to claim the minimum wage are as follows:

- anyone aged under 18
- apprentices aged 19-25 and in their first year of apprenticeship; in their second year, those under 22 are entitled to the 'youth rate' of minimum wage (see below), and those over 22 are entitled to the full rate; apprentices over the age of 26 qualify for the full rate of minimum wage regardless of which year of their apprenticeship they are serving

Workers from outside the UK

For information on coming to the UK to work, work permits, the dangers of employing illegal workers, etc., see pages 267–271.

- nannies and au pairs who 'live in', and whose board, lodging and other expenses are met by their employer, are not entitled to the minimum wage
- those living in the household who help to run the family business
- members of the armed forces; with the exception of civilian staff in administrative roles
- share fishermen
- those serving custodial (prison) sentences
- volunteer workers
- some trainees on government schemes
- those working as part of their first degree or teacher training course
- people who live and work in religious communities
- people who are self-employed
- those who are homeless or living in a hostel, are claiming certain benefits, and are taking part in a back-to-work scheme run by a charity.

There are variations in how much the minimum wage is, depending on age. At the time of writing:

- those aged 18-21 are entitled to the 'youth rate', £3.60 per hour
- those aged 22 and over are entitled to the 'standard rate' of £4.20 per hour, and

---

References

Employers are becoming increasingly wary about giving references for past employees. If you as a past employer give a poor reference, you may lay yourself open to allegations of defamation. If you fail to mention important facts (or misrepresent them), and the new employer, having relied on your reference subsequently suffers a loss relating to it, you may be liable in negligence. A good policy, therefore, is simply to confirm the objective facts of the employee's work: their job title, period of employment, etc., and state that it is a company policy not to comment on past employees' work or character.

♦ those aged 22 and over, but classed as trainees, are entitled to the 'trainee rate' of £3.60. This includes people who have been working for their employer for less than six months, and who are on a recognised ('accredited') training scheme.

The minimum wage changes from year to year, and some rules relating to it are very complicated, so check with Citizens Advice, your local law centre, or the government's own advice line (see page 313) if you are concerned that you are not being paid the minimum wage, or want to find out whether the training you are undertaking qualifies as a recognised training scheme.

Deductions and your payslip

As an employee, you have a right from day one of your employment to an account of your pay and of the money taken from your pay at source ('deductions'). Your payslip should give:

♦ your gross pay (the amount you would get before deductions)
♦ the amounts deducted for tax and National Insurance
♦ other agreed deductions, including for a pension, for charity donations, etc.

It is generally illegal for an employer to take money from your pay without your express agreement, but there are some exceptions, including deductions to compensate for previous overpayment.

Another exception to this rule is in the retail industry. A retail employer is entitled to stop wages if the till is found to be short or stock levels are lower than expected, but only if the employer can prove you have been dishonest or have been responsible for the loss in some way, and only if you agreed to this in your

Maternity pay

Every woman is entitled to a minimum income while she is on maternity leave. This may be paid in the form of statutory maternity pay or benefits. See page 186.

contract of employment. The maximum amount that can be deducted is 10%, but this limit is lifted in the employer's final period of employment after giving notice.

If you find deductions are being taken from your wages or salary that cannot be accounted for in the normal way, seek advice immediately.

Hours of work

Most employees are protected by law from working very long hours. There are some workers who are exempt, and these include trainee doctors, the self-employed and those working in transport and at sea. The following summary was correct at the time this book was written, but changes to the law are planned, so if you have any queries about your working hours, contact your local Citizens Advice Bureau, law centre or union representative.

If your employer makes you work more than an average of 48 hours in one week, unless you expressly agree to do this (called 'opting out'), you may be able to bring a claim against him. You may also be able to bring a claim if your employer dismisses you or victimises you for refusing to work longer. If you have agreed to work longer hours, and then change your mind, you can do so by giving your employer notice (up to three months, depending on your contract).

Note that the 48 hours is an average, and it is calculated over a period of 17 weeks.

If you work nights, the amount of time you work each night is limited to an average of eight hours, and if you do heavy work at night, your shift is limited to eight actual hours.

If you feel that you are being pressured to work longer hours, and you don't want to do this, or you are being treated unfairly because you don't wish to work longer hours, seek advice. You may be able to bring a claim against your employer.

Rest breaks

You are also entitled to rest breaks, both during the working day and during the working week. There are some exceptions, but the following is a broad outline of the rules. If you work more than six hours consecutively, you are entitled to a 20-minute rest-break. Obviously, this should be taken at a suitable time, not at the start or end of the shift. You should also be getting a break of at least 11 hours between each working day, and at least 24 consecutive hours off every week.

Lay-offs and short-time working

Most employers agree in their contracts of employment to pay the employee regardless of whether there is work for them to do. However, if this is not stipulated in your contract, your employer does have the right in some circumstances to lay the workforce off (i.e. to have them stop working). In the same way, employers may declare a period of short-time working, during which workers do fewer hours than normal. Short-time working is defined as a period during which the employee earns less than half a week's wages.

In both cases, employees will see their wages reduced, by 100% in the case of a lay-off and pro rata in the case of short-time working. However, regardless of whether there is work to do, the law stipulates that the employer must pay a minimum amount to:

- permanent workers (if they have been employed for more than a month)
- fixed-term workers with contracts for three months' work or more
- contract workers (if they have a contract for less than three months' work but have in fact worked more than that) regardless of whether there is work to do.

This payment is called the 'guarantee payment'. It is pitifully small and is payable only in limited circumstances and for a limited number of days.

If you are laid off or put on short-time for more than four

Equal pay

Every employee is entitled to be paid the same as other employees doing a substantially similar job or a job of similar value for the same company or an associated company, regardless of their sex, nationality or any disability. Claims for equal pay fall under the law on discrimination at work. See pages 194–196.

consecutive weeks (or any six weeks over a period of 13 weeks), you could declare that you have effectively been made redundant, and you could claim a redundancy payment. If you intend to do this, seek advice first.

Holidays

Every employee (apart from the special cases mentioned above under hours of work) is entitled to four weeks' paid holiday per year, including bank holidays, from the first day of their employment. Of course, your employer may offer you more holiday, but he is not allowed to give you less. If you work part-time, you should still get four weeks, but pro rata. So, if you work half-time (two-and-a-half days per week), you would be entitled to half the paid holiday - two weeks per year. If you are an agency or contract worker, you are also entitled to the same holiday (pro rata if appropriate), but who pays depends on who is actually employing you.

Your employer should tell you what dates the holiday year runs from. Most companies run the holiday year from January to December, but some start the holiday year in October, or, alternatively in April.

Employers are not under any obligation to carry over unused holiday from one year to the next, but often they will agree to carry over the contractual holiday entitlement (i.e. anything above the statutory 20 days). Neither are employers under any obligation to pay you in lieu of unused holiday. However, if you are leaving the company and have accrued holiday you have not taken, you should be paid in lieu.

You must give notice before taking a holiday. The rules for doing this are usually part of your employment agreement. However, if there are no specific agreements on this, the law kicks in, and according to the law the amount of notice you must give is double the length of the intended holiday. So, if you are planning two weeks' leave, you must give your employer four weeks' notice. The employer is quite within his rights to ask you not to take leave at the time you want, but only if he gives you notice of the same length as the intended holiday. To illustrate: you want to take two weeks off, and so you give your employer four weeks notice. He must make his refusal known to you two weeks before your proposed leave begins, and no later. Many of us now arrange our holidays months in advance, so it is important to get express permission from your employer before making ny firm bookings. This is usually possible because most employers operate a written permissions system.

Just as your employer can refuse you leave if the time is not right (perhaps the company is especially busy at certain times of year), so he can also ask you to arrange leave for certain times. Many companies close down during the Christmas period, and while many employers give a couple of extra days at Christmas as a goodwill gesture, some may ask that holiday is reserved to cover the shutdown period. Contracts of employment often include agreements about when holiday is to be taken.

Other time off

The law entitles you to further time off for the following:

◆　if you are a trade union official or representative (such as a health and safety representative), or other employee representative, you have the right to use a reasonable amount of paid company time to perform your duties or to attend training sessions. (If you are simply a member of the union, you have a right to meet, but not on company time.)

◆　if you are a trustee of an occupational pension scheme, you have the right to take paid time off to carry out your duties or to attend training sessions

◆　if you are pregnant, a new mother or a parent or carer, you are entitled to paid time off for a variety of reasons. See pages 184–188 for a résumé of the maternity leave entitlements and other entitlements related to caring for dependants

◆　if you are under 18 and have not achieved the government-stipulated minimum educational requirement, you are entitled to a reasonable amount of paid time off to pursue your studies. What courses of study qualify for this entitlement vary, so ask at the local Job Centre or Citizens Advice Bureau

◆　if you have been made redundant, you are entitled to take a reasonable amount of paid time off during your notice period to look for another job or to take training courses that will make you more employable

◆　if you are a member of a public body, such as a health

authority, you are entitled to reasonable time off to carry out your duties, but this time will be unpaid.

You are not by law automatically entitled to paid leave from work for jury service, although your employer may be held in contempt of court if he refuses to give you leave to perform this duty. Also, you are not automatically entitled by law to a sabbatical, although employers are beginning to offer this as a benefit to long-term members of staff.

Sick leave and sick pay

The majority of employees are entitled to statutory sick pay if they have to take time off because they are unwell. At the time of writing, statutory sick pay is £64.35 a week, and you are entitled to this if you are aged 16-65 and earn enough to pay National Insurance contributions. Statutory sick pay is payable only after the first three days of your illness.

Many companies have a written policy on sick leave. If you are sick, make sure you comply with the instructions laid down in your contract or company handbook. For example, you may be asked to call your immediate manager or the personnel department before midday on each day of your illness, and to fill in a self-certification form for the first few days of your illness. These instructions will also tell you how many days you can be ill before you need to supply a doctor's certificate.

If you are very often away from work because of short-term illnesses that are not part of a long-term or more serious condition, your employer may have the right to dismiss you, but not before investigating your absences and going through the standard disciplinary procedure, giving you an opportunity to defend yourself. If you are dismissed without any warning because of absenteeism, you might be able to claim for unfair dismissal.

If you have a more serious illness that forces you to take long periods off work or makes it impossible for you to do your job, you may find yourself dismissed. Check your contract of employment. While it may be within the law for an employer to sack an employee on these grounds, he has to be very careful indeed how he goes about it. In particular, he must do everything he reasonably can to accommodate an employee with a disability, even if it means moving the employee to a different type of job.

If you are dismissed because of an illness or medical condition, seek advice. You may be able to for unfair dismissal or for compensation under disability discrimination laws (see pages 192–193) or for unfair dismissal.

Working on a Sunday

Those who work in shops or betting offices are protected by law from being forced to work Sundays.

If you have worked in the same job since before August 1994, your employer cannot force you to work on a Sunday, unless you have signed an 'opting-in' form, stating that you are willing to work on a Sunday, and have actually worked on a Sunday.

All others working in retail and betting are similarly entitled to refuse to work on a Sunday, but they must fill in an 'opting-out' form, and then give the employer three months notice before ceasing to work on a Sunday. The exception is, of course, those who are employed only to work on a Sunday; they do not have the right to opt out of Sunday working.

The employer is entitled to reduce the wages of people not willing to work on Sundays, but you may have a claim against him if he dismisses you or victimises you for opting out.

Notice periods

Every employment agreement should contain information about notice periods. As with pay and working time laws, there are also statutory rights for notice periods, which protect most employees from dismissal at very short notice. According to the law, the minimum periods of notice are:

◆ if you have less than two years continuous service with the company, you are entitled to one week's notice

◆ if you have between two and 12 years continuous service with the company, the required notice period is one week for every year of service, so if, for example, you have worked for six full years, you are entitled to six weeks' notice

◆ if you have more than 12 years continuous service with the company, you are entitled to 12 weeks' notice.

In return for the statutory notice periods, the employee must give the employer a minimum of one week's notice after he has worked for the company for a month.

As always, these statutory requirements are minimums, and often they are varied – especially the notice period to be given by the employee. But any clause in your contract that reduces these minimums is void; the statutory minimum always applies. Note that those with less than one month's service are not entitled to a minimum amount of notice by law, but their contract may give them this entitlement.

If you are dismissed without notice, you should normally be entitled to compensation that is at least equivalent to your pay during the statutory period of notice, or the period agreed in your contract. For example, a worker is entitled to four weeks notice, having worked at a company for four-and-a-half years. She is dismissed without notice, and asked to leave the premises immediately. Either the employer will pay her for the period of the notice as if she were still working, or she may be able to make a claim for this amount at an employment tribunal. Time limits apply for making any claim, so if you are dismissed without notice or without enough notice, seek advice immediately.

Trade union representation

Every employee has the right to join a trade union. Every employee also has the right not to join a union, and it may be unlawful to discriminate against you when you apply for a job on the basis of whether you are or are not a union member. In addition, as mentioned above, if you are a trade union officer you are entitled to paid time off during working hours to carry out your duties.

If you are victimised, feel you have received poor treatment, or have been denied a job because you are or are not a union member, or because of your union activities, you may be able to complain to an employment tribunal. Seek advice as soon as you can.

If you work in a company employing more than 20 people you are entitled to have a union negotiate ('bargain') with the employer on your behalf, on such matters as redundancies, pay and benefits. The procedure for getting union recognition is complex. For more information and advice on union representation in the workplace, contact the Central Arbitration Committee.

If you are a member of a union, and that union is not recognised in the workplace, you are still entitled to have your union representative attend any grievance or disciplinary proceedings, or employment tribunal hearing.

Separate laws exist to regulate the conduct of the unions themselves. If you find yourself in conflict with a union, seek advice from your local Citizens Advice Bureau, law centre or a solicitor.

Health and safety at work

These days, employees have a measure of protection against poor working conditions and the threat of industrial accidents under health and safety legislation, and liability under the legislation extends beyond immediate employees to customers and others who may be affected by the company's working practices.

Under the legislation, your employer must take all reasonable steps to ensure your health, safety and welfare in the workplace. This includes:

- providing equipment that is safe to use and ensuring that it is adequately maintained
- ensuring that you are safe when you handle any materials in the course of your work
- ensuring that you are trained properly before you use any equipment or handle any materials, and in particular you are given all the instruction, training and supervision required to ensure your safety in the course of your work
- maintaining the workplace in such a way that it is without health risks and reaches a minimum standard of hygiene and comfort, and ensuring that workers are not exposed to risks to your health and safety as they enter

---

Accidents at work

For information on what the law says about accidents at work, see pages 126–128. For information on work-related illnesses, see page 128.

◆ or leave the workplace
◆ for companies employing more than five people, drawing up a written statement of policy as regards health and safety, and making sure that employees know of its contents
◆ discussing health and safety provisions with employees or with their representatives, union or otherwise.

In addition, employers have a duty to carry out 'risk assessments', and, if more than five people are employed, must record them. If you are pregnant, have just given birth or are breast-feeding, your employer must carry out special risk assessments to ensure that you and your child are not being harmed by workplace practices. Similarly, if you are under the age of 18, your employer must carry out further risk assessments, among other things paying particular attention to your relative inexperience of health and safety issues.

Your employer should also keep a record of accidents and injuries that take place in the workplace, and display a poster giving details of employee's rights under the health and safety legislation.

In return, as an employee you have a duty not to put other people in your workplace at risk by your actions and to ensure that you take notice of and act on all training, instructions and regulations regarding your own safety.

If you feel that there is something happening in your workplace that might prejudice your health and safety or that of your colleagues or other people, or you feel you are not being properly consulted on matters of health and safety, speak to your representatives (a staff association, trade union or safety committee) or to your employer. You have a right to raise issues

---

Smoking in the workplace

It is now generally agreed that passive smoking can harm one's health, and so a smoke-free workplace is considered to be safer than one in which smoking is allowed.

Employers who wish to should implement a new non-smoking policy with full consultation of the employees rather than simply imposing a rule at the drop of a hat.

of health and safety without being victimised or dismissed, and if you feel you are being ill-treated because you have spoken up about health and safety issues, you may be able to bring a claim at an employment tribunal. Seek independent advice as soon as is practicably possible.

Stress and work

Don't forget that your employer is responsible for your mental as well as your physical well-being at work, and that stress is considered to be just as important as physical injuries or disorders under Health and Safety legislation.

Corporate manslaughter

It is now possible to convict a responsible individual if someone dies as a result of health and safety negligence. This is very difficult to prove, but landmark cases have resulted in convictions.

Maternity rights and care of dependants

The law provides for a raft of rights surrounding pregnancy, giving birth, bringing up children and caring for dependants. But it is also a very complex area of the law, and here there is space only to give a broad outline. Use the government's interactive website www.tiger.gov.uk (Tailored Interactive Guidance on Employment Rights) to calculate your maternity leave and pay, speak to your personnel department or call in at your local Citizens Advice Bureau for advice on your specific circumstances.

Maternity leave

Every mother-to-be is entitled to maternity leave. How long the leave is depends on how long you have been working for your employer.

Compulsory maternity leave

It is positively illegal for your employer to allow you to work in the first two weeks after your child is born (four weeks if you work in a factory). This is known as 'compulsory maternity leave', and your employer could find himself in court if he forces you to work in that period.

Ordinary and additional maternity leave

All women, regardless of how long they have worked for an employer, are entitled to 26 weeks 'ordinary maternity leave'. If you have worked for your employer for one year or more by the eleventh week before your 'due date' (the date on which doctors estimate your baby is due to be born), you are also entitled to take 'additional maternity leave', giving you a total of 52 weeks maximum leave.

You must give your employer 21 days notice that you intend to take leave, and you will be asked for a certificate showing your due date. You do not need to give your employer notice that you intend to return to work (that is assumed), but you must give notice within 21 days of the end of your leave if you do not intend to return or if you intend to return part-time.

While you are away on ordinary maternity leave, you are entitled to be treated as if you were actually at work, apart from being paid (see below for information on maternity pay). So, all other terms and conditions still apply. If, for instance, you have a company car, you are entitled to continue using it. If you have a season ticket loan, you are still entitled to that benefit throughout your ordinary leave period. However, if you extend your leave to take the additional maternity leave period, your other benefits (with the exception of holiday entitlements) will disappear.

Time off for health care

In addition to maternity leave, you are also entitled to paid time off for ante-natal classes or for any other health care appointment that has been specifically ordered by your health care practitioner. However, if you are sick because of your pregnancy within the four weeks preceding the expected week of childbirth you may have to count the time you take off as part of your maternity leave.

Health and safety for new mothers

Your employer has a duty to carry out a special risk assessment for you if you are pregnant, have just given birth or are breast feeding. See page 183.

Victimisation and maternity rights

You are entitled to take your maternity leave without being victimised for doing so. If you are passed over for promotion, left out of training or made redundant without warning, simply because you are on maternity leave, you may have a claim against your employer. And your employer must hold your job open for you, or have a very good reason for moving you to another job when you return. Your employer must treat you in exactly the same way as every other employee. If you are ill-treated because of your maternity leave, or because you have taken any of your other maternity rights, you may be able to claim for constructive dismissal, unfair dismissal or sexual discrimination.

Maternity pay

New mothers are entitled to maternity pay. Statutory maternity pay is payable to mothers who have worked for their employer for at least 26 weeks before the 15th week before their due date and earn enough to pay National Insurance contributions.

Statutory maternity pay is payable for a total of 26 weeks. The first six weeks are paid at 90% of your usual wage or salary and the remaining 20 weeks are currently paid 90% of your usual wage or salary or £100 per week, whichever is less.

If you are not entitled to statutory maternity pay, you may be able to claim maternity allowance from the Benefits Agency. Contact the Agency as soon as your pregnancy is confirmed.

Rates of maternity pay change from year to year, so check your entitlement as soon as your pregnancy is confirmed.

Paternity leave

Some prospective fathers are now entitled to two weeks paid paternity leave, but they are not entitled to paid time off to accompany their pregnant partner to ante-natal classes or healthcare appointments. Employers are quite within their rights to ask that fathers use part of their annual leave entitlement for this purpose.

Statutory paternity pay is paid at a rate of 90% of average salary or wages or £100 per week (whichever is less). To be eligible, employees need to have worked for their employer for 26 weeks by the 15th week before the baby's due date, and they must give notice that they intend to take leave.

Adoptive parents

If you are adopting a child, one parent is entitled to elect to take up to 26 weeks paid leave on the same terms as new mothers. You will be paid at the lower rate of statutory maternity pay (at the time of writing, £100 per week) during this entire period.

Parental leave

If your child was born after 15 December 1999, and you have been employed by the same employer for at least a year, you will be entitled to take 13 weeks unpaid leave from your job to look after him or her. This 13 weeks extends until the child's fifth birthday. You will probably have to give 21 days notice that you intend to take parental leave, and your employer may decline if your absence could harm the business. The minimum period of parental leave is a week and the maximum is four weeks.

If you change your job, you can carry unused parental leave over into your new job, but will not be entitled to take the leave until you have worked for your employer for at least a year.

Adoptive parents are also entitled to this leave, and it extends for five years after the date you adopt.

Time off to care for dependants

You are entitled to take a reasonable amount of paid time off from your job to take care of your dependants.

Dependants are: your children, your spouse or parents, or someone who lives in your household (perhaps a partner or a young person who lives with you as part of your family). Lodgers, employees or tenants do not count as dependants.

Child-friendly working

On return to work, all new mothers may request that their hours are organised in a child-friendly way. Employers are not absolutely bound to change what was a full-time job into a part-time job, but they must give the request a hearing, and if they cannot offer more flexible working hours, there has to be a specific business reason.

You must give your employer a good reason for taking the time off, and tell him when you expect to return. The amount of time taken must be reasonable, and in many cases this may amount to only an hour or two. Your reason for taking leave should fall into one of the following categories:

◆ if your dependant falls ill, is injured or gives birth
◆ if you need to arrange to get care for your dependant, or if arrangements for the care of your dependant are disrupted
◆ because your dependant has died
◆ because you have to attend an unexpected crisis at your child's school.

Leaving your job

Any employee may leave employment as long as they give the required notice. See pages 180–181 for statutory notice periods. If you fail to give the appropriate period of notice, your employer could sue you for compensation (although this rarely happens). You may also agree with your employer to terminate your contract by mutual consent. However, if you choose to leave your job (either with or without notice) because of some intolerable situation, or if you are pressured into leaving your job, you may be able to claim for constructive dismissal (see page 197).

Dismissal

It is lawful for an employer to dismiss an employee on the following grounds:

◆ the employee is not qualified for the job
◆ the employee is or becomes incapable of doing the job for which he or she was employed, or is not performing as well as required
◆ misconduct (for example, committing theft or damage to company property, misuse of company equipment)
◆ redundancy (see below)
◆ 'breach of statutory provision', that is, you find yourself in a position where the law prevents you from doing your job. For example, a taxi driver loses his licence, and so it becomes illegal for him to carry out his duties.

◆   some other 'substantial reason', for example, criminal activity when you are not at work, or some behaviour that makes you repulsive to colleagues or customers.

However, if an employer is to dismiss a person 'fairly' then he must take care to consult with the employee, do everything in his power to follow through the standard disciplinary procedure, if appropriate, giving adequate time for the employee to improve where appropriate, and give the right amount of notice if dismissal becomes inevitable.

If you feel you have been unfairly treated when you were dismissed, seek advice immediately. You may be able to make a claim for unfair dismissal.

Redundancy

Employees can be made redundant for the following reasons:

◆   your employer is closing the business
◆   your employer is moving the business to a new location
◆   your employer has a reduced need for people doing your job.

Your employer may resort to laying you off for a period or going onto short-time working in an effort to prevent redundancies, but if you have been laid off for more than a certain period of time, you could consider yourself to have been made redundant and may therefore be eligible for a redundancy payment.

Your employer should consult with you as to your redundancy. Generally, the first time you hear about your impending redundancy should be in a statement telling you your job is at risk. There then should follow a period of consultation in which the employer should do everything in his power to find ways to avoid making you redundant, including finding suitable alternative work within the company. If your employer is making only a small number of people redundant, there is no legal minimum period of consultancy. If, however, he is making more than 20 people redundant in any 90-day period, he must consult for at least a month, and must in addition supply the at-risk employees' representatives (such as the union) with specific information about the redundancies. If the employer is making more than

100 people redundant in a 90-day period, the consultation period is 90 days.

Your employer should tell you (preferably in writing) the exact business reason you are being made redundant, and you should be able to appeal internally against redundancy. Your union representative, if you have one, should be able to advise in this respect.

Unless you are one of a number of groups of workers who are exempt, you are entitled to a redundancy payment if you have worked for your employer for two years or more. The law gives statutory amounts based on age and length of service, but your contract of employment may guarantee you more.

If your employer succeeds in finding you suitable alternative employment, you are allowed to take the alternative on a trial basis (usually four weeks). If you refuse to take a job offered to you, or turn it down after a trial, without justification, you may lose your right to a redundancy payment.

Once you are officially made redundant, you are generally entitled to the usual notice period: statutory notice (see pages 180–181) or contractual notice, whichever is the greater. Some employers require you to work your notice; others do not. If you leave your job without your employer's agreement before the end of your notice period you may lose your right to a redundancy payment.

Once you have agreed your redundancy with your employer, you are entitled to take a reasonable amount of time off during your notice period to seek alternative employment or to undertake training.

If you feel that your redundancy is in fact a pretext for what would be unfair dismissal, you may be able to make a claim to an employment tribunal. However, this kind of claim is very hard to prove.

Blowing the whistle

Is your employer using illegal migrant workers? Is he dumping toxic waste in a local forest? Are the company accountants fiddling the books? Is your colleague being asked to operate a dangerous piece of equipment without a safety guard?

All workers have a right to report illegal goings-on in the workplace to the authorities (and this includes agency and contract workers, as well as employees, but not people working in the Police Force or those working overseas). If you lose your job or are treated unfairly by your employer because you have 'blown the whistle' – disclosed sensitive information – on someone in the company, you are entitled to claim unfair dismissal or for the unfair treatment, and receive compensation.

However, if you are party to information that you feel should be disclosed, be very, very careful. First of all, be sure that you can answer 'yes' to at least one of the following questions:

◆　　　has a crime definitely been committed?
◆　　　has someone failed to comply with his or her legal obligations?
◆　　　has there been a miscarriage of justice?
◆　　　is there or could there be a risk to health and safety?
◆　　　is the environment is being damaged?
◆　　　is there a cover-up going on?

Be sure that the information you have is true to the best of your belief, and that you are acting in good faith by disclosing it. If it can be shown that you disclosed information about your employer's business for personal gain, you may be liable for damages.

You will be protected by the law in the following circumstances (this list is not exhaustive):

Monitoring your activities at work

Your employer has the right to monitor your activities at work, provided that this is given as one of the express terms of your employment (perhaps in the employer's handbook, for example). This can include listening in on or recording telephone calls, reading letters, monitoring e-mails and internet activity and recording your activities on a CCTV system. Of course, if such monitoring amounts to a breach of privacy or harrassment, employees should seek advice. The employer also has the right to limit use of communications equipment to business use only, and any restrictions of this sort should also appear in your handbook or contract.

- you disclose information to your employer or your manager in good faith
- you disclose information to an advisor (such as a solicitor) in the course of seeking advice
- you disclose information to a minister of the crown or a regulatory body such as the health and safety authorities
- you may disclose information outside the company if you feel that you will be victimised if you speak to someone inside the company, if you think that evidence will be destroyed, or if you have already spoken to someone within the company. You may also disclose information outside the company if the disclosure is exceptionally serious. Suitable people to talk to include: the police, your union representative, a relative of the person involved.

Seek legal advice before making any disclosure. Be particularly wary of disclosing information to the media!

Discrimination

It is unlawful to discriminate against anyone on grounds of their gender, race or nationality, or disability except in certain limited circumstances.

The discrimination laws cover many situations other than in the workplace, including at school or at college (see pages 93–94), when you buy goods or services (see page 50), or when you are buying or renting somewhere to live (see page 14).

At work, discrimination applies to all workers, including full-time and part-time employees, contract workers and agency workers.

If you are subject to discrimination because of your sex, race or disability, you may be able to bring a claim at an employment tribunal or to a court. Seek advice immediately - time limits apply.

Just as with other laws relating to work, if you complain of discrimination and are subsequently victimised or dismissed, you may be able to bring a claim at an employment tribunal.

Direct and indirect discrimination

The law distinguishes between two different types of discrimination: direct discrimination and indirect discrimination. If a person is treated differently because of her sex, race or disability, we say that she has been the subject of direct discrimination. Indirect discrimination takes place where a rule that applies to everyone has more bearing or effect on a particular group.

Sex discrimination

Sex discrimination is the treatment of men and women differently simply because of their sex. This applies in all aspects of your working life. When an employer recruits people, he must not be sexist in the job advertisement or in the job specification. He must offer equal terms and conditions to men and women, and he must consider equally applications from both sexes. So, for example, he cannot ask for a male to work in a specific job where a female could do just as well (for instance, asking for a woman to work as a secretary, or a man to work as a labourer doing heavy manual work), and he cannot seek to employ a single woman over a married woman because he believes that a married woman is more likely to take maternity leave. (In fact, the recruiting employer is well-advised not to ask about your family situation at all during the recruitment process.)

There are some exemptions to this, and these are to do with situations in which being someone of a certain sex would cause embarrassment or indecency, or just wouldn't work. In these cases, the employer can claim he has a 'genuine occupational qualification' (GOQ), and it should fall into one of the following categories:

◆ where there is genuine concern for decency, or when employing someone of a certain sex would cause embarrassment, for example, employing a female carer to bathe elderly women in residential care
◆ in the provision of personal welfare services, for instance, a counsellor in a women's refuge
◆ in situations where the employee lives in and there is no provision for separate sleeping arrangements for men and women, or where the employee lives in at the employer's own home (for example, a live-in careworker)
◆ in situations where there is a real need to be either a man or a woman - perhaps in portraying a woman in a

stage play, for example
◆ in situations where the job calls for a married couple.

In general, sex discrimination law applies if a person is treated in a certain way when a person of the opposite sex would be treated differently. For example, a man is promoted where a woman doing the same job for the same length of time and with the same skill is not; a man is dismissed for absenteeism where a woman absent the same amount is not.

Discriminating against part-time workers

Any company policy that means that part-time workers get fewer benefits than full-time workers could be shown to be discriminatory against women because it is a fact that most part-time workers are women.

Discrimination during maternity leave

It is not unlawful to make a woman redundant or to dismiss her during her maternity leave, but it is unlawful to do so if it can be shown that she was picked for redundancy or dismissal simply because she was on maternity leave. She would then most likely be able to make a claim for sexual discrimination.

Like pay for like work

It is unlawful to pay a person less than someone of the opposite sex in a situation where both people are doing the same work, substantially similar work, or work of equal value for the same or an associated company. To prove a case under the Equal Pay Act, you will need to find a 'comparator' - someone who is working for the same company as you and who is doing the

Relationships in the workplace

Some employers don't allow husbands and wives or partners to work together in the same workplace. In doing so, the employer must make sure that whatever action he takes, he would take the same action against a person of the opposite sex in a similar circumstance. Affected employees should take advice.

same job or something similar or a job of similar value, but is being paid differently.

If you believe you are being paid less than a member of the

Discrimination action plan

◆ If you feel you have been the subject of unlawful discrimination, the first thing to do is take advice. Talk to the Equal Opportunities Commission, the Commission for Racial Equality or the Disability Rights Commission (whichever applies), your union representative, your local Citizens Advice Bureau, a law centre or a solicitor. For sex discrimination cases, time limits apply (as little as three months in some cases), so you must be prepared to act quickly if your dispute cannot be resolved by other means.

◆ Decide what outcome you want: perhaps you want a promotion, or a raise in pay, or you want your job back, or you want an apology, or you want to prevent other people from being victims of the same kind of discrimination.

◆ Take steps to resolve the issue with your employer or the person who is discriminating against you.

◆ If your employer refuses to accept that discrimination has taken place or that you are entitled to some sort of compensation, you may both agree to take the case to ACAS, who will act as arbitrator.

◆ If arbitration fails, you may take a claim for discrimination to an employment tribunal or to court. If a tribunal finds you have been the subject of unlawful discrimination, it may award you compensation for: loss of earnings (actual or possible), hurt feelings, personal injury. You will require form IT1 to get the claim process moving, and you can get it from your local job centre, benefits office or the Equal Opportunities Commission. To start proceedings in a court of law, you will need to file claim form N1, which you can get from the court.

---

opposite sex who is doing the same job (and that includes benefits such as holidays, pensions, sick pay, etc., as well as salary or wages), talk to your employer before doing anything else. If the issue cannot be resolved by direct discussion, or through the grievance procedure if there is one, you may wish to take your claim to an employment tribunal. Take advice from your union, local Citizens Advice Bureau, a law centre or solicitor. The Equal Opportunities Commission should also be able to provide you with information and advice.

Sexual harrassment

Harrassment is considered to be a form of sexual discrimination because it generally involves treating a person of one sex differently from a person of the other sex.
Harrassment includes:

◆ unwelcome comments about the way you look
◆ indecent remarks which you find offensive
◆ outright requests for sex or sexual favours (sometimes in return for favours such as a promotion or pay rise)
◆ any other behaviour that makes you feel intimidated or humiliated.

If you feel you are being harassed by someone at work, the first step is to make it clear that their behaviour is offensive to you and ask them to stop. If the behaviour continues, speak to your manager, employer or personnel officer. If this fails to make an impression, take advice at your local Citizens Advice Bureau, your union, a law centre or from the Equal Opportunities Commission.

To help your case, record all incidents, including where and when it took place, who else was there, what the incident consisted of, how you responded and how it made you feel. A record like this could be useful evidence in court.

Key terms

additional maternity leave
This is a period of 26 weeks' unpaid leave in addition to ordinary maternity leave (see below). See page 185.

breach of contract

Breaking an agreement. Either party to a contract – in this case, the employer or the employee – may break its terms, and the other party may be able to sue in a court of law for breach of contract. An employee may bring a claim for breach of contract against her employer in the employment tribunal after termination of employment.

compulsory maternity leave

This is the period of two weeks (four if you work in a factory) immediately after the birth of a baby during which it is illegal for a new mother to go back to work. See page 184.

constructive dismissal

Situation in which an employer has failed to abide by the terms of the employment contract, forcing the employee to resign. The employee may, in these circumstances, claim for unfair dismissal at an employment tribunal. See page 166.

custom and practice

A practice that has taken place regularly for many years may be considered to have become part of an employee's contract of employment. It has become a part of that contract by 'custom and practice'. See page 171.

dismissal

Being told to leave your job. See pages 165–166.

employment tribunal

A body set up specifically to hear many cases to do with employment, including complaints of unfair dismissal. Previously called an industrial tribunal.

express terms

The terms of a contract that are specifically agreed between the two parties. See pages 170–171.

fixed term contract

An employment agreement in which the employee agrees to work for a certain period of time, say six months, rather than indefinitely.

genuine occupational qualification (GOQ)
A reason for employing a member of one sex rather than the other. Employers who can cite a GOQ may advertise and recruit in a way that may otherwise be discriminatory. See page 193.

gross misconduct
Behaviour that constitutes a breach of the employment contract and could therefore be grounds for instant dismissal. Such behaviour may include fighting or being drunk at work, for example.

industrial tribunal
The former name for an employment tribunal.

in lieu
"In place of". For example, 'payment in lieu' means that you are given extra pay, perhaps for working on a bank holiday.

implied terms
Agreements that may not have been written down, but which are implied in the day-to-day interaction between two parties, or by law. See pages 170–171.

lay-off
Being asked by the employer not to come to work during a period in which there is less work to do. See pages 176–177.

notice
Warning that you intend to do something. A notice period is the length of time between the notification and the actual event. For example, you contract states that you need to give four weeks' notice of your intention to leave your job, meaning that you must tell your employer four weeks in advance of your last day. See pages 180–181.

ordinary maternity leave
A period of 26 weeks' leave before or after the birth of a child. See page 185.

parental leave
Leave from work to take care of children. See page 187.

paternity leave
Leave of absence from work for a father whose child has just been born, or for someone (man or woman) who has just become an adoptive parent. See page 186.

pro rata
'In proportion'. For example, a part-time worker may have the same holiday rights as a full-time worker 'pro rata', meaning that where a full time worker might get 20 days holiday, someone working half the amount of time would get 10 days holiday.

redundancy
Being asked to leave your job because the employer no longer needs that job to be carried out. See pages 189–190.

sabbatical
A period of unpaid leave in which to pursue a period of training, study or other interest

short-time working
Being asked by the employer to work half time or less during a period in which there is less work to do. See pages 176–177.

statutory rights
Your minimum rights as laid down by law for all employees.

unfair dismissal
Terminating the employment of an employee for a reason other than those allowed in law. See page 166.

10 Motoring

Transportation, especially road transport by motor vehicles, is a huge part of modern life. This chapter covers how the law affects you when you take to the road, starting with your rights when you buy a motor vehicle, and then covering driver's licences and insurance requirements, the major motoring and parking offences and what action you must take if you are involved in an accident. Later in the chapter, information is given that may come in useful when motoring abroad.

Buying a motor vehicle

New motor vehicles

When you buy a new motor vehicle, your rights are protected by the same laws that protect you when buying any other consumer goods: the Sale and Supply of Goods Act 1994. And this is the case whether you buy new from a dealer or from the manufacturer direct. So, as for any other goods, the dealer must ensure that:

- the vehicle is fit for its normal purpose
- that the description given to you of the vehicle is accurate
- that the vehicle is of 'satisfactory quality'
- that the dealer has the right to sell the vehicle (e.g. it is not stolen).

If you have problems with a new car, return it immediately to the dealer and ask for a new one, preferably in writing. Speed is important here – if you continue to drive the vehicle, the dealer may be able to claim that you have 'accepted' the goods. Resist having repairs made to a new vehicle. But if you do have it repaired, this does not stop you returning the vehicle if the repair does not solve the problem.

Buying a used motor vehicle

There are three options for buying a used motor vehicle: from a dealer, from an auction or from a private individual. In each case, your rights of redress are very different.

Buying from a reputable dealer offers you the greatest legal protection. As someone who makes it his business to buy and sell vehicles, he must conform to the responsibilities set out in the Sale and Supply of Goods Act (1994), and he must also stick to his side of the contract you make between you in writing. Because he has a registered business, it is relatively easy to complain if something goes wrong.

Buying at auction is a different matter altogether, and only those who know a lot about vehicles should attempt to do so, despite the low prices. When you buy at auction, you have none of the usual protection, and often an auctioneer has terms and conditions making it very difficult indeed to return a vehicle or make a complaint.

Similarly, when you buy from a private individual, you are not protected by consumer law, but you may be able to sue for 'misrepresentation' if a fault becomes apparent immediately after the sale making the vehicle substantially different from the description given, or if the seller is in breach of contract (either verbal or written). That is, if you can find your seller!

Misrepresentation

As the buyer, you are expected to take account of any faults in the vehicle when you make the purchase, especially those defects pointed out by the seller. In law, you are also expected to take account of faults that are not pointed out, as far as is reasonable for a lay person. It is best, therefore to have a professional mechanic or other knowledgeable person inspect any used vehicle before you buy it and to act as a witness to any statements made by the seller about the vehicle.

Having said that, you may still have some redress if there turns out to be a problem – a court may rule that, as a lay person, you are not expected to diagnose non-obvious mechanical failings. Your rights in this respect cannot be waived, even if you sign a document saying that you are happy with the condition of the car at the time of purchase.

Always complain in writing as soon as a fault becomes apparent and ask for your money back. You are entitled to receive either the full cost of the vehicle back, or the difference in value between the cost of the vehicle you paid for and the one you actually bought. Speed is crucial – the longer you leave it, the more credible becomes the defence that you accepted the vehicle with all its faults. Stop using the vehicle immediately.

You may also wish to report the seller (if a dealer) to the Trading Standards authorities.

If the fault turns out to make the vehicle unroadworthy, the seller could be prosecuted under the Road Traffic Act 1988, and you should contact the police.

Past credit agreements

Another pitfall of buying a second-hand car is that it may still be subject to a credit agreement entered into by the previous owner. You may buy a vehicle only to find that its previous owner has not completed payments, and the credit company is now asking you to do so. If this happens, seek legal advice immediately. If you bought the car in good faith, you should be protected in law from having to pay off someone else's debt.

Stolen vehicles

If the vehicle you have bought turns out to be stolen, you will probably not be so lucky. In general, stolen goods are returned to their rightful owner or the insurance company that paid out for them. While you may be able to buy the vehicle from the insurance company, it still means you have to pay twice for the same vehicle. In the event you may be able to sue the seller for the cost of the vehicle.

Insurance write-offs

Vehicles that have been in major road traffic accidents and then repaired could be dangerous, particularly if the back of one vehicle has been welded to the front of another. It is illegal to sell such cars, and if you have suspicions, contact your local Trading Standards office or the police.

Checking a car's history

You can get information about a car's history from the Driver and Vehicle Licensing Agency (DVLA, see page 310). The DVLA can also tell you if a car's registration document is genuine.

'Clocking'

Winding back the odometer in a car is an offence, because the mileage is generally seen as being part of the description of the vehicle, and can therefore be judged as misrepresentation.

Dealers acting as private sellers

It is illegal for someone who makes a business out of buying and selling goods to represent himself as a private seller (thereby avoiding his responsibilities under the Sale and Supply of Goods Act). If you suspect a private seller of being a dealer, contact the police.

Before you drive

Drivers of most motor vehicles require a licence. In the UK, licences are divided into five separate categories, each of which carries a separate test:

- motor cars (separate licence for automatic or manual transmission)
- motor cycles
- medium/large vehicles over 3,500kg
- minibuses
- buses.

It is an offence to drive without the relevant licence.

The licence now has two parts, one with a photograph and a paper counterpart, which shows details of any endorsements. It is normally valid for 10 years, although after passing the relevant tests, the normal driving entitlement is until the driver's 70th birthday. The old-style paper licences are being phased out, but they are still valid until the driver's 70th birthday, when all drivers must re-test. After your 70th birthday, the licence is renewable every three years.

You must keep your licence up to date with your current

How old?

For information on what age you have to be to drive various vehicles, see page 81–83.

name and address. If you fail to do this you could receive a fine of up to £1,000. If you develop any medical condition that could impair your driving, you must report it to the DVLA. Not reporting it to the DVLA could result in a fine of £1,000.

Information on the various tests and licences is available from the DVLA (see page 310).

Provisional licence

This licence entitles you to drive certain vehicles before you have passed your driving test, but with certain restrictions. You must:

- be accompanied by a licensed driver over the age of 21 and with at least three years' driving experience
- be correctly insured
- display 'L' plates on the front and rear of the vehicle.

Insurance

It is an offence to drive a motor vehicle without being properly insured, and you should get at least third-party insurance, and ensure that it is kept up to date. As the owner of the vehicle, you are responsible for insuring it, even if you are not the person driving.

The Motor Insurer's Bureau exists to compensate those who have suffered injury or damage by drivers who are not insured and cannot afford to pay compensation or hit-and-run drivers who cannot be traced. See page 312 for details.

Road tax

It is an offence not to pay the relevant road tax for your vehicle. It can be paid at a post office, and you will receive a disc, which must be displayed on the front windscreen of the vehicle. If your vehicle is not going to be driven, however, or is not kept on the

Defining the driver

In law, the driver is defined as the person in control of (or in charge of) the vehicle. Thus, you may be considered the driver if you are found approaching a vehicle with the keys in your hand, or even if you have stepped out of the car for a short period during your journey.

public highway, you may be able to declare a Statutory Off Road Notification, which exempts you from paying the full tax. You can get information from the DVLA or at a post office.

Paperwork

You must have and be able to present the following documents:

- valid driver's licence
- car registration document (should not be kept in the car itself)
- up-to-date car insurance policy
- current tax disc
- current MOT certificate if your car is more than three years old.

Vehicle maintenance

You are required by law to maintain your vehicle for the sake of your own safety and that of others. Police officers are at liberty to inspect any vehicle, regardless of whether or not it is being driven at the time, and may issue you with a 'vehicle defect notice'. This requires you to put right the defect within a certain period of time. If you fail to do so, you may find your MOT invalidated (making it illegal to drive your vehicle). Such maintenance includes the condition of:

- tyres (including the spare)
- windscreen, wipers, washers and demisters
- mirrors
- brakes
- steering
- seat belts
- exhaust and silencer.

The Highway Code

The Highway Code is not enforceable in law, but it may be used to back up claims that you were driving carelessly or, on the other hand, that you were driving competently and with due care and attention.

Seat belts

In all cases, it is the driver's responsibility to ensure that seat belts are used in the front and back seats of the vehicle where fitted. In addition, young children must be secured with appropriate child restraints. Children under three years of age should be wearing appropriate restraints (such as a booster seat); children from the age of three years to 11 years should be using a restraint or a normal adult seat belt if they are more than about 5ft (1.5m) tall. From the age of 12, a child should be using an adult seat belt.

Traffic accidents

If you are involved in a traffic accident you must stop and remain on the scene if any of the following apply:

- anyone is injured
- a vehicle, or property is damaged (including property inside the vehicle)
- an animal is injured (either crossing the road or inside another vehicle, but not including a cat or poultry)
- any item of 'street furniture' is damaged (e.g. a street light).

As the driver of the vehicle, you have a duty to give certain information to anyone involved in the accident (the other driver, a pedestrian, the police, for example), including:

- name and address of the driver
- name and address of the owner of the vehicle, if different
- registration number of the vehicle.

All accidents involving injury or damage as listed above must be reported in person at a police station within 24 hours. If someone

---

Accidents involving emergency vehicles

Emergency vehicles are not above the law. Drivers of emergency vehicles must observe all legal requirements in the event of an accident, and are liable in just the same way as other motorists.

has been injured, the driver must give his insurance details, either at the scene or at a police station within seven days.

Failing to stop at the scene of an accident, or to report an accident, carries a possible six months' prison sentence or a £5,000 fine. The offender may be disqualified, particularly in a case of hit and run, but in any event will receive between five and 10 penalty points.

Action following traffic accidents

Most traffic accidents are minor, leading to small damage to vehicles or property. In the vast majority of these cases, the insurance companies settle claims without you having to go to court to claim directly from the other driver. However, where there is uninsured liability or where the police have ascertained that the driver or drivers were breaking the law, there may be a claim for compensation in the civil court, or a prosecution brought in the criminal court.

Traffic Accident Action Plan

◆ First, do not accept or admit liability for the accident

◆ At the time of the accident, make a note of the damage or injury caused

◆ Look around for people willing to act as witnesses and take their names and addresses; ask them to write down what they saw and heard as soon as possible

◆ Find out about the insurance held by the other party or parties; note that if a person is driving a company vehicle, the person you may need to pursue for compensation may be the employer rather than the individual driving

◆ Make notes as soon as possible of how the accident happened; a sketched map showing the 'before' and 'after' is always useful in explaining what happened; going back to the scene can help to refresh your memory

◆ Find out if any action is being threatened, either civil or criminal.

Motoring offences

There is a wide range of motoring offences on the statute books – they have been passed in an effort to protect the millions of drivers on the roads and ensure that the traffic keeps moving. Many of the most minor offences, such as moving traffic offences, can be dealt with by a simple warning from a uniformed police officer at the kerbside. Offences such as parking violations or failure to maintain a vehicle can be dealt with using fixed penalty tickets (usually attracting small fines) or vehicle defect notices (requiring the owner to undertake maintenance work). You are asked either to pay the fine or undertake the work, or you can contest the ticket and take the case to a magistrates' court if you think you have a good defence. If you are contemplating contesting a ticket, the first step is to get legal advice from a local law centre or Citizens Advice Bureau.

In the most serious of cases, you may be arrested at the roadside or on a warrant at some other time. You may then be charged with an offence and tried either at the magistrates' court or in the county court, depending on the offence. In this case, you are entitled to legal advice, and your solicitor may also arrange a barrister to represent you in court if necessary.

Endorsements and disqualification

If you are convicted of a motoring offence, you may at worst be disqualified, or your licence may be endorsed with penalty points. If you accumulate 12 points in three years (called 'totting up'), your licence is likely to be revoked for at least six months unless there are exceptional circumstances. If you accumulate six or more penalty points within the first two years of driving, your licence will be automatically revoked and you will need to retake all tests as if you had never had a licence.

If you are disqualified for a period that is less than 56 days, your licence will be stamped with the date on which the disqualification expires. You do not need to apply for a new licence after the disqualification expires.

If you are disqualified for a period of more than 56 days, you will have to apply for a new licence.

If you are disqualified for one of the following offences, you will not get your licence back until the DVLA has completed medical enquiries to ensure that you are fit to drive:

- blood alcohol level more than 200mg/100ml (or equivalent in breath or urine)
- disqualified twice in 10 years for serious alcohol-related offences
- disqualified for failing or refusing to give a specimen.

If you are disqualified for more than two years, you can go back to court to ask that the disqualification be lifted after a certain period of time. If you were disqualified for two–four years, you can ask to have the disqualification lifted after two years. If you were disqualified for four–10 years, you can ask to have the disqualification lifted after half the disqualification period. If you were disqualified for more than 10 years, you can ask to have the disqualification lifted after five years. Contact the court that disqualified you if you are not certain when you can get your disqualification lifted.

Endorsements stay on the licence for either four or 11 years, depending on the offence. The 11-year period is for the following offences:

- drinking/taking drugs and driving
- causing death by careless driving while under the influence of drink or drugs
- causing death by careless driving and the failing or refusing to give a specimen.

You can apply to the DVLA to have endorsements removed from your licence after they have expired. Further information is available from post offices or the DVLA.

Causing death by dangerous driving

Attracts a maximum penalty of 10 years' imprisonment, an unlimited fine and an obligatory minimum disqualification of two years followed by an extended driving test. If the defendant is not disqualified (and he has to have 'special reasons' to be able to mount a defence against disqualification), then three–11 penalty points apply. In some cases where it is uncertain whether a prosecution for causing death by dangerous driving will succeed, the charge may be reduced to dangerous driving or careless/inconsiderate driving. Charges of causing death by dangerous driving are always heard in the Crown Court.

Dangerous driving

If heard in the Crown Court, this charge attracts a penalty of two years' imprisonment, an unlimited fine and obligatory disqualification. If the defendant is not disqualified, then three–11 penalty points apply. If heard in the magistrates' court, it carries a maximum prison sentence of six months and/or a fine of up to £5,000. With an obligatory disqualification period of a minimum of 12 months, or three–11 penalty points if the defendant is not disqualified. In some cases where it is uncertain whether the case will succeed, the charge may be reduced to careless/inconsiderate driving.

Causing death by careless driving while under the influence

The full name for this offence is 'Causing death by careless driving while under the influence of drink or drugs or with excess alcohol in the body'. It attracts a maximum penalty of 10 years' imprisonment, an unlimited fine and obligatory disqualification. After the end of the disqualification period, the defendant must undertake and pass an extended driving test. If the defendant is not disqualified (and he has to have 'special reasons' to be able to mount a defence against disqualification), then three–11 penalty points apply. This charge may be reduced to the one of the following if the prosecution believe this charge will not apply: careless/inconsiderate driving; driving when unfit through drink or drugs; driving with excess alcohol; failure to provide a specimen. This charge is always heard in the Crown Court.

Careless/inconsiderate driving

This charge is heard in the Magistrates' Court and attracts a fine up to £5,000. Disqualification is at the discretion of the magistrates and may be replaced by three–nine penalty points.

Driving with excess alcohol

Drink driving charges for incidents that do not involve death or injury are brought in the Magistrates' Court and carry a maximum six-month prison sentence or £5,000 fine. The magistrate will also disqualify the defendant for a minimum period of a year. If the defendant is not disqualified, three–11 penalty points apply.

Driving while unfit through drink or drugs
This charge attracts the same penalties as drink driving (above).

Refusing to take a breath test at the kerbside
Attracts a £1,000 fine, possible disqualification and 4 points.

Refusing to give a specimen
Can attract a prison sentence of six months and/or a £5,000 fine. The Magistrate must disqualify the defendant for a minimum of 12 months.

Driving when disqualified
Attracts a six-month prison sentence and/or a fine of up to £5,000. Magistrates may disqualify the defendant or apply six penalty points.

Driving without insurance
Attracts a fine of up to £5,000 and the possibility of disqualification or six–eight penalty points.

Alcohol limits

The law requires that we do not drink and drive. It has laid down limits to alcohol in the body, tested in the breath, and the blood or the urine. The limits are:

- 35 microgrammes of alcohol in 100ml of breath
- 80 milligrammes of alcohol in 100ml of blood
- 107 milligrammes of alcohol in 100ml of urine.

In order to take a sample of blood or urine, the police should normally have 'screened' the motorist using a breath test, and should ask the motorist at the time of the blood or urine test for permission, and whether he knows any reason why he should not be tested in this way. Refusing to give a sample of breath, blood or urine without good reason is an offence.

Seat-belt offences
Attract a fine of £500.

Failure to stop after an accident
Attracts a possible six-month prison sentence and/or a fine of up to £5,000. You may be disqualified or receive five–10 penalty points.

Failure to report an accident
Attracts the same penalties as failing to stop after an accident, above.

Failure to produce documents after an accident
Attracts the same penalties as failing to stop after an accident, above.

Failure to stop when required by a uniformed police officer
Attracts a fine of up to £1,000.

Failure to produce a driver's licence
Attracts a fine of up to £1,000.

Failure to give name and address
Attracts a fine of up to £1,000.

Speeding on a road
Magistrates may hand down a fine of up to £1,000 and may disqualify you at their discretion or apply three–six penalty points.

Speeding on a motorway
Fines can be as high as £2,500, and you may find yourself disqualified or with three–six penalty points.

Parking offences
Generally carry fines of up to £1,000, or a fixed penalty ticket. Some also attract tow-away fees.

Joy-riding
This is the popular term for taking a vehicle without the owner's consent with the intention of driving and then

abandoning it. Car-theft, on the other hand, is the taking of a vehicle without the owner's consent with the intention of permanently depriving the owner of it. Joy-riding accompanied by damage or injury is, in law, called 'aggravated vehicle-taking', and is applicable as an offence not only to the driver of any vehicle taken in this way, but also to any passengers. The maximum penalty for aggravated vehicle-taking is a two-year prison sentence and a minimum 12-month disqualification. If someone is killed while joy-riding or by a joy-rider, the driver and passengers could face up to five years in prison. Cases of aggravated vehicle-taking are always tried in the Crown Court.

Bicycles, motor cycles, mopeds

All laws relating to driving a car relate in the same way to driving any other vehicle, including bicycles. It is an offence to ride a bicycle on the pavement or to ride it carelessly or while intoxicated.

Road rage

The phrase 'road rage', coined recently in the United States, is used to cover a range of aggressive driving styles, from angry words and gestures to full-blown attacks on other road users. There is no offence of road rage, but incidents that result from losing your temper can lead to charges ranging from a breach of the peace to grievous bodily harm.

Mobile phones

There is currently no specific law against using a mobile phone while driving. However, you could be charged under related

---

Accidents caused by a sudden illness

Drivers are not usually held responsible for injury or damage caused if they are rendered incapable at the wheel by a sudden illness (perhaps a heart attack or a stroke). However, an illness that reduces the driver's ability to drive safely should be discussed with a doctor and may need to be reported to the DVLA. Drivers should also take their doctor's advice on when it is safe for them to drive after surgery or if taking medicinal drugs.

offences (such as careless/inconsiderate driving) if you are not in proper control of your vehicle at all times.

Nuisance

It is an offence to cause a nuisance, and this can cover playing loud music on your car stereo or having a car alarm that is frequently going off for no good reason. In theory your car alarm should not sound for more than five minutes at a time. This offence falls under the Noise and Statutory Nuisances Act 1993, and an environmental health officer could have your vehicle towed away if it causes enough of a nuisance.

Driving abroad

If you wish to drive in other countries, you will need to note differences in regulations, including licence regulations. There is not enough space in this book to cover the differences between the laws of other countries and the UK, and the best place to get information about the country you are travelling to is a motoring organisation such as the AA or the RAC or the tourist office for the country you are intending to visit.

Papers you will need

When driving abroad, always take with you your:

- car registration documents
- UK driver's licence
- insurance documents.

If you have a new photocard-type driver's licence, you should take both parts with you. If you do not have a photocard licence, ensure you also take with you a form of identity that includes a photograph, such as your passport.

Check with your insurance company that your insurance covers you to drive in the country you intend to visit. When hiring a car that you wish to take abroad, check with the hire company that it is insured outside the UK. A Green Card is an internationally recognised certificate that you are insured to drive (called the International Motor Insurance Certificate), and while it is not compulsory in the EU, it could be useful where language barriers may prevent understanding of your English policy documents.

A licence to drive abroad

If you are planning to drive in any of the countries of the European Economic Area (all the countries of the EU plus Iceland, Liechtenstein and Norway), you may do so on your full UK driver's licence. Equally, if you go to live in any of the countries of the EU, you may simply exchange your UK driver's licence for a licence for that country. Indeed, you may be required to do so, and there may be time limits.

If you wish to drive outside the EU, you may require an International Driving Permit, a photocard permit obtainable from the AA or the RAC, or the Post Office. You are not entitled to an International Driving Permit unless you have a full UK driver's licence.

If you have been living outside the EU and you do not have a UK driver's licence, you are entitled to drive on your non-EU licence for a period of 12 months, as long as you can show a valid foreign licence. After this time, you must apply for a UK driver's licence, and will receive one only if you are normally resident in the UK.

Other requirements for motoring abroad

Many countries, whether in the EU or not, have other requirements. You may be required to display a GB sticker on your vehicle, for instance. Such requirements may include:

- displaying a GB sticker on rear of car
- carrying a first aid kit
- carrying a fire extinguisher
- carrying a spare set of light bulbs
- carrying a warning triangle.

Your motoring organisation can give you details for the country or countries you are planning to visit, or, failing that, check with the relevant embassy, consulate or tourist office before you travel.

If you have an accident abroad

Laws vary from one country to another, but advice given for an accident situation in the UK applies just as well to similar situations abroad (see page 207). It is particularly important to photograph or sketch the scene before leaving it (getting back there may be costly).

Foreigners driving in the UK

If you carry a valid EU driver's licence, you can use it until your 70th birthday or until 3 years after you become a resident in the UK, whichever is the longer. If you intend to live permanently in the UK, you may simply exchange the licence from your home country for a UK licence. Contact the DVLA for further information.

The same applies to those from the following 'designated' countries:

◆ Australia
◆ Barbados
◆ British Virgin Islands
◆ Canada
◆ Cyprus
◆ Gibraltar
◆ Hong Kong
◆ Japan
◆ Malta
◆ New Zealand
◆ Singapore
◆ South Africa
◆ Switzerland
◆ Zimbabwe.

If you carry a valid driver's licence from a country outside the EU and from any country other than a designated country, you will be permitted to drive in the UK using your valid home licence or International Driving Permit for up to one year. You will then need to take a driving test, using a provisional UK driver's licence. Contact the DVLA or the Post Office for further information.

There are different rules for those who drive for a living, and anyone in this category should contact the DVLA for a list of requirements and entitlements.

Vehicles other than cars

The majority of the information given in this chapter could be said to be true for all motor vehicles, but some groups of vehicles have their own laws.

Mopeds are defined as any motorcycle below 50cc and with a maximum speed of 50kph (30mph). If the vehicle was manufactured before 1977, it must also have pedals. You must have completed a basic training course in order to ride a moped and be in possession of a valid provisional moped licence. You must always wear a helmet while riding a moped on the public highway.

Light motorcycles are defined as those under 125cc. Again, you must complete basic training before you can drive a motorcycle on the road. The minimum age to ride a light motorcycle is 17 years.

Heavy motorcycles are defined as those over 125cc, and you have to be 21 or older to ride one. Again, you must complete basic training before you can get a licence.

For all motorcycles and mopeds, it is illegal to carry pillion passengers while still in basic training.

Trailers (including caravans) are subject to licensing regulations as for other vehicles. In general, you may tow a 750kg (1650lb) trailer after passing the standard car driving test. It must be in a roadworthy condition just as for a car, and you should observe regulations about carrying passengers and securing loads. Trailers and caravans must also observe lower speed restrictions:

- In urban/built-up areas   30mph (48kph)
- On single carriageways   50mph (80kph)
- On dual carriageways   60mph (96kph)
- On motorways   60mph (96kph)

Camper vans ('RV's') are not subject to such restrictions.

Coaches and mini-buses (collectively known as passenger service vehicles or PSVs), tractors, heavy-goods vehicles (HGVs) and electrically assisted vehicles all attract their own regulations. Contact the DVLA for information.

Key terms

breathalyser
Equipment used by the police to determine the amount of alcohol in a motorist's bloodstream.

damages
A sum of money awarded by the courts when damage has been caused to property or person.

disqualification
Being prohibited from driving (usually for a given period of time) if convicted of a driving offence.

DVLA
The Driver Vehicle Licensing Agency, the body which issues driver's licences, registers vehicles and records endorsements. See page 310.

endorsement
Penalty points recorded on a driver's licence when convicted of a driving offence. See page 208–209.

full driver's licence
A licence that entitles a motorist to drive on the public highway after passing a theory and a practical driving test. See page 203–204.

Motor Insurers' Bureau
Organisation that deals with cases where accidents have been caused by uninsured or foreign motorists. See page 204.

provisional driver's licence
A licence that entitles learner drivers to train on the public highway prior to passing a driving test.

speeding
Exceeding the speed limit. Speed limits vary, and penalties for exceeding speed limits depend on how much faster the motorist is travelling and, in the event of an accident, whether any damage has been caused.

summons
A document summoning a person to court.

totting up
The practice of adding up a motorist's penalty points. See page 208.

traffic accident
An accident that takes place on the public highway.

11 Leisure and Travel

This chapter looks at the laws that come into play when we are playing. It starts with an evening or lunchtime out, perhaps having a meal – an activity that has grown enormously in the UK in the last 30 years or so – and looks at our rights as consumers of food cooked and served by others. Alcoholic drinks are frequently present at meals, so it seems natural to go on to discuss the various laws relating to the consumption of alcohol, particularly for young people. The government has recently acknowledged that alcohol-related crime is a significant problem in our society, and there is an outline of some of the government's plans to change the law related to alcohol consumption, not yet law at the time of writing.

Alcohol is a drug – one drug among many that are consumed in today's society. The next part of this chapter looks at how the law regulates the use of certain 'controlled' drugs, such as cannabis, ecstasy, heroin, cocaine and various others.

Many people like to spend their leisure time out and about, walking, perhaps, or taking part in other countryside pursuits. But how does a city-dweller know when they are trespassing on a farmer's land, and where exactly do visitors to the countryside have a right to walk? Moving further afield, this chapter takes a detailed look at the laws that affect us when we travel abroad, from problems with unsatisfactory package holidays, to buying timeshares, to getting into trouble in a foreign country. It closes with a résumé of the rules on film classification.

Eating out

Eating out has become big business in today's Britain. Big cities and small provincial towns alike are littered with restaurants serving every cuisine imaginable, Mediterranean-style street cafés with seats outside (despite the less-than-Mediterranean weather), pubs serving good home-cooked food in separate dining rooms and food-vendors of all sizes and persuasions. When a customer takes advantage of these wide-ranging eating options, he can usually rely on the law to provide a remedy if his experience has proved dangerous to his health or merely unsatisfactory. Here are some of the problems that may arise, and what the law says you can do about them. (In the following, the word 'restaurant' is used to mean any establishment serving food either for consumption on the premises or takeaway.)

Reserving a table

When a customer reserves a table in a restaurant or other eatery, he is entering into a contract with the restaurant – to be there at a certain time and to purchase a meal for the given number of people. In turn, the restaurant agrees to make space available for the party and to serve a meal. If the customer fails to turn up, arrives with fewer people than expected, or turns up so late that the restaurant has lost the opportunity of making money from other customers, the restaurant-owner may be able to sue for breach of contract, making a small claim in the Small Claims Court to cover her losses. Of course, if the restaurant is able to fill the vacant spaces from customers arriving at the door without reservations, then no loss has been incurred, and there should not be any claim for compensation.

Restaurants are within their rights to ask for a credit card number as security against the customer's failure to arrive, and may indeed debit the card a certain amount to cover her losses in this event. Simply by giving the credit card number, the customer may be seen to be agreeing to a charge being debited in this way.

What if the situation is reversed? The customer reserves a table, only to arrive at the appointed hour to find that the table has been given to someone else, and the restaurant has no space left. Again, there is a contract between the customer and the restaurant in which the restaurant agrees to reserve a table. The customer may therefore be able to make a claim for compensation, usually limited to expenses incurred in getting to the restaurant. It may also be possible to claim for disappointment, especially if the meal was planned as a special occasion.

Disabled access

Under the discrimination laws in force in England and Wales, establishments offering goods or services for sale should not discriminate on the grounds of race, sex or disability. This means that everyone should be treated in the same way, and if they are not, there are avenues open to the victim to pursue a claim for compensation.

Disability discrimination may include not providing access and facilities for people with disabilities, for instance, wide doors and ramps for wheelchair access, specially-designed toilet facilities, etc. At present, the law only requires such places as restaurants to provide a 'reasonable degree of access' – a temporary ramp, for instance – and where this is blatantly possible and the restaurant-owner has not done so, a disabled person effectively barred from using the restaurant because of this neglect may have a claim. By 2004, all restaurants will have to have made disabled access possible, and this means that they will be breaking the law if they do not.

Smoking in restaurants

There is no legal requirement for restaurants or other eateries to set aside a space reserved for non-smokers, although many do. If an establishment has a non-smoking area and customers are smoking in that area, a non-smoking customer affected by tobacco smoke may be able to ask that the smokers are moved, or that they are asked to stop smoking. If this doesn't happen, then he may feel the need to deduct a small amount from the bill to compensate for loss of enjoyment.

This is legally possible because the restaurant has entered into a contract with the customer to provide a smoke-free area; not doing so may be a breach of this contract. Restaurants that do not advertise a smoke-free area cannot be said to have included this in their contract with the customer and so it is unlikely that he could do anything about a loss of enjoyment because of smokers nearby.

Service

Many restaurants offer delicious meals at honest prices served in a pleasant and efficient manner by well-trained staff. But once in a while, the poor behaviour or incompetence of restaurant staff can spoil the enjoyment of the meal. Poor service might include:

- ◆ unreasonable slowness in serving the meal
- ◆ unreasonable haste in serving the meal
- ◆ rude or abusive behaviour on the part of the waiter or other staff
- ◆ incompetence of staff leading, perhaps, to spillages.

Where the restaurant leaves the tip to the discretion of the customer, he may wish to pay no gratuity at all where there is poor service. If the restaurant policy is to add a fixed service charge to the bill of all customers, and this fact is advertised properly, then a customer faced with poor service has two options: to pay the service charge under protest and claim it back at a later date; or to refuse to pay the service charge altogether. The restaurant has an obligation under the Supply of Goods and Services Act (1982) to provide a satisfactory service, so if the customer can show that the service has been far from satisfactory, he may have a case. See page 223 for advice on how to go about refusing to pay or paying under protest.

We've all seen slapstick comedy in which the surly or awkward diner is rewarded with spaghetti in his lap or wine down her blouse. However, when this happens to you (perhaps dressed in a special outfit for a special occasion), it's no laughing matter. If ever customers' clothing or goods are damaged by careless restaurant staff, the customer has the right to claim the cost of repairing the damage, such as cleaning. If an injury is sustained, perhaps a burn from hot food, the consequences could be more serious. See chapter six on personal injuries for more information.

Problems with the product

The sale of food is governed by various acts. Under the Supply of Goods and Services Act (1982), all goods must be of satisfactory quality. They must also be 'as described' by the vendor and, in the case of food, prepared with 'reasonable care'. Under the Food Safety Act 1990, restaurants are obliged to ensure that food served is fit for human consumption.

If a restaurant indicates in its advertising (its menu, for example) that a dish is of a certain kind, then that's what the customer should get. Restaurants that advertise homemade meals should supply just that – dishes made on the premises. Vegetarian dishes should be made without meat products. A customer who is served a dish that is clearly not as advertised (a 'vegetarian' soup, made with chicken stock, for example) should not eat the food, but complain to the waiter immediately, and consider deducting the charge for that part of the meal from the bill (see page 223 for advice on how to go about doing this).

If a restaurant serves food that is inedible, perhaps because it has not been properly cooked, or shows signs that it has been contaminated (the old phrase, 'waiter, there's a fly in my soup', comes to mind), the customer should send it back to the kitchen. If, after another attempt to get it right, the cook still fails, then the customer is again at liberty to deduct an amount for this part of the meal from the bill. The key is to refuse to eat any more of the meal as soon as it becomes clear that it is not of satisfactory quality. No customer really has a case if he has wolfed down the plateful and only then complains.

If the food offered is alarmingly poor all round, the customer may have a case for suing for breach of contract, claiming back the cost of the meal (if anything was paid) plus travel expenses and possibly even a sum for disappointment.

Serving food that is unfit for human consumption is an offence. Restaurants that do not keep food-preparation areas clean or allow unhygienic or dangerous food preparation practises to go on could be closed by Environmental Health

Restaurant bills

If some part of a meal has been unsatisfactory, the customer may be able to take one of two courses of action. He may pay the full bill, but indicate to the restaurant that further action will be taken. In this case, he should make it quite clear that he is not happy to be paying for an unsatisfactory meal. The Consumer's Association advises that he should write on the credit card slip or on the back of the cheque the words 'Under Protest'. Later, he may then be able to pursue a claim against the restaurant to claw back part of the cost of the meal.

An alternative is to deduct a reasonable amount from the bill at the time of paying, making it clear to the restaurant manager why this is the case. If a customer opts to do this, he should leave his name and address with the restaurant manager so that the situation can be discussed further if the manager feels this is necessary. Managers who threaten to call the police in an effort to force the customer to pay are misguided. As long as the above steps are taken, the police will generally not interfere.

In all this, staying cool and stating the case firmly but politely can help to keep things on a civilised footing.

officers. Customers who suffer a bout of food poisoning after eating out may be able to sue the restaurant for the cost of the meal and for the suffering involved in the sickness. However, they will have to be able to show 'causation' (see pages 116–117): that eating the meal led directly to the sickness. Of course, if all six people in your party have the same symptoms after eating the same meal, there may be quite a strong case. Those troubled by food poisoning should go to their GP immediately to record the details of the symptoms.

Prices

Every restaurant is obliged by law to display an accurate list of prices (inclusive of VAT), either at the door or at the place where a meal is ordered – at the bar, for instance, in a pub. If a service charge is automatically added to the bill, this should be noted on the price list, as should any minimum charges. These details should also be given on the menu. Breaches of this regulation fall under Consumer Protection legislation which says that prices should be clearly and accurately displayed, and customers who notice that a restaurant is not advertising its prices accurately should complain to the Trading Standards department of their local authority. Deliberately advertising inaccurate prices is a criminal offence.

If faced with a charge that has not been properly advertised by the restaurant, the customer may be within his rights to deduct this amount from the bill. See the advice on page 223.

If you have booked a table at a restaurant, and sit down, you may be obliged under the terms of your agreement with the restaurant to order a meal or compensate the restaurant for loss of business if you subsequently decide not to order a meal. Make sure you check the price list and menu before sitting down to order.

Alcohol

The laws regarding the purchase and consumption of alcohol are many and various; some of them go back as far as the first half of the 19th century. Many people enjoy a drink in pubs, bars, restaurants and at home without a problem. However, alcohol is implicated as an element in a wide range of offences, including assaults, damage to property, public order offences, rape and domestic violence. At the time of writing, the government was considering a wide range of changes to legislation that would target what were perceived as increasing social problems related to alcohol. What follows is a survey of the law as it stands at the time of writing. On pages 229–230 there is a brief overview of the planned changes.

Home brewing

Anyone is entitled to make wines, beers and other forms of alcohol (excluding spirits) without regulation, as long as it is for private consumption. It is against the law to produce alcoholic drinks for sale without a licence.

Licensed premises

Alcohol may be sold only by licensed vendors. Ordinarily, there are two types of licence:

◆ on-licence, which allows the licensee to sell alcohol for consumption on the premises, e.g. pubs, bars, restaurants, nightclubs, etc.
◆ off-licence, which allows the licensee to sell alcohol only for consumption elsewhere, e.g. supermarkets, wine merchants, off-licenses, etc.

In addition, licensees may apply for special licenses in some circumstances, which allow for different opening hours, for example, for nightclubs or restaurants.

Licences are currently granted and renewed by local magistrates, who take into account such matters as any offences committed on the premises, and the impact of its presence on the local community. Local residents may object to the granting or renewal of a licence at the court hearing.

Licensees are responsible for what goes on in their premises. They are committing an offence if they:

Alcohol consumption in restaurants

For details of the law regarding the consumption of alcohol in restaurants, especially by young people under the age of 18, see page 226–227.

- serve alcohol to people who are under the legal drinking age
- allow under-age people into the bar in contravention of the law
- serve alcohol to someone who is already drunk
- allow drunken behaviour to continue on the premises
- flout the rules on drinking hours by continuing to sell alcohol after closing time.

Drinking hours

The times at which alcohol may be sold or served by licensed premises are as follows:

- Mondays–Saturdays (except for Christmas Day): 11:00–23:00
- Sundays (except for Christmas Day): 12:00–22:30
- Christmas Day: 12:00–15:00 and 19:00–22:30.

A period of ten minutes after closing time is earmarked as 'drinking-up time' during which customers should finish their drinks and leave the premises. Some premises may obtain special licences, and can then extend their drinking hours beyond these times.

For off-licenses, the hours are:

- Mondays–Saturdays (except for Christmas Day): 08:00–23:00
- Sundays (except for Christmas Day): 10:00–22:30
- Christmas Day: closed.

Legal drinking age

The law gives the following regulations for children and young people under the age of 18:

- children and young people of any age may enter a registered private members' club where alcohol is sold

---

Did you know?

It is an offence to be drunk while in charge of a child under the age of 7.

- ◆ under-5s should not be given any alcohol to drink unless on medical instructions
- ◆ 5–13 years inclusive: children of this age may drink alcohol as long as they are not on licensed premises. This means they can drink at home, in public places (unless there are local bye-laws prohibiting the consumption of alcohol in certain public places), and in registered private members' clubs
- ◆ under 14: children under 14 are allowed into licensed premises (but not to drink alcohol), but they must be accompanied by an adult over the age of 18, the premises (e.g. the garden or family room in a pub) must have a license for children, and they must leave at 21:00
- ◆ 14–18 years: young people may enter the bar of any licensed premises unaccompanied, but they must not buy or consume alcohol
- ◆ 16 years and older: young people after their 16th birthday may buy and consume beer, cider and some other kinds of alcohol (excluding spirits) in a part of licensed premises set aside for food service, and only when consuming a meal
- ◆ below 18 years: young people below this age may not buy or consume alcohol in a bar on licensed premises; they cannot buy alcohol from off-licenses. It is also an offence for licensees to sell alcohol to people under the age of 18 in a bar or off-license. In addition, young people under the age of 18 may not work in licensed premises.

Police are empowered to confiscate alcohol from young people under the age of 18 who are drinking in a public place and inform their parents of the situation.

Drinking in the streets

In England and Wales it is generally not against the law to consume alcohol in public places – that is, in the street, parks and public buildings. However, the Licensing Acts of 1892 and 1902 make it an offence to be drunk in a public place, and an even older law (the Metropolitan Police Act 1839) makes it an offence to be drunk in the street or to behave 'riotously' because you are the worse for wear, but this is limited to the area covered by the Metropolitan Police Force. Some local councils have taken the unusual step of using local bye-laws to make it an offence to drink in the streets in certain parts of their area. Police have the power to confiscate alcohol if they find a person who is drunk and disorderly in a public place.

Some places, typically where a number of drinking establishments disgorge their entire clientele at the same time, for example, 23:00 on a Saturday night, are considered to be 'flashpoints'. Drunkenness leads to aggression, particularly, or so the statistics say, among young men aged 18–32. Where alcohol misuse leads to assault, damage to property and other offences major or minor, the drunk and disorderly offence may be augmented by other more serious offences.

Importing alcohol from abroad

Private individuals may import a reasonable amount of alcohol for private consumption from other parts of the European Union without paying customs duty. The definition of a 'reasonable quantity for personal consumption' does get stretched in the case of individuals buying alcohol from abroad and selling them to friends, or even, in the most blatant cases, through an off-licence. For a list of quantities above which customs officers will raise an eyebrow, see page 245.

If customs decides that an individual is bringing in alcohol in order to sell it on (even if not for cash but for goods or services in kind), they have the power to confiscate the goods and impound the vehicle used. In serious cases, offenders may be liable to imprisonment, a fine and/or disqualification from driving.

Those bringing alcohol from outside the EU should observe duty-free allowances (see page 245), and if they bring larger quantities than the regulations allow should declare the extra bottles at customs and pay the appropriate amount of duty.

For further information, go to the website of HM Customs and Excise (see page 311).

Drinking and driving

For information on offences relating to drink-driving, see pages 210–211. For a list of the alcohol limits for drivers, see page 211.

Work and alcohol

If an employee comes to work drunk he may be in breach of his contract of employment. Some employers consider drunkenness at work to be so serious that it is a good reason for summary dismissal (i.e. being sacked without going through the usual disciplinary procedures).

In addition, all employers have an obligation to provide their employees with a safe place to work (see pages 182–184), and this includes providing any one employee with competent co-workers. If an employee comes to work drunk, and causes an accident involving another member of staff, the employer may be liable to pay compensation to the injured staff member under Health and Safety law.

People employed in the transport system are in a position of responsibility as regards their passengers. Under the Transport and Works Act (1992), drivers of public transport vehicles (such as train drivers) and support staff are governed by a specific set of legislation concerning coming to work after drinking. In general, the legislation is similar to that governing drink-driving.

Alcohol and sporting events

The Public Order Act (1986) made it an offence to carry or consume alcohol while travelling to and from various sporting events. This legislation was enacted in an effort to reduce violence and disorderly conduct at events such as football matches.

Changes to the alcohol laws

Recent statistics have shown that alcohol is present in a large number of criminal offences, and most people walking in the streets of town centres on Friday and Saturday nights would testify to the detrimental effect of large numbers of people forced onto the streets simultaneously at closing time. Reform of the licensing laws is currently under consideration as this book goes to press, and may include:

◆ stronger enforcement of existing laws, such as the prohibition on selling alcohol to young people under 18, including extending the prohibition on selling alcohol to under-18s to all employees and not just the licensee himself

- changes to opening times, possibly instituting 24-hour opening in an effort to make drinking a more relaxed activity, and reducing the effect of the simultaneous closing of a number of establishments in the same area
- more widespread use of voluntary proof-of-age schemes whereby licensees refuse to serve anyone who looks under age without a proof of identity card
- better and more widespread use of laws that enable police officers to confiscate alcohol from under-age drinkers in public places
- strengthening the powers of the courts to order a convicted offender to stay away from certain licensed premises
- backing up local bye-laws (e.g. against drinking in certain places) by giving the police powers to arrest offenders.

For up-to-date information on the law on alcohol and licensing, check the Home Office website (see page 311).

Controlled drugs

Many people in the UK use, or have used, drugs other than alcohol and tobacco to while away their leisure hours. Youth dance culture has, in the past 15 or so years, become inextricably linked (rightly or wrongly) with psychedelics and other kinds of drugs. However, the danger of addiction, the detrimental effects on health and the connection between the use and supply of drugs and serious criminal offences has led to the regulation of a range of drugs. As this book went to press, a number of details in the law were about to change, including the re-classification of cannabis as a class C drug, rather than a

Drugs abroad

Many countries around the world impose very severe penalties for those caught in possession of drugs. In some cases, smuggling drugs can attract the death penalty. In some countries it is also an offence to consume alcohol and/or smoke in public.

class A drug and far heavier penalties for those caught dealing certain types of drug.

What the law says

The law covering the possession, production, sale and importation of 'controlled substances' includes a number of separate pieces of legislation, but the principal act is the Misuse of Drugs Act 1971. This Act classifies various substances according to what the government of the time saw as their dangers, and lays down penalties. Under the Act, it is a criminal offence to:

- be in possession of a controlled substance (including having it on the person, in one's home, luggage or car – anywhere the offender could be said to be 'in control' of the drug)
- produce, grow or process (including cooking, drying, etc.) a controlled substance
- be in possession of a controlled substance with the intention to supply it to someone else (this can include selling, but also giving it to someone)
- supply someone else with a controlled substance (even if no cash changes hands, and there is no profit involved)
- offering to supply someone else with a controlled substance
- importing or exporting a controlled substance.

Drug classes

The 1971 Act gives three classes of controlled substance. Class A is the highest, including drugs that are perceived as being the most dangerous, and carrying the heaviest penalties. Class C is the lowest. Some of these drugs (for example, tranquillisers) are available on prescription, and if they are supplied on prescription their possession and use is not illegal. In addition, some drugs are controlled under the Medicines Act 1968, which regulates where drugs usually used for medicinal purposes can be sold, and whether they require a prescription. This complicates the law as regards certain drugs, so the following should be used only as a broad outline.

Class A drugs include:

- cannabis oil

- cocaine
- crack
- ecstasy
- heroin
- LSD
- methadone
- magic mushrooms (but only if they are 'processed', which could mean crushed, added to a dish, made into a tea, dried, etc.).

Class B drugs include:

- amphetamines (speed)
- barbiturates
- cannabis (herb and resin) – shortly to be downgraded to class C
- codeine.

Any of the above drugs move up into the Class A category if they have been prepared for intravenous injection.

Class C drugs include:

- anabolic steroids
- mild amphetamines
- minor tranquillisers.

Some drugs are not classified as controlled substances at all. These include:

- poppers (amyl or butyl nitrite)
- magic mushrooms ('unprocessed')
- solvents such as glue (although it is an offence to sell solvents to young people knowing that there is a fair chance they will be misused).

Penalties related to controlled substances

The law lays down maximum penalties for possession, supply and importing of controlled substances, but there is wide variation in the application of these penalties. Whether a person is arrested and prosecuted for the possession of cannabis or merely cautioned informally, for example, depends on the policy of the local police force. The severity of the penalty imposed on offenders who are found guilty depends on the views of the local courts, and these have been found to differ widely. It also depends on the past record of the offender, and in minor cases, on the offender's personal circumstances. However, here are the maximum penalties attached to each class of drug:

Class A drugs – maximum penalties

- possession: seven years and/or a fine
- supply, intent to supply, import/export: life imprisonment and/or unlimited fine.

New legislation will make it possible to force offenders convicted of offences in this class to attend for rehabilitation and to be tested for the drug in question.

Class B drugs – maximum penalties

- possession: five years imprisonment and/or a fine
- supply, intent to supply, import/export: 14 years and/or a fine.

With the new legislation, police will no longer be able to arrest those found in possession of cannabis; instead, offenders will be sent a court summons in the same way as those breaking traffic laws. However those caught trafficking in cannabis are unlikely to see a similar reduction in the maximum penalty. In fact, the penalty looks set to stay at 14 years.

Class C drugs – maximum penalties

- possession: it is not a criminal offence to be in

'Paraphernalia'

It is not only an offence to possess and sell controlled substances. It is also an offence to offer for sale any of the paraphernalia that is used to prepare and take them. The ownership of scales and other bits and pieces may act as evidence that a person was intending to supply drugs.

---

possession of most class C drugs (the exception is tamezepam, a minor tranquilliser, the unlawful possession of which carries a maximum sentence of two years and/or a fine)

◆ supply, intent to supply, import/export: five years imprisonment and/ora fine (but see the note on cannabis trafficking, above).

Drugs on the premises

In addition to possessing, using, producing or trafficking in controlled substances, it is an offence knowingly to allow your home or other premises to be used for drugs-related activities. The responsible person (i.e. the one liable for prosecution) may be the owner-occupier of a house or flat or a person in authority in commercial premises, or the landlord of a bar, nightclub or pub. The key to identifying the responsible person is that in general they are the one with legal power to refuse entry to certain people.

This area is fraught with difficulty. A responsible person who finds someone engaged in such activities should confiscate the controlled substances and either destroy them immediately or pass them on to the police, or he risks being prosecuted. If he is told by a reliable source that such activities are taking place, he again risks prosecution unless he takes immediate action to exclude the offender from the premises or ensure the activity is brought to a halt.

Leisure in rural areas

Britain's laws on land ownership and use have grown up over ten centuries, with their roots in the ancient feudal system. Many of Britain's forests, moors, mountains, hills and beaches are in the hands of private owners. On the other hand, millions of people every year flock to Britain's beautiful wide open spaces to walk or hike, to camp, to cycle.

Rights of way

While a large proportion of the English and Welsh countryside is in private hands, and much of it is under cultivation, the law allows for paths to be designated as rights of way. Visitors may use such paths at any time, and the law seeks to preserve this right. There are three types of path designated as rights of way:

- public footpaths (sometimes signposted with yellow arrows) are for the use of walkers only. Walkers may bring dogs with them, but must keep them on a lead at certain times of the year and always when passing through fields in which farmers are keeping livestock
- public bridleways (sometimes signposted with blue arrows) may be used by walkers, those riding horses and ponies and those on push-bikes
- public byways (sometimes signposted with red arrows) are open to all vehicles.

In addition to these, there are paths known as 'permissive routes'. These have not been designated in one of the above categories, but the landowner has made it clear that he is happy to have people use the route.

Obviously, those using rights of way do not have the right to deviate, for example, onto pasture or into forests (although they may stop to rest or to picnic close to the path). Motor vehicles are mostly prohibited from public footpaths and bridleways, although they may be allowed to use the part of paths closest to roads to turn or park.

The freedom to roam

A recent law, the Countryside and Rights of Way Act 2001, has given new rights to the general public (within limits) to roam across certain parts of the countryside that is not under cultivation, without having to stick to the public byways. The law covers such places as moors, mountainsides, common land, heaths and downs. It does not yet cover forests, beaches or coastline, or river- and canal-sides. The right of access to such places will not come into force until they have been mapped, and interested landowners have had an opportunity to protest if they have a good reason for not allowing a right of access on certain pieces of land.

While allowing new rights of access to huge swathes of the countryside, the law does limit the activities of people while on the land. It does not include people using any kind of vehicle (including bicycles), or horse riders, and walkers may not, for instance:

- bathe in non-tidal waters
- light fires

- take part in organised games
- interfere with livestock, or damage property or plants.

Those found breaching these regulations may be ejected from the area by the landowner as trespassers. In addition, landowners may have the right to close areas of land at certain times of the year.

Trespass

People deviating from designated paths and entering land that is not covered by the 'freedom to roam' legislation may be guilty of trespass. (Those who flout the rules prohibiting certain activities on open-access land also become trespassers in the eyes of the law.) A landowner has the right to ask a trespasser to leave, and to use reasonable force to get a trespasser to do just that. In the courts, a landowner may only be able to claim compensation in the civil courts against a trespasser if crops, livestock or other property, such as buildings, have been damaged (and this includes causing anxiety among livestock so that they produce less). See pages 252–253 for information on the law regarding the activities of dogs on private property.

In addition, the police have various rights to ask certain groups of people entering private land to move on and to arrest those who do not.

Conservation

There are various laws regulating our activities in the countryside which are aimed at protecting fragile environments and endangered species of birds, animals and plants. A general rule is to stay away from wildlife and not to pick or uproot any plants (many of our most familiar plants are now protected by law). Following the Country Code should go a long way to keeping visitors to the countryside out of trouble:

- enjoy the country side and respect its life and work
- guard against all risk of fire
- fasten all gates
- keep your dogs under close control
- keep to public paths across farmland
- use gates and stiles to cross fences, hedges and walls
- leave livestock, crops and machinery alone
- take your litter home

◆ help to keep all water clean
◆ protect wildlife, plants and trees
◆ take special care on country roads
◆ make no unnecessary noise.

Travelling abroad

More and more people these days are taking their holidays and breaks abroad, taking full advantage of cheap flights and bargain-basement package deals. The vast majority of people travelling abroad have happy experiences. Others are not so lucky. Their dream package holiday has not lived up to expectations raised by glossy advertising, flights are overbooked, luggage goes missing or the hotel is noisy. Here is a summary of some of the laws that might come into play in certain situations.

Problems with holiday services

These days, the media are full of holiday horror stories, and it seems that all too often, holidaymakers are disappointed with their holidays, either because their expectations were too high or because of the failings of one or more of the organisations involved in the arrangements.

Holidays are governed by consumer laws, just as any other service or goods we buy. So, if any part of the experience fall below expectations, you may be able to make a claim for compensation.

As for restaurants, when you make a reservation at a hotel, you enter into a contract with that establishment. So, if you arrive and things are not as agreed, you may be able to claim for breach of contract.

If you feel that your holiday has been misleadingly described, the organiser may conceivably be breaking laws that make it a criminal offence to actively give a misleading description of a

Rough camping

Rough camping on private land is generally illegal in England and Wales, although some landowners tolerate it. If you can't use a campsite, it's always best to ask before setting up your tent.

product. The same is true of organisers who give a misleading price. In cases like these, you should inform your local Trading Standards department, who may investigate.

The first step to take is to complain as soon as you can, giving the hotel or tour representative an opportunity to put things right. However, if you feel things do not improve, you may be able to claim in the Small Claims Court for a sum to cover that part of your holiday which was unsatisfactory. Barring a complete disaster, it is unlikely that you will be able to claim more than the full amount you paid.

Package holidays

Package holidays are covered by specific laws, set down in the Package Travel Regulations (1992). Under these regulations, those who organise package holidays have certain responsibilities towards their customers, and if things go wrong, customers have certain avenues for action.

A package holiday is defined as a group of services which may include:

- transport
- accommodation
- other travel services.

The package must include at least two of these services to qualify under the Regulations. If you book a hotel through a travel agent, for example, this is not a package holiday.

The Regulations say that an organiser must provide an accurate description of the holiday; if a brochure is produced, this must give an accurate representation of the holiday. The customer must receive a contract from the organiser, and this should include:

- a clear indication of the dates of travel and the destination(s)
- a clear indication of the transport with relevant dates
- details of the accommodation
- details of meals
- details of the itinerary
- what the organiser will do in the event of a change to any of these details
- a deadline for the customer to cancel the package

- whether a minimum number of customers is required for the package to go ahead
- the deadline for the organiser to cancel the trip should it fail to have enough bookings
- anything else that is included in the price
- the price of the package and a note on what will happen if the prices change
- full contact details for the organiser, and their insurer.

In addition, organisers should supply the holidaymaker with a host of other information, including, among other things, passport and visa requirements.

Package holidays – insurance

Under the Regulations, all organisers of package holidays must protect holidaymakers in the event that the company becomes insolvent. In theory, if this happens, the company should be able to either transport holidaymakers home or enable them to complete their holiday before travelling home. Package holiday organisers must do this either by: taking out an insurance policy; being a member of ABTA (see page 308); by holding an Air Travel Organisers Licence (ATOL) or by putting funds paid by customers into a separate account.

Those who book package holidays should check that the business concerned is a member of the relevant organisation.

Package holidays – price changes

Many package organisers reserve the right to change the price of a package before travel. This is due usually to changes in exchange rates. The organiser is required to absorb the first 2% of any change in the cost of a package but can pass on to the customer anything over this. Check the contract.

Problems with package holidays

As for all services, if any part of the package does not come up to standard, consumers may have a case for a small claim. Again, a case is unlikely to succeed unless you have informed the organisers as soon as possible, and given them an opportunity to put things right. If the situation does not change, contact the package organiser as soon as possible on your return. If this does not bring a satisfactory outcome, the Regulations allow a consumer to take a case to the Small Claims Court, to claim for actual losses (for example, the part of the price of the holiday that covered accommodation) but also for lost enjoyment. In order to back up such a case, put together evidence, including photographs of dirty rooms and the names and addresses of other holidaymakers who may be able to act as witnesses. A small claim can be pursued through the courts without the help of a solicitor.

In addition, the Regulations lay more responsibilities on travel organisers than are listed here. Contact your local Citizens Advice Bureau for guidance if you are unhappy with any aspect of your travel arrangements. They should be able to tell you whether you have a valid claim.

Problems with flights

With the skies getting so full these days, air travel seems to be becoming more and more fraught. The most frequent complaint is about delays. Airlines have a duty to get their passengers where they are going within a reasonable time of the advertised time of arrival. This 'window' depends on the length of the journey, and airlines cannot be asked to compensate travellers if circumstances out of their control caused the delay (for example, bad weather).

Another problem is overbooking of flights. Airlines lose money if they don't fly full, so they tend to overbook flights, relying on a few people not to turn up on the day. Unhappily, sometimes, everyone turns up, and the airline must ask people to fly later. They must, however, offer compensation. If you are one of the unhappy few and are not happy with the compensation offered, don't take it, reserving your right to make a claim at a later date.

Timeshares

Timeshare organisations have been portrayed as notorious villains in the popular press for pressure-selling fresh air to

Warning!

Some travel organisers have a time limit for complaints – if your holiday has gone wrong, don't wait too long before making a complaint to the organiser. Do it as soon as you return.

unsuspecting members of the public. Of course, many organisations who build and run timeshare developments offer a bona fide place in the sun, and adhere to a professional code of conduct. Some, however, do not.

A timeshare is by law defined as an interest in a property by which the purchaser has the right to use the property for a certain time period each year for a minimum of three years. Holiday plans that do not offer for sale an interest in property or for the minimum of three years, are not timeshares. Any product that involves buying a share in a floating vessel, such as a boat, is not classified as a timeshare. The difference is very important: timeshare selling is covered by statute, both in the UK and in all the countries in Europe. Selling other holiday 'products' that look like timeshares is not covered by such legislation, and consumers may in some cases find themselves without any legal protection.

Selling of timeshares is governed in the UK by the Timeshare Act (1992) and the Timeshare Regulations (1997). Across the European Economic Area (EEA, see page 264 for a list of EEA countries), selling timeshares is governed by the Timeshare Directive (94/47/EC). These rules are designed to give some measure of protection to consumers. They say:

- anyone sold a timeshare scheme has 10 days in which to consider the deal after signing (in the UK the cooling-off period is 14 days), and may cancel at any time during that period.
- those selling timeshare deals are not permitted to take any form of payment, even a deposit, until the cooling-off period is over.
- prospective purchasers must be given adequate documentation describing the property accurately, and giving other important information. Information must

---

OTE

Reputable timeshare organisations are usually members of an organisation called The Organisation for Timeshare in Europe (OTE). They offer a conciliation and advice service for timeshare buyers. See page 313 for contact details.

be in the language of the country the prospective buyer comes from.

If you feel you have been mis-sold a timeshare in the UK, contact your local Trading Standards department. If the selling has taken place abroad, you are advised to contact the equivalent department in the relevant country.

Readers are advised not to purchase timeshares on the spur of the moment, but to take all written information away and consider the purchase very carefully before signing up. Take advice before making a commitment.

Passports

Any UK citizen who wishes to travel beyond these shores will require a valid passport. The exceptions are if you are travelling to Eire, the Channel Islands or the Isle of Man, but you will still need valid photo-identification.

A normal British passport is valid for 10 years and entitles the holder to travel to any destination provided she satisfies the entry criteria of the country to which she is travelling, such as acquiring a valid visa.

Even babies now have to have a passport. Previously, infants and children travelled on the passport of one of their parents, but the law changed recently so that every individual now needs his or her own document. If you are a parent and you have a passport issued before October 1998 that includes a child or children, the children can continue to travel on your passport as long as they travel with you. When your passport expires, needs to be re-issued, or the child turns 16, you will need to apply for separate passports.

Those under 18 who wish to apply for a passport will need the permission of one of their parents.

Issuing a passport can take a surprisingly long time. If you are planning a trip, apply for a passport in good time. Contact the Passport Service (see page 313 for contact details) for up-to-date information on how long the process takes.

Visas

British citizens do not require special permission to travel to any of the EEA countries (for a list of these countries, see page 264), even if you are planning to work. However, if you are travelling to any other country, it is wise to check in good time whether you need a visa. Contact the relevant embassy or consulate, or your travel agent.

Carriers, such as airlines, will refuse to transport you if you do not have the correct documentation for entry to your destination country.

Getting into trouble while abroad

Travellers should always be aware that the law of the land in Britain is not necessarily duplicated in other countries. In general, and particularly when compared to non-Western countries, Britain is a relatively permissive society. Other countries' legal systems are not so forgiving. Be prepared for penalties to be more severe than in the UK. Capital and corporal punishment may not be used in this country, but abroad it is still relatively common. In some cases, life sentences mean exactly that.

Also, be prepared for laws to be different. British travellers sometimes fall foul of laws regarding dress codes, alcohol and drunkenness, and the use of drugs (for which penalties can be very harsh indeed). It is very difficult to give specific warnings for every country, but it is wise to know something of the country you are visiting before you go. On general modes of behaviour, such as dress and drinking in public, take your cue from local people. If your visit involves specific activities, such as plane spotting, hitch-hiking or hiking, get as much information as you can about legal restrictions you travel.

If you do get into trouble when abroad, you will be subject to the legal system of the country you are in, regardless of how different it may be to the British system. The British government is unlikely to be able to intervene on your behalf (but see the section on the Consular Service, below). If you are found guilty of a crime and given a prison sentence, it may be possible to be transferred to a British prison, but government agreements relating to this exist with a very few countries (including Egypt and Thailand).

Pets abroad

See pages 255–257 for information on travelling with your pet and the new 'pet passport' scheme.

If you are the victim of a crime while overseas, you should seek advice from the British consulate in that country. It is not likely that they will be able to intervene legally, but they may be able to provide useful advice and subsidiary help. In general, you will need to employ the services of a local lawyer if you wish to claim compensation, for example.

The Consular Service

The British government has consulates around the world. In countries where there is no British representation, travellers may make use of the services of consulates from any of the EU countries. The Consular Service can provide only limited help to travellers abroad, and it does charge a fee for its services. It can among other things:

- contact friends or family at home if you need help, for example, extra cash for an emergency
- cash a sterling cheque up to £100 in an emergency (it cannot lend money to travellers in trouble)
- help you to get documents with which to travel if you have lost your passport or it has been stolen
- give advice in emergency situations, such as a death or illness while abroad
- help you to find an English-speaking local lawyer (and/or an interpreter), and, if you cannot afford legal service, advise on local 'legal aid' schemes, if these exist
- if you are on trial abroad, it can intervene only in cases where your human rights have been violated or your conviction may be unfair, and in the latter case, only when you have exhausted all other avenues, such as the appeals process
- intervene in cases where British citizens in prison in a foreign country have been mistreated; monitor the healthcare of prisoners and pass on personal items (such as toiletries, newspapers, etc.) sent by families.

Driving abroad

For information on driving outside the UK, see pages 214–215.

Duty-free

Any person or company that imports goods from abroad for commercial purposes is liable to pay an import duty, which is levied by HM Customs and Excise. Individual travellers who are importing goods purely for private use (or as gifts) and not for sale are allowed to bring into the UK certain quantities before they must start paying duty. Customs Officer who believe that travellers are trying to smuggle goods into the country without paying duty for commercial purposes are empowered to confiscate goods and vehicles and impose penalties.

Travellers whose point of departure was one of the EU countries are allowed to bring into the country a reasonable quantity of goods for personal use without paying duty. Customs Officers will become suspicious that you are flouting the rules (and actually bringing in goods for commercial purposes) if you are carrying more than the following quantities:

- 3,200 cigarettes or
- 400 cigarillos or
- 200 cigars or
- 3 kg pipe or rolling tobacco
- 110 litres beer
- 10 litres spirits
- 90 litres wine
- 20 litres fortified wine.

Travellers whose point of departure was outside the EU have strict duty-free limits:

- 200 cigarettes or
- 100 cigarillos or
- 50 cigars or
- 250 g pipe or rolling tobacco.
- 60 ml perfume
- 250 ml toilet water
- 2 litres wine
- 2 litres fortified wine, sparkling wine or liqueurs
- 1 litre spirits (or liqueurs over 22% volume)
- £145 worth of other goods.

Film classification

The British Board of Film Censors is a body set up to classify films as suitable for consumption by certain members of society in an effort to protect the more vulnerable from inappropriate material, such as pornography or excessive violence. It uses the following classification system, which is enforced by law.

- **Uc**
  Particularly suitable for pre-school children
- **U (Universal)**
  Suitable for children of four years old and older
- **PG (parental guidance)**
  Films classified as PG should not be disturbing to a child of about the age of eight or older. Children over the age of eight may be admitted to a cinema to view a PG film without being accompanied by an adult. Parental guidance is required for children under this age
- **12a**
  No-one under the age of 12 may see a 12a film unless they are accompanied by an adult
- **12**
  No child under the age of 12 may rent or buy a 12 rated-video or DVD
- **15**
  No-one under the age of 15 may be allowed to see a 15-rated film in the cinema, or rent or buy the video or DVD
- **18**
  Only adults over the age of 18 may be admitted to a cinema to see 18-rated films, and only adults may buy or rent the video or DVD
- **R18**
  Only available in licensed sex shops (to adults over the age of 18) and not to be sold by mail order.

Key terms

ABTA

Short for Association of British Travel Agents. The professional association for travel agents. See page 308.

ATOL
Short for Air Travel Organisers' Licence. Scheme operated by the Civil Aviation Authority (see page 309) which protects holidaymakers by ensuring operators have a sound financial base and that a bond is posted to cover customers in the event that an operator goes out of business.

bridleway
Right of way through private land for the use of walkers, cyclists and those riding horses. See page 235.

controlled substance
Any of a number of drugs whose possession, use and trade are controlled under legislation including the Misuse of Drugs Act (1971) and the Medicines Act (1968). See pages 230–234.

duty-free
Bringing goods into the UK without needing to pay excise duty. See page 245.

freedom to roam
Term that covers new laws enabling the general public access to specific parts of Britain's open country. See pages 235–236.

licensed premises
A bar, nightclub, restaurant, off-licence or other premises for which there is a licence to sell or serve alcohol.

licensee
The individual who applies for and holds a licence, e.g. to serve or to sell alcohol.

PETS
The government scheme that enables some travellers to bring their pets into the UK without the necessity for quarantine. See pages 255–256.

public byway
Right of way through private land for the use of wheeled vehicles, riders and cyclists. See page 235.

public footpath
Right of way through private land for the use of walkers (their dogs and prams) only. See page 235.

right of way
The right of ordinary people (not the landowner) to 'pass and re-pass' along a certain route. See pages 234–235.

12 Pets and other Animals

It is estimated that more than half of the households in the UK keep some sort of pet. The vast majority of them are dogs and cats, but we also have developed an affection for other species, including reptiles and big cats. The laws that cover animals kept in normal households (rather than on farms, for instance) are aimed at ensuring they are well-treated, and that they present no problems for the health and safety of the people living with and around them. This chapter looks at how we acquire our pets, and what responsibilities we have for them when they are living with us at home as well as when they are taken outside the home, in the UK and abroad. It also looks at requirements for establishments that make a business out of looking after our pets, such as kennels.

Buying a pet

The law restricts the sale of animals in order to provide for their welfare. In general, pets may only be sold by shops with a licence from the local authority. The licensing system is there to ensure that animals for sale are kept in humane and hygienic conditions, that they are fed properly and that they are protected from fire risks and from disease. If you feel that any shop selling animals is mistreating them, contact your local branch of the RSPCA or the local authority. Pets may not be sold in local markets or in the streets.

Buying from a recognised shop or breeder will go some way towards ensuring you have recourse if the animal turns out to be unhealthy or unfit in some other way. Your purchase is covered by the general laws relating to the sale of goods (see page 39–41). The animal should be 'fit for the purpose' for which it was purchased and of satisfactory quality. If your hamster becomes unwell shortly after its purchase, you are generally entitled to return the animal and ask for your money back if you can show that it was not of saleable quality.

Pedigree dogs and cats that have been bred in a breeding establishment and are sold through a licensed pet shop will come with certified information about where and when they were bred. Breeders must themselves be licensed by the local authority under similar terms to pet shops.

Incidentally, it is illegal for anyone under the age of 12 to buy and own a pet. Of course, many children 'own' pets, but in law, the head of the household is ultimately responsible for the animal's welfare and behaviour.

Animal welfare

Cruelty to animals is a subject close to the hearts of many Britons, and the law reflects this. Under the law it is an offence to mistreat any animal kept in captivity, whether a family pet, a wild animal or livestock. Mistreating an animal can bring a fine of up to £5,000 and/or a maximum prison sentence of six months. Additionally, a mistreated animal may be taken away from its owner, and if its suffering is too great for it to be moved or treated, the authorities may order it put down.

'Mistreatment' includes the following:

◆ beating or kicking, overburdening, torturing, infuriating or terrifying the animal
◆ abandoning the animal in circumstances that are likely to cause it suffering
◆ causing unnecessary suffering during transportation
◆ administering substances that will harm the animal without a good reason (scientific experimentation, where licensed, is exempt from this), and causing an animal undue suffering while operating on it
◆ causing unnecessary suffering while the animal is being slaughtered
◆ forcing animals to fight, or taking part in animal baiting
◆ hunting an animal that has been previously reduced to an injured or exhausted state and then released
◆ hunting an animal that is confined in an area from which it cannot escape.

There are additional laws covering the treatment of horses, the prohibition of cock fighting, and the licensing of establishments where animals are trained and exhibited.

Specific laws for dogs

Many of us keep dogs as pets, and the different breeds are as numerous as their temperaments. Dogs have been with us for centuries, and they can be used to work for us, to act as friends and companions, but also to guard and in some cases to intimidate and do damage. A large body of legislation has, understandably, grown up around the keeping of dogs.

All dogs in a public place should have a collar with an identifying tag which clearly gives the owner's name and contact details. When in a public place with a keeper, dogs should be kept under control and on a lead.

Controlling your dog

It is an offence to allow a dog to become out of control in a public place.

A public place is defined as any area where the public is permitted access, and can include parks, streets and shopping centres, but also public transport and the common parts of shared housing such as blocks of flats or the garden of a private house (if the animal is threatening people in a neighbouring garden, for example, or people who have business at your front door).

The term 'out of control' is defined in a range of ways. The animal could be obstructing or annoying people around it, or putting them in danger. Such danger does not have to be real danger. If a ferociously-barking dog is enough to make a person believe he or his own animal is about to be attacked, the law considers the barking dog to be out of control, and an offence has been committed. It is also an offence to set a dog onto someone or someone else's animal, or (again) to make another person think he or his own animal is about to be attacked. Your dog doesn't actually have to bite to be considered 'out of control'.

Get advice

The RSPCA (see page 314) has a series of factsheets on the purchase and care of various popular household pets. If you are contemplating buying a pedigree dog or cat, contact either the Kennel Club or the Governing Council of the Cat Fancy.

Anyone may make a complaint that a dog is dangerous and out of control. In response, the court may order one or more of the following actions:

- ◆ that the dog is kept under control in future (including being muzzled, being kept tethered, and being banned from certain places)
- ◆ that a male dog is neutered
- ◆ that the animal is put down ('destroyed').

If a dog causes injury to a person while out of control in a public place, then its keeper may be guilty of an 'aggravated' offence, and this could bring a prison sentence and/or a fine. In addition, the offender may be disqualified from keeping dogs in the future.

Dogs and livestock

If your dog 'worries' livestock on someone else's farm, you may be charged with a criminal offence under the Dogs (Protection of Livestock) Act 1953. Under this Act, 'worrying' means attacking or chasing, causing injury, threatening to cause injury or reducing the livestock's yield of young through anxiety. Under this Act, 'livestock' means cattle, sheep, goats, pigs, horses and poultry.

Under the Animals Act 1971, if your dog injures or kills livestock on someone else's farm, then you can be sued for damages in the civil courts. Under this Act, the definition of 'livestock' includes captive pheasants, poultry, grouse and other animals as well as those animals listed under the 1953 Act.

A farmer who kills your dog while it is in the act of worrying or attacking his livestock can in certain circumstances defend that action in civil proceedings if he can show that there was no other way of stopping the dog's attack or that he had no way of finding the dog's owner.

Beware of the dog

Signs that warn visitors to beware of the dog will not act as a defence in court; in fact they will only serve to prove that you were aware that your dog was in the habit of biting people and you failed to restrain him!

If, however, your dog worries or kills livestock that has strayed onto your land, you would not be held responsible as long as you can show that you did not incite the dog to attack.

It is a criminal offence for the owner of a dog to be out of control in a field of sheep. In addition, it is an offence to send a dog onto someone else's land to catch game without the consent of the landowner. This would be an act of trespass. However, if the dog is not sent, but enters someone else's land of its own accord and does not kill, worry or injure any livestock, the owner cannot be sued for trespass under civil law.

Dangerous dogs

The Dangerous Dogs Act was enacted in 1991 and amended in 1997 in response to a growing number of attacks on people by individual dogs from a number of specific breeds. These Acts cover the following breeds:

- pit bull terrier
- Japanese tosa
- Dogo argentino
- Fila braziliero.

It is unlawful to breed, sell, exchange or give as a gift or even to offer to sell, exchange or give as a gift dogs of these breeds. A court may order that a dangerous dog of one of these breeds is destroyed, or that it is muzzled and/or kept on a lead. However, if the court feels the dog is not a danger then it can order it to be registered on the index of exempted dogs.

Dog fouling

It is illegal to allow your dog to defecate in any public place, and all dog owners are advised to carry equipment with which to remove dirt. Allowing your dog to foul the environment could bring an instant fine or prosecution. The definition of a public place is wide. Many local authorities display signs warning

Guard dogs

For information on the law about keeping and using guard dogs, see page 161.

against dog fouling, but it is unwise to assume that the absence of a sign means that you should not clear up after your dog wherever you are.

Animals and accidents

If you as a motorist are involved in an accident involving an animal (excluding cats), you should stop. You are also required by law to report the accident to the police within 24 hours. You may be liable for damages if you injure an animal in a traffic accident on the public highway, but you may be able to counter-sue if the animal has strayed into the road through the negligence of its owner (e.g. if the owner has allowed fencing designed to keep animals off the road to fall into disrepair).

Wild animals

It has become fashionable in recent decades to make pets of all sorts of wild animals, including spiders, reptiles of all sorts and even big cats. The law requires all owners of wild animals to be licensed by the local authority if they are to be kept in private premises, and the licensing system seeks to ensure that the authorities are aware of the presence of potentially dangerous animals and that they are being cared for in suitable circumstances.

Of course, owners are liable for the activities of their pets, and keepers of dangerous species who cause injury or damage may be liable for damages regardless of whether they are aware of the animal's dangerous characteristics.

Boarding your pet

It is your responsibility to see that any pets are looked after if you are absent, for example, on holiday. Leaving a pet unattended at home while you are away could amount to neglect.

All boarding establishments – kennels, catteries, etc. – must be licensed by the local authority and are governed by Act of Parliament. The relevant Act requires that boarding establishments:

- meet certain standards as to hygiene and accommodation
- provide adequate and suitable food and drink
- are active in stopping the spread of disease from one

animal to another, and specifically have suitable facilities with which to isolate diseased animals from the other 'boarders'

◆ keep appropriate records about the animals in their care

◆ employ a qualified vet to look after the health of the animals in their care

◆ take appropriate steps to protect the animals in the event of a fire or some other emergency.

Travelling with your pet

Until very recently any family pet entering the UK had to endure six months quarantine before it was allowed to go home. This period of quarantine was enforced in an effort to prevent the spread of diseases such as rabies. In recent years, however, the government has established a pet 'passport' scheme which enables travellers from some countries to bring their pets into the country without putting them into quarantine. The scheme is known as the Pet Travel Scheme (PETS). PETS covers only dogs (including guide dogs and hearing dogs) and cats. Only pets entering the UK from the following countries are eligible (pets that have been in any other country within six months of entering the UK have to go into quarantine):

Andorra	Antigua and Barbuda
Ascension Island	Australia
Austria	Bahrain
Barbados	Belgium
Bermuda	Canada
Cayman Islands	Cyprus
Denmark	Falkland Islands
Fiji	Finland
France	French Polynesia
Germany	Gibraltar
Greece	Guadeloupe
Hawaii	Iceland
Italy	Jamaica
Japan	Liechtenstein
Luxembourg	Malta
Martinique	Mauritius
Mayotte	Monaco
Montserrat	Netherlands

New Caledonia   New Zealand
Norway   Portugal
Réunion   St Helena
St Kitts & Nevis   St Vincent
San Marino   Singapore
Spain   Sweden
Switzerland   USA
Vanuatu   Vatican City
Wallis and Futuna

Note: some of these countries have special requirements, and as time moves on, the regulations may change, so get advice from DEFRA (see page 310) if you are considering travelling with your pet.

In order to enable your pet to be part of the scheme it would need:

- to be microchipped in order for the authorities to make a positive identification of the animal
- to be vaccinated against rabies within a certain time period and treated for tapeworm and ticks
- to have passed a blood test proving that it is free of disease, and be accompanied by certificates to this effect
- to be accompanied by a document in which you declare that the animal has not been taken to any country other than those on the list above in the previous six months
- to be transported by a recognised carrier and enter the UK via a recognised route.

The procedure needs to be carried out in a certain order and within a certain time period, and these rules change depending on the country in which the animal starts its journey.

Quarantine

If your pet does not qualify for the PETS scheme, you will have to place it in quarantine for six months. To do this you will need to have chosen the quarantine premises and carrier in advance, you will need an import licence so that the animal can be cleared through customs, and you will need to import your pet through certain routes. Contact DEFRA (see page 310) for further information on procedures.

If you import an animal without going through the necessary

procedures you could be prosecuted. You may be faced with an unlimited fine or a prison sentence. Your pet may be returned to its point of departure, put into quarantine or even put down.

Premises used for quarantine must comply with the laws laid down to ensure animal welfare as for other animal boarding establishments. They will employ a qualified vet who will vaccinate each quarantined animal against rabies on arrival.

Taking your pet abroad

A number of countries, including some in the European Union, place strict requirements on the pets of travellers from the UK before they will be allowed to enter. If you are planning to travel abroad with your pet, contact the relevant country's embassy or consulate as soon as possible.

Key terms

boarding establishment
Any premises where the main business is the boarding of animals. See pages 254–255.

breeder
Any person who makes a business out of the breeding and selling of animals. See page 250.

dangerous dogs
Officially, dogs from certain breeds, which UK law has made subject to special regulation because of their generally aggressive temperament. See page 253.

livestock
In general, animals farmed for financial gain.

PETS
A scheme set up by the British government to enable travellers from some countries to import their pet into the UK without having to put them in quarantine. See pages 255–256.

quarantine
Keeping an animal in isolation for a period of time in order to prevent the spread of disease. See page 256.

13 Immigration, Nationality and Identity

Today's Britain is a vibrant multiracial, multicultural society. By virtue of its global language and historical links with many countries around the world, Britain continues to attract visitors, workers, students, settlers and those seeking asylum. This chapter looks at the legal framework for regulating immigration, starting with the primary question of who is eligibile for British citizenship. It goes on to cover regulations for those who want to visit, work or study in the UK, and those who wish to take up residence in the country. It also covers briefly the current laws on asylum and how best to get immigration advice. Finally, this chapter looks at issues of personal identity, how to register the birth of a chid (the most fundamental step in establishing identity) how to prove your identity and how to change your name.

In the law relating to immigration and nationality, the word 'British' is frequently used. It is important to say at the outset that when Britain/British appear in this context, it actually refers to the whole of the United Kingdom, which comprises: England, Scotland, Wales and Northern Ireland, plus the Channel Islands and the Isle of Man.

British citizenship and nationality

The terms 'citizenship' and 'nationality' have different meanings. To be a citizen is to have nationality, but a British national doesn't necessarily have a right to British citizenship. There are six categories of British national: British citizens; British Overseas territories citizens; British Overseas Citizens; British Subjects; British Nationals (Overseas); British Protected Persons. All are entitled to carry a British passport, but not all have the same residency rights. British nationals who are not British citizens may require visas for countries that generally waive the need for visas, e.g. currently the USA and Japan.

IMMIGRATION, NATIONALITY AND IDENTITY

British citizens

British citizens have the right to live and work in the UK – they are said to have 'right of abode'. British citizens are allowed to travel freely in the UK and to live and work within the EEA (the European Economic Area, see pages 263–264 for a list of EEA countries). British citizens fall into two categories, and these are important in determining the rights of their children to British citizenship:

◆ 'British citizens otherwise than by descent' are generally people who were born, adopted, naturalised (see pages 261–262) or registered (see page 261) in the UK or a British Overseas Territory (BOT, see below). If you are a British citizen otherwise than by descent, and are settled in the UK, and your child is born in the UK (or, after 21 May 2002, a BOT), then she is a British citizen otherwise than by descent. If your child is born outside the UK or a BOT, she will be a British citizen by descent. It is not necessary to register a child born in this case before she can become a citizen (except of course, you will need to register her birth in the usual way, see pages 276–277).

◆ 'British citizens by descent' are generally people born outside the UK to at least one parent who is a British citizen. If you are a British citizen by descent and your child was born in the UK between 1 January 1983 and before 21 May 2002, or in the UK or a BOT after 21 May 2002, she is automatically a British citizens otherwise than by descent.

Changes in the law

The detail of immigration law is subject to change, and this book can only give information on the law at the time of writing. If you are uncertain about your immigration rights or those of your family and friends, or you need to act in some way, you should ask at your local Citizens Advice Bureau or law centre. The Home Office's own website gives large amounts of up-to-date information as well as downloadable application forms. See page 311 for details.

If you are outside the UK or any BOT when your child is born, she is not automatically entitled to British citizenship. Regulations governing the circumstances in which your child is entitled to become a citizen relate to the strength of her connection with the UK. The parent who is a British citizen by descent needs him- or herself to have had a parent who was a British citizen otherwise than by descent (or would have been entitled to be so on 1 January 1983) and to have lived in the UK for at least three years at some stage. Alternatively, the child may be entitled to British citizenship if she is born stateless. Children who qualify will need to be registered with the Home Office in order to become British citizens.

British Overseas Territories Citizens

Citizens of British Overseas Territories are citizens of a British dependency such as Bermuda or Gibraltar (but not including the Sovereign Base Areas of Akrotiri and Dhekelia in Cyprus). The BOT were formerly called the British Dependent Territories.

Since 2002, BOT citizens have been entitled to be both British citizens and BOT citizens. Children born to those settled in a BOT or to BOT citizens generally become BOT citizens and British citizens at birth (see above).

British Overseas Citizens

People connected to countries that were once British colonies (e.g. Kenya) and who did not take up citizenship of that country when it became an independent state. British Overseas Citizens are not automatically entitled to British citizenship.

British Subjects

People born before 1 January 1949 and with a connection to British India or the republic of Ireland. British Subjects are not automatically entitled to British citizenship.

Women's rights

Surprisingly, it was only in 1981 that the law enabled women to pass on their British citizenship to children born outside the UK. Up until then, only male citizens were entitled to do so.

IMMIGRATION, NATIONALITY AND IDENTITY

British Nationals (Overseas)

People connected with Hong Kong, a former British Dependent Territory. British Nationals (Overseas) are not automatically entitled to British citizenship.

British Protected Persons

People connected with former British Protectorates, Protected States and Trust Territories. British Protected Persons are not automatically entitled to British citizenship.

Becoming a British citizen

The vast majority of British citizens are entitled to that right when they are born. However, it is possible to become a British citizen by two other methods: by registration, or by naturalisation.

Registration

This process generally only applies to people under the age of 18 (although a small number of adults acquire citizenship by this means) who are British nationals (see above) and either:

- have been resident in the UK for five years as for the naturalisation process below, or
- have worked in the Crown service and satisfy certain criteria, or
- have been settled in the UK (with indefinite leave to remain) for at least a year, or
- are children whose parents are not British citizens and were not permanently settled in the UK at the time of their birth, but who have subsequently become settled, or
- are children who have been in the UK (lawfully or unlawfully) for a consecutive period of 90 days since 1983, or
- are children who are citizens by descent but were not born in the UK or a BOT.

Some of these categories rely on the discretion of the Home Secretary, and if registration is refused, there is no right of appeal.

Naturalisation

Those who have no connection to the UK through a parent

who is a citizen can acquire British citizenship by a process known as naturalisation.

To be naturalised, a person would normally have to satisfy the following criteria:

- he must have been resident in the UK continuously for a period of at least five years, perhaps on a work permit or as a resident from an EEA country
- he must be competent in at least one of the following languages: English, Welsh or Scots Gaelic
- he must be 'of good character', that is, without criminal convictions
- he must be genuinely intending to make the UK his home.

(The rules on language competency and the swearing of an oath of allegiance were under consideration at the time of writing.)

Those who become British citizens and are then convicted of a serious crime within five years may be stripped of their citizenship and deported.

People who marry British citizens are eligible to become naturalised after they have been resident ('settled') in this country for three years. The language competency requirement does not apply to those who marry British citizens.

If you become a British citizen, you may apply for an existing spouse and children to become citizens as well.

If you apply for British citizenship and your application is refused for any reason, there is no right of appeal.

Illegitimacy and British citizenship

If a child is born to unmarried parents in the UK and the mother is a British citizen, then the child would take on the mother's citizenship rights. However, if the parents are unmarried and the mother is not a British citizen and is not officially 'settled' in the UK, the child is not automatically entitled to citizenship. Parents in such circumstances should seek advice from a Citizens Advice Bureau or the IND (see page 311).

IMMIGRATION, NATIONALITY AND IDENTITY

Dual Nationality

British law allows its nationals to hold passports from more than one country. So, if you become a British citizen, for example, you are not forced by the UK authorities to give up your former citizenship. However, if you are a British Subject, or a British Protected Person, in most cases you will be required to give up your British nationality if you become a citizen of any other country.

You may also be required to give up your British nationality/citizenship by another government if you become a citizen of a country that does not allow dual nationality.

If you have taken on British citizenship, you may automatically have cancelled your citizenship of your former homeland. It may also be the case that your children and spouse automatically lost their citizenship of your homeland when you acquired your citizenship of the UK, even if they have not formally become British citizens themselves. If you wish to visit your former homeland and are not sure what the situation is, check with the consulate or embassy of your former homeland before travelling.

Giving up British citizenship

Any British citizen or BOT citizen is entitled to renounce his British citizenship. It is also possible to take citizenship back, but only once. It is also possible to renounce other forms of British nationality, but in this case, you will have no right to resume your nationality if you change your mind.

Coming and going

British law divides the world into different categories for the purposes of regulating those who wish to visit the UK or to work, study or settle here.

At the top of the pile, as may be expected, come British citizens. People in this group are said to have 'right of abode' in the UK (i.e. they have the right to live here), and may in general come and go as they please.

Next come people who are citizens of the group of countries called the European Economic Area (EEA). This group includes all the countries of the European Union plus four others. They are:

Austria   Belgium   Denmark

Eire	Finland	France
Greece	Germany	Iceland
Italy	Liechtenstein	Luxembourg
Netherlands	Norway	Portugal
Spain	Sweden	Switzerland

At the time of writing, the following countries were due to join the EU in 2004:

Cyprus	Czech Republic	Estonia
Hungary	Latvia	Lithuania
Malta	Poland	Slovakia
Slovenia		

Citizens of these countries and their families may enter the UK, work, study and settle here without special permission, although they may be 'removed' (deported) if they are convicted of a serious crime.

The citizens of the third group of countries do not require visas to visit the UK, or to take a course of study, but they do require permission to conduct business, to get work or to settle. Such countries include the USA.

The fourth group of countries is by far the biggest. It is made up of countries called 'visa national countries', and regardless of the reason for coming to the UK (to visit, to study, to work, or to settle), 'visa nationals' (citizens of the visa national countries) require permission in the form of a visa. Some even need visas simply to pass through (transit) the UK without stopping.

Visa national countries

Citizens of countries on the following list require visas for entry into the UK. Those marked ★ also require a visa to land in the UK even if they are bound for an alternative destination, although the majority of visa nationals may 'transit without visa' (TWOV).

Afghanistan★	Albania
Algeria	Angola
Armenia	Azerbaijan
Bahrain	Bangladesh
Belarus	Benin
Bhutan	Bosnia Herzegovina

Bulgaria

Burundi

Cameroon

Central African Rep.

China (People's Rep.)★

Comoros

Congo Democratic
    Rep. (Zaire)★

Djibouti

Ecuador★

Equatorial Guinea

Ethiopia★

Gabon

Georgia

Guinea

Guyana

India

Iran★

Jamaica

Jordan

Kenya

Kuwait

Laos

Liberia

Macau

Madagascar

Mali

Mauritius

Burkina Faso

Cambodia

Cape Verde

Chad

Colombia★

Congo

Croatia★

Cuba

Dominican Rep.

Egypt

Eritrea★

Fiji

Gambia

Ghana★

Guinea-Bissau

Haiti

Indonesia

Iraq★

Ivory Coast

Kazakhstan

Korea (Dem. People's Rep.)

Kyrgyzstan

Lebanon

Libya★

Macedonia

Maldives

Mauritania

Moldova

Getting a visa

Travellers who are not British citizens or citizens of an EEA country are advised to check whether they need a visa with their local British consular post (an embassy or consulate) before travelling. Transport companies such as airlines may be fined if they bring someone to the UK who is not entitled to enter, and they may also be required to transport that person back to the point of departure. Those without the correct visas for their destination will generally be refused by the carrier at the point of departure.

Mongolia	Morocco
Mozambique	Myanmar (Burma)
Nepal	Niger
Nigeria★	Oman
Pakistan	Palestinian Authority
Papua New Guinea	Peru
Philippines	Qatar
Romania	Russia
Rwanda	São Tomé e Principe
Saudi Arabia	Senegal
Sierra Leone	Slovak Republic★
Somalia★	Sri Lanka★
Sudan	Surinam
Syria	Taiwan
Tajikistan	Tanzania
Thailand	Togo
Tunisia	Turkey★
Turkish Rep. of N. Cyprus (TRNC)★	Turkmenistan
Ukraine	Uganda★
Uzbekistan	United Arab Emirates
Vietnam	Vatican City
Yugoslavia★	Yemen
Zimbabwe★	Zambia

Visiting the UK

Visitors to the UK are generally defined as those who come for tourism or to visit friends and family. British citizens and nationals, and citizens of the EEU may visit the UK as often and for as long as they wish. Non-visa nationals do not need a visa to visit the UK, but may only stay for six months from the date of entry into the UK.

Visa nationals require a visa if visiting the UK, and, again, the length of stay is limited. It is illegal to remain in the UK once the visa has expired, or to engage in study or work if the visa is for a visit only.

Studying in the UK

EEU citizens and non-visa nationals may all engage in a course of study in the UK without special permission. Again, visa nationals require a visa for this purpose and may not change the purpose of the stay or overstay the visa time period.

In general, visa nationals studying in the UK may be permitted to work full time during holidays and part-time during term, or to undertake full time work during term if the work is part of an internship or work experience component of the course.

Employers who need to check that a student has the correct permissions to work should seek advice from the Immigration and Nationality Directorate (see page 311).

It is possible for UK employers to take on students from overseas educational institutions, such as universities, as part of an internship, training or work experience programme. In general, such students will need a work permit, and the employer should seek advice from the Immigration and Nationality Directorate.

Working in the UK

EEU citizens are permitted to work in the UK without special permission. EEU citizens must be able to support themselves and their families 'without recourse to public funds' (i.e. without claiming social security benefits such as job seeker's allowance).

Visa nationals and non-visa nationals require work permits, and these would need to be acquired by the employer rather than the worker. In general, the worker should not be in the UK while the application process is taking place, and the employer will need to show that the individual has special skills that would be difficult to find in a worker already in the EEA (called a 'resident worker'). The employer also has to show that

---

Switching

In general, the immigration authorities do not look kindly on those who come to the UK with one type of visa and then wish to change their reason for being here (called 'switching'). For instance, you may have arrived here on a tourist visa, then married a British citizen and then wish to apply to remain. If you wish to change the nature of your visa, it is generally advised that you leave the UK and make a new visa application from abroad. For advice, ask at your local Citizens Advice Bureau or at the Home Office Immigration and Nationality Directorate.

the vacancy is genuine and has been advertised in the UK without yielding a suitably qualified. The rules governing work permit length of duration and renewal vary. For further information and application forms, contact the Immigration and Nationality Directorate (see page 311).

Categories of work permit

The UK authorities have defined six separate types of work permit: business and commercial, covering many forms of business; GATS work permits; sportspeople and entertainers (including engineers and back-up workers in some instances); internships; training and work experience; and highly skilled migrants. Each defines a group of circumstances in which a UK employer can apply for a work permit for someone outside the EEA.

GATS work permits

The General Agreement on Trade and Services (GATS) allows a company based outside the UK which has sold a service to a UK-based client to send its own employees to the UK to work for a period of time in connection with that sale.

Highly Skilled Migrants

This UK Highly Skilled Migrants Programme offers work permits to outstanding individuals. This enables people with extraordinary personal and specialist skills to come to the UK in search of employment without first having a contract and a sponsoring employer.

Shortage occupations

From time to time the UK government publishes a list of occupations for which there appears to be a shortage of workers in the EEA. These occupations are considered a priority for work permits. They include: various occupations under the umbrella term 'engineering'; a large number of occupations in the health sector; all teachers qualified to teach in the primary and secondary education system; vets; actuaries; and aircraft engineers. This list changes from time to time, so check with the IND for further information (see page 311).

IMMIGRATION, NATIONALITY AND IDENTITY

Working holidaymakers

This term refers to citizens of Commonwealth countries between the ages of 17 and 27, who are entitled to work in the UK for a period of two years without a work permit. The principle is that such young people are on holiday and they therefore should be taking part-time or casual work, rather than pursuing a career in the UK.

Au pairs

An au pair is a young single person (aged 17–27) who comes to the UK principally to learn English. Au pairs may stay with an English-speaking family for up to two years. The work they do is limited to work within the household, five hours a day maximum and five days a week maximum. Au pairs may change families during their two-year stay, but they are not permitted to take a job outside the home and they must not pursue any career while in the UK.

UK ancestry status

Commonwealth citizens over the age of 17 who can prove that one of their grandparents was a British citizen are entitled to come to the UK to work for a period of four years. After that time they may apply for residency.

Domestic workers

This category of workers includes people who travel to the UK with their employers and undertake domestic duties in the home. Such people are normally given entry clearance for 12 months, and must leave the country if their employer does so, or at the end of the period of permission if they have not been granted permission to remain for a further period.

Domestic workers are entitled to change employers while in the UK, but not the nature of the work they do. Even though their employers are from another country, domestic workers are entitled to all the protection of British law, including employment rights conferred by British employment law, health care and protection from abuse.

Domestic workers are, technically, permit-free because they travel on the permission obtained by their employer.

Business visitors

Visa nationals and non-visa nationals are allowed to enter the

UK to undertake certain business activities that are not classified as 'working'. The visitor will need to show that he has enough money to support himself during his stay, that his main business is based abroad, that he does not intend to move his business base to the UK, and that his salary is paid abroad. An entry permit for this reason is for a period of six months only, but if you come to the UK frequently for business, you may be issued with a multiple-entry visa, which means you do not have to apply for a new visa every time you visit.

The following are some of the activities that come under this heading:

- to attend conferences, trade shows and exhibitions
- to undertake market research and negotiate contracts
- to undertake training and instruction related to your business (not including practical training, but limited to observation and classroom training only)
- to deliver and install goods from abroad
- to service or repair a product (such as a machine or computer software) delivered from abroad
- to act as a consultant or trainer.

There are other categories that come under this heading. Check with the Immigration and Nationality Directorate (see page 311) for a comprehensive list.

Employing illegal workers

Employers can be fined up to £35,000 per worker if they are found to be employing workers who do not have the right to work in the UK.

Specifically, the law states that it is a criminal offence for an employer to employ anyone over the age of 16 who does not have permission to work in the UK. However, as the employer you are only responsible if the employee was taken on after 27 January 1997. You are also only responsible for employees, and not responsible for agency, contract or freelance workers or those employed by sub-contractors. (For more information on definitions of employees, see pages 166–167.)

Checking prospective candidates' right to work is a minefield, however, because insensitive behaviour in your application procedure – behaviour that could be classed as racist – could land you with an unlimited fine for racial discrimination.

IMMIGRATION, NATIONALITY AND IDENTITY

All employers can defend themselves against charges of employing illegal workers by asking for documentation. They can avoid charges of racial discrimination by asking for and copying such documentation from all prospective employees, regardless of race or nationality.

If a candidate cannot produce proof that they are entitled to work in the UK, the prospective employer should suggest that they contact Citizens Advice or a local law centre for advice on obtaining it, rather than assuming that they are attempting to get work illegally.

Making these steps part of a written employment policy will create a strong defence for the employer if accused of racial discrimination or of knowingly employing illegal workers. Documentation can include, but is not limited to:

◆ a document such as a P45, which shows the applicant's name and, most importantly, national insurance number

◆ a document which says the applicant has leave to remain in the UK indefinitely or is not forbidden to work in the UK; this can be in the form of a passport stamp or a letter from the Home Office

◆ a work permit or other permission to carry on employment

◆ a document showing that the applicant has the right to live in the UK ('right of abode') or that he or she is a UK citizen; this could include a passport, birth certificate or a 'naturalisation' document

◆ a document showing that the applicant is a citizen of one of the European Economic Area countries (see the list on pages 263–264), including a passport or an identity card.

The government has issued a code of conduct for employers, and being able to show that you have followed the code will be a good defence if you are charged with employing an illegal worker or with racial discrimination. Contact the Immigration and Nationality Directorate (see page 311) for further information. The IND's website shows examples of stamps an employer may encounter when dealing with workers from abroad, and a host of other useful information.

Leave to remain

British citizens and EEA citizens may settle in the UK without any special permission. If an EEA citizen wanted to settle permanently in the UK, she can apply to the Home Office for a certificate proving the length of time she has lived in the UK. While this document could be useful (e.g. for acquiring citizenship in the fullness of time), it is not essential.

Those from any other country wishing to stay permanently in the UK need to apply for 'indefinite leave to remain' from the Home Office. They must be able to show that they have lived in the UK for the past four years in one of the following categories:

- with a work permit
- as a business person or self-employed person
- as a retired person with his or her own financial resources
- as someone who is 'permit-free' (see page 283).

If you are given indefinite leave to remain, you become a 'resident' of the UK and are allowed to travel freely, live and work in the UK without restrictions. However, your residency may be withdrawn if you are convicted of a serious crime or stay away from the UK for more than two years. In the latter case, you will need to prove your intention to settle in the UK if you wish to have your residency reinstated.

If you have permission to stay, your children and spouse, a person to whom you are engaged, a gay partner, your parents and grandparents are also entitled to stay in the UK on the same terms.

The non-EEA family permit

Citizens of EEA countries and their families who are also citizens have an automatic right of residence in the UK, and may come

British citizenship

For information on how settling in the UK can lead to British citizenship, see pages 261–262.

here to live and work without restriction. Members of the family who are not citizens of an EEA country may be given permission to come to the UK, but they must apply for permission before they arrive. The permission is limited to the length of stay of the EEA citizen. If the EEA citizen leaves the UK permanently, then so must the non-EEA family members, and if family members cease to be so (e.g. a non-EEA spouse is divorced), they do not have an automatic right to stay in the UK.

For these purposes, 'family-members' refers to the spouse, dependent children under the age of 18, dependent parents and grandparents. It does not automatically cover siblings or more distant relatives such as cousins, aunts and uncles.

Of course, family-members who are staying less than six months and are not planning to settle may enter the UK on a visitor's visa rather than a non-EEA family permit.

If you wish to obtain a non-EEA family permit, you can get information from the Home Office Immigration and Nationality Directorate (see page 311).

Bringing visa-national relatives to the UK

Those who are citizens of the UK or who are permanently settled here have the right to bring visa-national family members to settle here with them. They are automatically entitled to bring a spouse and any dependent children under the age of 18, but they may also be able to bring other 'dependent relatives':

- a widowed parent over the age of 65
- both parents or grandparents travelling together as a couple if one is over the age of 65
- in exceptional circumstances where the dependent relative is suffering extreme hardship, children over the age of 18, parents and grandparents under the age of 65 and various other relatives, including aunts, uncles and siblings.

Those settled in the UK (the 'sponsor') must be able to show that such relatives are totally dependent financially and that they are able to support them once they arrive in the UK without applying for help from public sources ('without recourse to public funds', in the jargon).

Those wishing to come to the UK to settle as dependent relatives must get entry clearance before travelling to the UK.

IMMIGRATION, NATIONALITY AND IDENTITY

Asylum-seekers

Under the 1951 United Nations Convention Relating to the Status of Refugees, an 'asylum-seeker' (or refugee) is someone who, "owing to a well-founded fear of being persecuted for reasons of race, religion, nationality, membership of a particular social group or political opinion, is outside his country of origin and is unable or, owing to such fear unwilling to avail himself of the protection of that country". The law on the process for claiming and granting asylum in the UK was under consideration as this book was written, so anyone who requires up-to-date information should contact either the Refugee Council or the Immigration and Nationality Directorate.

The asylum process

At present, someone wishing to make a claim for asylum in the UK may do so either at the place where they enter the country, or to the Immigration and Nationality Directorate at the Home Office. However, it seems certain that this will shortly change, and that only claims made at the point of entry will be considered.

The application is considered on the basis of documentation or verbal evidence given during an interview with the claimant, and in the light of information gathered by the UK authorities regarding the country of origin the asylum-seeker is fleeing and according to the requirements set out in the 1951 Convention. During the interview process, the asylum-seeker is not automatically entitled to legal representation, but translators are available. While the application is being considered, the asylum-seeker will either be detained or will be asked to register his or her presence at regular intervals during the process.

Racially motivated attacks

It is a criminal offence to attack or abuse a person because of their race or religious beliefs or to incite racial hatred. Such attacks and abuse include attacking a person or their family, attacking or damaging their property, threatening or abusing them verbally, or publishing abusive material. If you have been the victim of an attack of the sort described above, you should contact the police immediately.

IMMIGRATION, NATIONALITY AND IDENTITY

It is a criminal offence for an asylum-seeker to give false information when making a claim for asylum, and conviction can carry with it a prison sentence of up to two years. On the other hand, the authorities have a duty to hear any claim for asylum fairly and thoroughly.

If the application is accepted, the asylum-seeker is granted indefinite leave to remain in the UK, and may look for work and bring their family to the country.

If the application is refused, the asylum-seeker is required to leave the UK, and may be removed if he does not do so. However, it is possible to lodge an appeal against a decision, and to remain in the UK while the appeal is being heard. It may also be that an asylum-seeker who is refused indefinite leave to remain is given exceptional leave to remain for a short period, usually on humanitarian grounds.

Asylum-seekers and work

Asylum-seekers are generally permitted to work in the UK after they have been in the country for six months awaiting processing of their application or any appeal. Asylum-seekers with permission to work should be in possession of a letter from the Home Office acknowledging their application, with a stamp on the back stating that they are entitled to work. If the individual asylum-seeker is granted leave to remain in the UK, he or she will usually also have permission to work here.

Getting immigration advice

In the UK, specialist immigration advice is usually free of charge. If you need immigration advice, you should first go to a Citizens Advice Bureau or your local law centre. There are many lawyers who specialise in immigration matters, and the vast majority are suitably qualified and very competent. But there is also a small number of individuals who are not qualified to do so, and may give poor advice or actively seek to deceive you. If you do decide to use a lawyer to advise you on immigration matters, he should by law tell you in writing:

- what kind of service you can expect from him
- how to complain if you are not happy with his services
- whether you will have to pay for the service, and how the fee will be worked out

◆   how to contact him when you need to
◆   that it is possible to get free advice from other sources.

If you use a lawyer for immigration advice, check with the Immigration Law Practitioners Association (see page 311) that he or she has a good reputation. If you feel that a lawyer has overcharged you for advice or has not given you a good service, contact the Office of the Immigration Services Commissioner (see page 313).

Personal identity

Many Britons have hitherto been proud of the fact that they are not (except in times of war) forced by law to carry proof of their identity with them. However, slowly but surely, what is affectionately termed in some circles the 'right to anonymity' is being eroded. Driving licences now need a photograph and the rules on which documents are acceptable as primary identification (e.g. for opening a bank account) are being tightened up. At the time of writing, 'entitlement cards' were being discussed by those in government as a way to control illegal immigration, benefit fraud and identity theft (see pages 280–282). However, there is no sign as yet that it would be an offence not to carry such a card.

For most of us, our identity is established at birth when our parents register the fact of our existence, and many carry that identity through life without giving it much thought. But a small minority of people choose to change their name. This section looks at how to register a birth, what documentation qualifies as primary identification, how to legally change your name and how 'identity theft' is dealt with.

Registering a child's birth

When a child is born, it is a legal requirement that its parent or parents register its birth within 42 days. If a doctor or midwife is in attendance at the birth, they will already have notified the local health authority. If the parents are married, either of the parents may register the birth. If the parents are not married, the mother alone is entitled to register the birth, and she does not need to give the name of the child's father if she does not wish to. If the unmarried father of a child wants to register his paternity, he will either have to go to the registry with the child's mother or both parents must sign a statutory declaration (in the presence of a solicitor) stating that he is the child's father.

The name given to the child at his or her registration does not need to include the surname of either of the child's parents, and any words or names may be chosen as forenames (although the registrar may draw the line at names that are blasphemous or profane).

Parents may change the child's forename at any time within 12 months of the original registration, and the register will be changed so that the child's birth certificate, an important piece of primary identification, reflects the new name. If they want to change the child's surname on his or her birth certificate because, say, they have subsequently married, they must apply to the registrar to do so within three months of their marriage.

Primary identification

For official purposes, most of us at some time or other need to be able to prove who we are. Such proof is called 'primary identification, and may be used to apply for such documents as a UK passport or driver's licence. They may also be used to open bank accounts, apply for credit and all sorts of other purposes. For instance, to apply for a driver's licence you will need to prove who you are with one or more of the following documents:

- ◆ full valid current passport
- ◆ birth certificate
- ◆ certificate of registry of birth which shows your name
- ◆ adoption certificate
- ◆ identity card from an EEA (see pages 263–264) country
- ◆ travel documents issued by the Home Office
- ◆ a certificate of naturalisation or registration (see pages 261–262).

Applying for a passport

For information on applying for a British passport, see page 242.

If your name has changed, you would also need to prove the change by showing a marriage certificate, decree absolute, deed poll or statutory declaration (see below). Similar documents would need to be shown when applying for a UK passport.

Note that most authorities (e.g. banks and building societies) will not accept a provisional driver's licence as primary identification.

Secondary identification

Secondary identification is proof of your address. This is required when applying for all sorts of things, from a bank account to a public library ticket. A good form of secondary identification is a utility bill or correspondence relating to council tax).

Changing your name

It is generally very easy to change your name, and indeed, there is no restriction as to how many times you can change your name as long as you can show that you intend to stop using your former name. How you change your name depends on what you want to achieve and your circumstances. Anyone seeking to change their name legally with the intention to defraud is committing an offence.

- Name change by usage: a person who is over the age of 16 can simply choose to use another name. No-one under 16 can do this without their parents' consent. If you wish to establish your new name a little more formally, you could advertise in a newspaper (keep the advert with details of its date and the newspaper it appeared in as evidence should it be needed in the future), or you could get a letter confirming that you have changed your name from an upstanding and prominent member of your community. This person could be a minister of religion or an MP, but they must be able to say that they have known you when you used your previous name, and that they can confirm you have changed your name by usage.
- Name change by 'deed poll' or 'statutory declaration': a deed poll is a standard and straightforward document drawn up by a solicitor and witnessed, in which you certify that you wish to change your name. A statutory declaration is a similar document that is drawn up by a

solicitor and then sworn before a Justice of the Peace or a Commissioner for Oaths. For most purposes there is no legal difference between a deed poll and a statutory declaration. Both are accepted by the UK Passport authorities and the Driver Vehicle Licensing Authority as evidence of a change of name. Changing your birth certificate and existing legal documentation such as a marriage certificate is a different matter, and is only possible in a small number of exceptional circumstances.

- By marriage: a woman who wants to take her husband's surname on marriage may do so automatically. To change official documentation, she simply produces her marriage certificate. On the other hand, a man wishing to change his name to his wife's name on marriage must do so by deed poll (British law is still riddled with such sexist archaisms). If a couple wish to join their two names together to make a double-barrelled name, they will both have to draw up a deed poll.

- By divorce or death of a spouse: a woman who has taken her husband's name on marriage and wishes to revert to her maiden name may do so on official documentation simply by producing her decree absolute (see page 78). Similarly, if she wishes to revert to her maiden name on the death of her husband, she produces her husband's death certificate.

If you wish to change the name of a child under the age of 16, you may do so simply by usage, as above, or, if you want the change to carry through to official documentation, you may do so by deed poll or statutory declaration. If you as parents are married and both of you consent to the name change, there should be no problem getting a deed poll or statutory declaration. However, if you as parents are separated or divorced, were never married, or there are custody orders in place, changing the name of your child becomes more complicated, and you are advised to contact your local Citizens Advice Bureau, law centre or a solicitor. In general, the following rules apply:

- If the child's parents were married at the time the child was born or have been married since, you will need the consent of both parents to effect a deed poll or statutory declaration. Where one parent is not contactable, it is possible to get the deed poll or declaration as long as it can be shown that all reasonable steps were taken to contact the absent parent. If one parent refuses to give consent without a good reason a deed poll or statutory declaration may still be possible, but the other parent may have to apply to the County Court for a court order.

◆ If the child's parents have never been married, then the parent with parental responsibility for the child (this does not automatically include a custody order), is (in general) entitled to change the child's name without the consent of the other parent.

◆ If you are adopting a child, the adoption orders will make the change of name to the adoptive family's surname valid in law.

In all changes of name, it is necessary to intend to stop using your old name altogether in order to make your name change 'stick'. You cannot, for instance, apply for a passport with your new name while still using your old name for other purposes.

Identity theft

In this modern world, our very identities are becoming more and more valuable, and identity theft is a thoroughly modern, worldwide problem growing by between 200 and 500 per cent each year. In 2001 more than 40,000 cases of identity theft were counted in the UK, and there must have been many more that were reported as ordinary thefts or fraud. While there is as yet no law against stealing another person's identity, fraud and deception can carry heavy penalties.

Stealing a person's identity (details of name and address, principally, but also bank, credit card, personal details such as date of birth, and tax and National Insurance details) can enable a thief to fraudulently apply for credit, run up debts, buy goods, even commit crimes, in that person's name. Often, a person may have had his identity stolen and not even realise it until the bailiffs appear at the door.

Steps to prevent identity theft

◆ Take care of documents that can prove your identity and your credit cards and other identification cards.

Don't carry unnecessary items around with you, and keep them secure and out of sight when at home. Never leave your wallet, handbag or brief case unattended, even in a locked car.

- Keep a separate record of all credit card and account information in case you have to report cards and documents missing, and make sure you know what numbers to call in the event of loss or theft. A service that informs all relevant organisations after a single telephone call can seriously reduce your stress!

- Never write down a pin in association with a particular card, and never tell anyone else what your PIN is. When using a PIN or password, take steps to ensure that no-one can see or hear you.

- Do not put the following in the rubbish (the most prevalent way of acquiring information about someone else is to get it from documents you have thrown away): bank statements, credit card bills, official correspondence such as tax bills, utility bills, anything that gives your personal details, including unsolicited offers of credit. Always ensure that credit card receipts and electronic till receipts are destroyed before you dispose of them.

- Do not give any of the following information to people on the telephone unless you are absolutely sure they are who you think they are: credit card details, bank details, personal information such as your date of birth, address, telephone number.

- When thinking up passwords, use a combination of letters and numbers, and change your passwords frequently.

- When you move house, get your mail redirected by the Royal Mail. Do this for at least a year to prevent someone at your old address receiving sensitive information about you. Make sure that your postman deals with your mail in a secure fashion; leaving letters sticking out of the box is a temptation to any passing fraudster. Complain to the Royal Mail if you feel your security is being put at risk.

- Stay on top of your regular bills and statements. Be aware when they are due to arrive and contact the organisation in question if they do not appear or if your mail seems a little thin on the ground. If you have difficulty doing this, reduce the number of accounts you have to the bare minimum.

- Always check any statement or bill from your bank, building society or credit company. Make sure that every item can be accounted for. Do this as soon as the statement or bill arrives.

- Avoid organisations that purport to be able to repair your credit rating. Contact your local Citizens Advice Bureau if you are having difficulties with credit.

- Every year, contact the major credit reference agencies, Experian and Equifax (see page 310) for a copy of your file. Follow up any unusual activity.

- If you are buying something online, make sure the site sends you to a secure room. A padlock should appear on your screen if the information you are sending is secure.

What to do if you suspect identity theft

- Stop any related credit cards and inform the relevant organisations immediately. Arrange to have sensitive documents held at a branch for you to collect rather than having them mailed.

- Contact the police and fill out a crime report.

- Keep a record of every action you take: who you called (the name of the individual you spoke to), when, letters you wrote, correspondence received. Always follow up a telephone call with a letter.

- If you lose your passport or driver's licence, you must report it to the DVLA (see page 310) or the Passport Service (see page 313) immediately.

- Change all account numbers, credit cards, PINs and passwords.

- If you think that someone is stealing your mail or someone has arranged for your mail to be redirected, contact the Royal Mail, who should investigate.

- Contact the CIFAS Protective Registration Service and ask that they flag your address. See page 309.

Key terms

common travel area
England, Wales, Scotland, Northern Ireland, the Channel Islands

and the Isle of Man. Those entering the UK at one of these points does not require a visa to travel to any other part of the common travel area.

deed poll

A document that is used to officially declare that you intend to use a different name to that registered with the authorities. See page 278.

EEA

European Economic Area. This group of countries includes those of the European Union and three others. See pages 263–264.

entry clearance visa

Proof that you have been given permission to come to the UK by the British authorities. It is not, however, an absolute guarantee that you will not be prevented from entering at the border.

indefinite leave to remain

Permission from the Home Office to stay in the UK permanently. This can generally be seen as a resident's permit and usually entitles the holder to live and work in the UK and to bring relatives here.

naturalisation

Method of acquiring British citizenship for those who are not born to parents who are British citizens or settled in the UK. See pages 261–262.

overstayer

Someone who remains in the UK after their permission to stay has expired.

permit-free

Someone whose profession entitles them to enter the UK and carry on their business without requiring a work permit. The profession of minister of religion is considered 'permit-free'.

recourse to public funds

Applying for financial aid from the state in the form of benefits such as job-seeker's allowance.

removal

Home Office euphemism for 'deportation'.

right of abode

The right to live and work in the UK without obtaining special permission.

Schengen visa

A visa issued by any one of a group of countries in European, with which a traveller may enter any of the countries in the group. The 15 Schengen countries are: Austria, Belgium, Denmark, Finland, France, Germany, Iceland, Italy, Greece, Luxembourg, Netherlands, Norway, Portugal, Spain and Sweden.

settlement

Remaining in the UK permanently as a resident but not as a citizen.

statutory declaration

A legal document, sworn in from of a Justice of the Peace or a Commissioner for Oaths, in which you make a declaration, e.g. that you intend to use a new name. See pages 278–279.

subject to control

Refers to people who need to have permission to enter the UK. The authorities are entitled to check the documentation of such people.

switching

Seeking to change the basis on which a person remains in the UK. For instance, a person on a visitor's visa may seek to get married here, or may seek to work or study here. See page 267.

temporary release

Allowing a person to enter the UK while their application to stay here is decided.

visa national country

One of a number of countries whose citizens require visas for entry into the UK. See page 264.

14 Navigating the Legal System

This chapter looks at how the legal system in England and Wales works. It starts by giving some information on the police, and what may happen if you are arrested. There is a section on getting legal help, followed by information on what, to an outsider, might appear to be a bewildering array of courts, and suggests several ways in which you may be able to avoid going to court in the first place. The chapter ends with a substantial Key Terms section, with definitions of some of the many legal terms you may come across in any encounter with the law.

Dealing with the police

The legal system in this country is partly grounded on the principle that it is better for the guilty to go free than for a single innocent person to be wrongfully convicted, and part of the system that ensures this is made up of a latticework of rights that individuals have when dealing with the law. It is important that all members of the public are aware of the powers of the police (or more specifically, the powers the police don't have) and their individual rights if they are arrested.

Stop and search

The police have limited powers in England and Wales to stop and search members of the public and their vehicles. These powers are now defined by two pieces of legislation: the Police and Criminal Evidence Act (1984) and the Misuse of Drugs Act (1971). Police may stop and search only if:

- the police suspect that person or vehicle is carrying controlled substances (see pages 230–234)
- the police suspect the individual or vehicle of carrying a prohibited object, such as an offensive weapon, or equipment to commit a criminal offence, such as poaching
- the police suspect the individual or vehicle is carrying

stolen goods or goods on which excise duty has not been paid
- the person or vehicle is going to a designated sports ground or event, and the police suspect the transportation of alcoholic drink
- the police suspect the person or vehicle of carrying articles that could be used to commit terrorist offences.

In all the above cases, the suspicion of the police must be based on reasonable grounds. Police wanting to make a search without a warrant must show identification (if they are not in uniform), identify themselves and their station and give the reason for the search. All searches must be reported in a written document, and individuals are entitled to receive a copy.

The police can only detain a member of the public for a few minutes, or what amounts to a reasonable amount of time. Searches carried out in a public place must be limited to outer clothing. Any further searches must be carried out in private, and only in the presence of a constable of the same sex as the person being searched.

Entering premises

The police may only enter premises without the permission of the owner or occupier with a search warrant or an arrest warrant. The only exception to this is if the police have reason to believe that a criminal offence has been committed or is in the process of being committed.

Arrest

The police have significant power to arrest members of the public. They can do so with or without a warrant.

Warrants can be issued in all sorts of circumstances – when a serious criminal offence has been committed, when a person has failed to turn up at a police station when asked to do so, or when she has failed to turn up at court or pay a fine. In order to gain a warrant for somebody's arrest, the police have to prove they have good reasons, including strong evidence that the person they want to arrest has committed an offence. Warrants may be issued not only to the police, but also to officers of Customs and Excise.

In order to make a lawful arrest without a warrant, the police need to show that they have good grounds for making the arrest. For example (and this list is not complete), a member of the public may be arrested:

- because he has committed an offence or has attempted to commit an offence
- if he fails to give his name and address (or if the police believe he has given a false name or address)
- if he is behaving in such a way that the police fear violence if he is not arrested
- so that the police may take fingerprints or a sample, for example of urine or blood.

Helping the police

Sometimes, a suspect may be asked to accompany the police to the station for questioning. No person can be forced to accompany the police without being arrested. If you have not been arrested, and are helping the police with their enquiries by attending an interview, you have the right to leave the station at any time, or to ask the police to leave your property (unless they have a warrant), if this is where the interview is taking place. You also have the right to demand that a legal advisor or friend is present at your interview.

The right to legal advice

Most importantly, every person arrested has the right to free legal advice from the moment they are arrested. This may manifest itself as the right to call your own solicitor, or to speak to the duty solicitor. Arrested individuals are booked in to police stations by a 'custody officer'. She should ask if you wish to see a solicitor. If you do not say 'yes' at this point, this does not mean that you no longer have a right to legal advice. You can ask to talk to a solicitor at any time.

In most cases, a duty solicitor will talk by telephone to someone who has been arrested, and only later, when a police interview is arranged, will she come to the station in person. The duty solicitor should be on call 24 hours a day, however. The initial consultation with the solicitor must be conducted in private.

If the interview is 'urgent' – that is, if a police officer of at least the rank of superintendent decides that a delay would be harmful – it may begin before the solicitor arrives.

The police will record everything a person says from the point of his arrest. Those who are arrested are advised to say nothing at all to the police until they have taken legal advice. Even passing comments may be interpreted against you in a court of law. Say nothing until there is a solicitor present. If you find yourself in an interview room before a solicitor has put in an appearance, make sure that you say on tape that there is no solicitor present and that you do not wish to answer any questions without a solicitor.

The right to silence

In the vast majority of cases, every person arrested has the right to refuse to answer any of the questions the police ask. Every person arrested should be informed of this right at the point at which they are arrested, and the police should make sure that this is understood. However, the Criminal Justice and Public Order Act (1994) allows a court to come to its own conclusions if a person fails to mention a fact when questioned but then later relies on it for his defence in court. Even ten years after the Act was enacted there is still controversy over this fundamental change in the law. Because it is not likely that a person will be convicted solely on the refusal to answer questions or give information, the advice remains to say nothing until you have talked to a solicitor.

Informing someone of your arrest

People who have been arrested have the right to have someone else told that they have been arrested.

Detention

Usually, the police have the power to detain those they have arrested for up to 24 hours. After this time, the detainee must be charged. After the detainee has been charged, he may no longer be questioned by the police. If the detainee has not been charged with an offence after 24 hours, he should be allowed to leave the station.

There are a few exceptions to this. For example, police have the power to detain people under Prevention of Terrorism legislation for up to 96 hours, provided that they have good reason.

Citizen's arrest

For information on citizen's arrest, see page 160.

Remand

After a charge has been brought, the accused is 'remanded'. This means that he is either committed into custody (kept in detention) or allowed to go on bail. If he is allowed to leave on bail, he must show that he can pay the amount of the bail (or someone else will) and will comply with the rules of bail (e.g. appearing at the police station or in court on a certain date).

Those who are remanded in custody are generally kept in the cells at the police station until they can be seen by magistrates. After the hearing in the Magistrates' Court, the accused is generally remanded in custody at a remand centre or prison until his court hearing. Periods of remand should not be excessive. The first period of remand is set at eight days, and if necessary there are further periods of 28 days each. If the remand period does become excessive – the total time ranges from 56 to 70 days – the accused may be successful with a bail application.

Young people and the police

Special regulations apply if the person arrested is under 17:

- ◆ the youth's parents (or a person with parental responsibility) must be informed
- ◆ an 'appropriate adult' must be present when the young person is cautioned, searched and interviewed.

For more on young people and the law, see chapter four.

Complaints against the police

The police force works to a strict code of conduct. If a member of the public has a complaint, it is usually taken seriously from the start. If you have a complaint against the police that you consider very serious (for example, if you have sustained an injury while in police custody), it might be wise first of all to discuss it with a legal advisor. She can tell you which course of action to take: pursuing your complaint via the police force's own complaints procedure or bringing a court action. You may be able to sue the police if you have been the victim of:

- ◆ wrongful arrest
- ◆ false imprisonment
- ◆ assault

- ◆ trespass
- ◆ negligence
- ◆ malicious prosecution.

Minor complaints against the police should be started with a letter to the force's chief constable. It is important to be able to identify the officer concerned, and to give as many details as possible of the incident. The force should respond by interviewing the person who is complaining and then following up the complaint with the officer or officers concerned. For more serious complaints that you do not wish to pursue through the courts, you may wish to approach the Police Complaints Authority (see page 313), who may start a formal investigation, usually run by someone of the rank of chief inspector.

Under arrest: action plan

- ◆ Try not to lose your temper; avoid becoming violent
- ◆ Speak politely to the police, telling them your name and address and answering with a simple 'yes' if you are asked whether you understand what is happening
- ◆ Ask to see solicitor as soon as you are arrested
- ◆ If you have not been told why you have been arrested, ask that this is explained to you
- ◆ If you do not understand English well enough to follow what is happening, try to make this clear; a translator should be provided
- ◆ Do not under any circumstances answer any questions (beyond giving your name and address), or indeed say anything to the police, without first speaking to a solicitor
- ◆ Stay cool and calm, ask the solicitor for all the information you need to help you to understand the situation; ask questions if you are not sure of something
- ◆ While under arrest, do not make any decisions without first getting legal advice and thinking very carefully about the possible consequences.

Getting legal help

Anyone who is considering legal action or who is in trouble with the law should seek 'live' information and advice from a properly-qualified specialist advisor. No book, website or leaflet can be a substitute for face-to-face advice on your specific case, and it is not wise to embark on a course of action without first getting advice.

Informal legal advice

The first port of call in many situations (short of having been arrested) is usually one of two networks of advice centres in the UK.

The National Association of Citizens Advice Bureaux deals with some five million legal and semi-legal queries every year. Its network of offices is staffed with sympathetic and knowledgeable advisors who can give guidance and information. This may include methods of alternative dispute resolution (ADR), the legality of the steps you are intending to take, and your rights in certain situations. CAB staff may also be able to recommend specialist legal practitioners who can take your case further. See page 312 for contact details.

The Community Legal Service is part of the Legal Services Commission, a government organisation charged with ensuring that everyone in the community has access to clear and informative legal advice. It recommends local advice centres and legal firms, and produces a wide range of information, distributed, for example, through local libraries. The CLS also administers a scheme that pays for some civil actions in the event that the claimant cannot herself afford to do so. This scheme – which is known as 'public funding' or 'state funding' – took the place of Legal Aid. See page 309 for contact details.

You may also be able to get advice from other organisations, such as your trade union, insurance company or motoring organisation.

Using a solicitor

Solicitors take on legal work from members of the public. They generally group together into firms (although some practice independently) and many specialise in certain areas of the law, such as conveyancing, family law, personal injury, immigration, etc. Solicitors are regulated by the Law Society, which has laid down guidelines for their conduct and which would investigate complaints about specific practices from members of the public (see page 311 for contact details), including complaints about fees.

Solicitors are entitled to represent their clients in Magistrates' Courts, County Courts and in some parts of the High Court. They are not normally entitled to represent their clients in Crown Courts, in some parts of the High Court, the Court of Appeal or the House of Lords, and they must engage the services of a barrister if a client's case appears in one of these courts.

When attending a meeting with a chosen solicitor, it is always a good idea to do some preparation. Put together all the documentation relating to the matter you wish to discuss, and think through what you want to say. Make notes if this will help you to make the meeting effective. At the first meeting, the solicitor should tell you:

- how he intends to handle your case
- how long the case might take
- what costs you are likely to have to pay
- whether you might be able to have the costs covered by public funds
- whether the legal work could be done free of charge by another organisation.

If you have been arrested, you are entitled to free on-the-spot legal advice from the duty solicitor. See pages 287–288 for details.

The courts in England and Wales

The English court structure is a product of hundreds of years of evolution. It has within it a number of inconsistencies and overlaps, where two different courts may be able to deal with the same kind of case, for example. In addition, the last century saw a new kind of legal forum come into being – the tribunal. At present there are many different tribunals, mostly able to deal with special kinds of case such as employment-related disputes, which are covered by the employment tribunal. In 2003, however, the Lord Chancellor's Department published plans to create a single, unified tribunal service within a few years.

County Courts
These courts deal only with cases in civil law, such as:

debts and other credit-related disputes

consumer disputes often related to faulty goods, poor service, etc.

family cases, such as some divorces (but only certain County Courts deal with divorces, known as Divorce County Courts), matrimonial disputes and cases involving the protection of children

personal injury claims (see pages 115–131)

race relations matters, other than those occurring in the course of employment

sex discrimination cases, other than those occurring in the course of employment

bankruptcies.

Small claims in the County Courts

A civil law claim is usually allocated to one of three 'tracks' (the small claims track, the fast track and the multi-track), depending on the amount claimed and the complexity of the case:

the small claims track is for most claims under £5,000, but it does not include: accusations of dishonesty; claims for repair to residential premises amounting to more than £1,000; cases of unlawful eviction or landlord harassment; or personal injury claims over £1,000.

the fast track deals with cases under £15,000 that can be dispatched within a day.

the multi-track deals with cases amounting to more than £15,000 or ones that may take more than a day to hear.

Small claims are processed through the County Courts and can sometimes be made without the aid of a solicitor. To start a small claim, collect a form from your local County Court (or download a form from the Court Service website, see page 309). You may be able to get help with filling in the form from your Citizens Advice Bureau or law centre. Gather all the evidence you can before submitting a claim to the Court – you must at least have tried to resolve the dispute in person before going to Court. Take the form back to the County Court, where a clerk will go through it and take the fee.

In due course a summons will be issued to the person you are claiming against, who must return a defence within 14 days. If the summons is not defended in that time, the case will be decided in your favour. If the case is defended, you may have to go to Court, and the case is usually heard by a single judge, whose decision is final (unless he has made a mistake on a point of law). The Court will tell you how to proceed from there.

Of course, winning a case in court is very different to actually extracting payment from your adversary!

Magistrates' Courts

These local courts deal with a combination of civil cases and minor criminal cases.

Magistrates dispose of up to 95% of all criminal cases heard in England and Wales. These criminal cases are called 'summary cases' (because they are started with a summons) and the sentence is a maximum of six months imprisonment and/or a fine of up to £5,000. In 'triable either way' cases, those accused of a criminal offence may be able to choose whether they are tried by judge and jury in the Crown Court (see below) or in the Magistrates' Courts. All those accused of such offences should seek legal advice before making the decision. It is not always better to opt for a Magistrates' Court simply because the sentence is likely to be less severe.

Many criminal cases involving young people and children 17 and under are tried in Youth Courts, which are run by magistrates. See page 95.

Magistrates are also responsible for granting and renewing licenses – for example – for gambling or to sell and serve alcohol. They issue search warrants and arrest warrants, and deal with applications for bail. They also deal with the recovery of debts, such as council tax and utilities bills. They act as 'family proceedings courts', hearing applications for adoption, residence and contact orders (see page 85), financial maintenance and non-molestation orders (see page 72).

In general, Magistrates' Courts are presided over by a group of 'lay justices'. Often called Justices of the Peace, these magistrates

---

Divorce County Courts

For a list of Divorce County Courts, see the website of the Court Service (page 309 for details).

are taken from the local community and are paid very little. They generally have no professional legal background, but they are given a certain amount of training. They rely on their court clerks to advise on points of law. In general, these clerks have at least five years' professional legal experience.

Some Magistrates' Courts, however, are presided over by professional magistrates. These people were formerly known as stipendiary magistrates and are now called District Judges (Magistrates' Court). These magistrates have at least seven years' legal training and practice.

The Crown Court

This court is technically one court with many different centres around the country. The Old Bailey in central London is probably the most famous of these centres. The Crown Court handles serious criminal cases, including both offences triable-either-way, or indictable offences, which can only be heard in the Crown Court. It also handles cases passed by the Magistrates' Courts for tougher sentencing and appeals made against a Magistrates' Court decision.

In the Crown Court, cases are generally dealt with by judge and jury. Solicitors are not normally allowed to be heard in a Crown Court, and have to hire barristers to make their clients' case.

The High Court

This court hears civil cases and appeals against decisions made in the Crown Court. It also monitors the operation of the other courts to ensure they work properly. It is divided into several divisions, the most familiar of which will probably be the Family Division, which looks at contested divorces and adoption, among other things. The Chancery Division takes care of such matters as contested wills and bankruptcies. The Divisional Court of the Queen's Bench Division hears certain types of appeals from magistrates' and Crown Courts. The High Court also includes a number of courts that cover specialist areas, such as the Restrictive Practices Court, and the Court of Protection, which handles cases where people are so incapacitated that they can no longer look after their own affairs (see pages 111–112).

Other courts

There are a number of other courts, including the Court of

Jury Service

Crown Courts rely on ordinary members of the public to form juries of (usually) 12 people to decide cases. In some cases, juries also sit in coroners' courts, and, once in a while, in the civil courts.

All those on the electoral register are liable to be called for service, unless they are in an exempt category, or in a category with the right to be excused. Such categories include members of the clergy, MPs, members of health professions, the armed forces, those in the law enforcement professions, etc. It is also possible to be excused jury service if this might cause undue hardship (e.g. if your fledgling business would fail if you had to leave it for any length of time), or if you have some kind of personal involvement in the case (e.g. you know the defendant). (Recent proposals, though, may change the rules on who may be excused jury service.) Individuals on jury service are usually paid travelling and subsistence expenses and some compensation for lost earnings.

Once selected from the electoral register, jurors may be vetted. Vetting is carried out either by the police (for a criminal record, for example), or on the request of the Attorney-General in certain types of cases. Groups of jurors (including possibly as many as 100 people) are then presented to all parties concerned, and may be rejected if it is felt that the selection is biased.

Then, 15 members of the panel of 100 are called to hear a certain case, and eventually 12 are chosen. The prosecution has an opportunity to reject individual members, replacing them with others from the panel. Jury members may only be rejected if they are clearly very unsuitable given the case in hand. Challenges of this sort are quite rare in the English courts.

Jury service is a serious business, and it is a legal requirement that jurors do not speak about the case to anyone either while it is being tried or afterwards.

The Criminal Justice Service website has more information for people who have been called for jusry service, including a virtual tour of a court. See page 309.

Appeal and the House of Lords, which consider appeals from the lower courts and deal with matters of public importance or interest.

Any court may ask the European Court of Justice (ECJ) for a ruling on how to interpret a point of European law, but the case between the parties will be decided by the UK court. Individuals cannot take private grievances to the ECJ.

Cases involving infringements of the European Convention on Human Rights may be heard in the European Court of Human Rights. This court has the power to award damages, but UK courts do not have to abide by its decisions.

Alternative dispute resolution (ADR)

Going to court is costly and time-consuming, and often does not bring a lasting peace, particularly in marital disputes or rows between neighbours, where sometimes everyone feels unjustly treated. These days, there are lower-cost alternatives to going to court, which can lead in some cases to a binding agreement. These include:

- ◆ **mediation:** In mediation, both parties agree to attend sessions with a professional whose role it is to provide a safe environment in which to talk and reach an agreement. The mediator has no powers to make the clients come to an agreement, and certainly should not suggest a resolution, but should simply act as a facilitator. Mediation can be useful for, among other things, cases of divorce or separation where the couple need to agree on arrangements for their children.
- ◆ **conciliation:** In conciliation, sessions go on very much as for mediation, but the difference is that the professional facilitator may suggest a way forward and even broker an agreement between the two parties.
- ◆ **arbitration:** In this form of ADR, both sides agree to go to an arbitrator who hears both sides of the story. In taking up arbitration, both sides agree to be bound by whatever judgement the arbitrator makes. If parties agree to arbitration and a decision is made by the arbitrator, the parties are not usually free to pursue the case further into the courts. Many contracts have a clause in which both parties agree that any disagreement over the contract will be dealt with by an

♦ arbitrator rather than through the courts.

♦ **complaints procedures:** Many companies and other organisations (such as the police, government departments, etc.) have a fixed complaints procedure by which a person's complaint is properly investigated and an outcome reached. All complaints and grievances against organisations should start with the complaints procedure if there is one.

♦ **the ombudsman system:** This is a network of independent officers, each charged with dealing with complaints in a certain sector. So, for example, complaints against the National Health Service are dealt with by the Health Service Ombudsman, and complaints against estate agents are dealt with by the Estate Agents Ombudsman. Ombudsmen will usually not deal with a complaint that has not first been through the complaints procedure of the organisation involved. If the complainant is unhappy with the decision of an Ombudsman, he can still go to court if he chooses to do so.

A criminal record

Anyone who is convicted of a criminal offence, even if it is a speeding ticket, gets a criminal record. The fact of having a criminal record can affect every part of your life, from getting a job to travelling abroad.

Under the Rehabilitation of Offenders Act (1974) those who have served certain sentences may apply after a certain period of time to have the slate wiped clean – the fact of the sentence

---

Warning!

No-one should replace legal action through the courts with ADR without getting legal advice first (and possibly also after an agreement has been reached). ADR is in most cases about resolving differences rather than exercising legal rights, and some clients may be throwing away the possibility of a more favourable outcome if they enter into a mediated agreement without having it checked by a solicitor.

may no longer be disclosed except in certain circumstances. So, after the sentence has been 'spent' the offender may not need to mention it when, for example, applying to travel to certain countries, or for certain jobs.

Whether it is possible to remove a sentence from a person's record depends on the type of sentence it is. Here are some examples (this is by no means an exhaustive list):

- for someone who was 18 or over when convicted, a prison sentence of less than two-and-a-half years but more than six months is removed after 10 years
- for someone who was under 18 when convicted, a custodial sentence of less than two-and-a-half years but more than six months is removed after five years
- for someone who was 18 or over when convicted, a prison sentence of up to six months is removed after seven years
- for someone who was under 18 when convicted, a custodial sentence of up to six months is removed after three years
- disqualification, for example, from driving, is removed on the day the disqualification expires
- a fine is removed from the record of a person who was 18 or over when convicted after five years and from the record of a person who was under 18 when convicted juvenile after two years
- a community service order is removed from the record of a person who was 18 or over when convicted after five years, and from the record of a person who was under 18 when convicted after two years.

However, for some purposes, a criminal record may never be erased. These include applying for jobs that involve children, and entering some professions, such as dentistry and accountancy.

Equally, those who have been sentenced to imprisonment for any period exceeding two-and-a-half years can never have their record erased, for whatever reason.

Key terms

absolute discharge
The defendant is found guilty but the court imposes no sentence.

action plan order
Order handed down by a Youth Court which can combine a variety of specified activities to be carried out by the offender over a period of three months.

adversarial process
The term used to describe the legal process in which two sides argue a case as opponents, or adversaries.

advocate
A person who speaks for another. This term is sometimes informally used to mean a barrister, and indeed, under the Scottish legal system, barristers are called advocates.

alternative dispute resolution (ADR)
Any method of coming to an agreement in a dispute without taking it to court. See pages 297–298.

anti-social behaviour order
Order handed down by a Youth Court to any offender aged 10 or over, spanning a minimum duration of two years, during which the offender must desist from the anti-social behaviour described. Breaking such an order is a criminal offence.

appeal
Taking a case that has already been decided to a higher court. The appeal court will decide whether a mistake was made at the earlier trial and, if it does, may overturn the earlier decision.

attendance centre order
Form of sentence for offenders aged under 21, which requires them to take part in activities at an attendance centre at weekends.

bail
Release from custody of a person accused of a crime before trial, or of a person convicted of a crime and awaiting sentencing or an appeal.

barrister
Professional lawyer who has the right to be heard in any court. Usually used to argue criminal cases in the Crown Court and

the High Court. May be instructed only by a solicitor, not by the parties themselves.

care order
A court order that places a child into the care of the local authority.

civil law
The body of law that relates to private individuals rather than to offences against the community as a whole.

civil wrong
Infringement of the rights of a private individual, for which the claimant may sue.

claimant
The party who brings a civil action to court.

clerk
In a court of law, particularly in a Magistrates' Court, the clerk is an individual who monitors proceedings and advises on points of law.

combination order
A form of sentence for young people over the age of 16, which combines community service (see below) with elements of a probation order (see page 305).

common law
A body of law established by previous cases, and so representing the customary practices of a community.

community punishment order
Court order specifying that the offender must undertake useful, unpaid work in the community.

community rehabilitation order
Court order specifying that the offender must undergo a period of supervision and rehabilitation in the community.

community service
A form of sentence in which a person is required to carry out

unpaid work that is of benefit to the community. Community service is generally a minimum of 40 hours and a maximum of 240 hours.

compensation
Financial payment made to someone who has suffered a loss or damage.

compensation order
Court order that the offender should pay compensation to the victim of the offence.

conditional discharge
See discharge (page 303).

County Court
Court that hears only civil cases.

Court of Appeal
Court that has the power to look into verdicts made by other courts and overturn them if a mistake has been made.

criminal law
The body of law that deals with offences that are considered to be against the community as a whole, rather than against private individuals, e.g. murder, robbery, rape, etc.

Crown Court
A court that deals with serious criminal cases, tried by judge and jury.

Crown Prosecution Service
Public organisation that prosecutes offenders in criminal cases on behalf of the community as a whole.

curfew order
Form of sentence in which the offender is required to remain in a certain place at certain times of the day.

custodial sentence
A term of imprisonment.

damages
A sum of money ordered to be paid by a defendant to a claimant because a legal right was infringed.

defendant
The party against whom a civil case is brought by a claimant, or who is prosecuted in a criminal case.

discharge
The offender is allowed to go free even though he has been found guilty of an offence. A conditional discharge is the release of an offender after conviction, but on condition that if a further offence is committed the court will sentence him for the original offence.

District Judge (Magistrates' Court)
A legally qualified magistrate, who presides over a large Magistrates' Court.

Divorce County Court
One of a number of County Courts that hear divorce cases. See page 294.

drug treatment and testing order
Court order that is aimed at helping those convicted of offences relating to drugs or drug-taking change their drug use and reduce their offending.

Family Division of the High Court
One of several divisions of the High Court, dealing with cases to do with the family, in particular cases affecting children.

family law
A legal specialism that includes such matters as, for example, divorce and adoption.

fine
Sentence in which the offender is required to pay a specific sum of money to the court.

injunction
A court order that prohibits a certain act on the part of a certain person.

judicial review
The process whereby the courts may investigate the workings of public organisations.

jury
A group of 12 people selected at random from the general population to hear the facts of a case and decide on a verdict.

lawful
Something, such as an action, that is permitted under the law.

lawyer
Umbrella term for anyone who has studied the law and practices within the legal system in some way.

legal
Something that is required by the law or recognized by the law.

magistrate
A person who presides over a Magistrates' Court. See pages 294–295.

Magistrates' Court
A local court that hears both civil and criminal cases. See pages 294–295.

miscarriage of justice
An incorrect verdict delivered by a criminal court, usually resulting in the punishment of an innocent person.

negligence
An act or omission on the part of a person with a duty to take care that leads to a loss or injury.

nuisance
An act or state of affairs that interferes with a person's right to quiet enjoyment of land or property. Nuisance can also be

extended to mean interference with the comfort, safety and health of the local community.

ombudsman

A person who investigates the complaints of the general public. There are ombudsman offices for many sectors of the commercial and governmental world. See page 298.

parole

Releasing a convicted offender before his sentence has been completed.

probation order

Any offender over 16 years of age may be required to be supervised by a probation officer. This may involve, among other requirements, regular meetings, attendance for drug rehabilitation treatment, attendance at a day centre, etc.

prosecution

Bringing a criminal case to court; or the group of lawyers that do so.

quash

To overturn a verdict of a lower court.

referral order

Order referring a young offender (who pleads guilty to what is her first offence) to a Youth Offender Panel.

remand

Either committing an accused person to custody or to release him on bail, pending trial or, after the trial, while awaiting sentencing.

reparation order

Court order that requires a young offender to repair the damage she has done, either through mediation with the victim of her offence, or through work in the community in general.

solicitor

Legal professional who gives legal advice, carries out legal work and takes legal action on the part of members of the public.

statute law
The body of law that is set down in Acts of Parliament.

stipendiary magistrate
Former term for a District Judge (Magistrates' Court).

sue
To bring a case against someone in a civil court.

supervision order
Similar to a probation order (see page 305), but for young people under the age of 17.

suspended sentence
Custodial sentence that is not acted upon for a period of time. If the offender is convicted of an offence during the period of suspension, the original sentence comes into force.

tort
A breach of civil duty that usually leads to a liability for damages.

trespass
Wrongfully entering another person's property, or interfering with his goods or person.

tribunal
A legal body that hears certain specialist disputes. An example would be an employment tribunal which hears disputes between employers and employees.

unlawful
Against the law.

Youth Court
Part of a Magistrates' Court that deals with young offenders.

Youth Offender Panel (YOP)
Panel made up of two members of the local community and a member of the Youth Offending Team. It deals with young offenders (aged between 10 and 17) who have pleaded guilty in court on their first offence, and is aimed at preventing further offending.

15 Further Reading and Useful Addresses

This book gives readers a general overview of the law as it stands at the time of writing. Of course, the law is changing every day, and this book cannot ever be a substitute for legal advice given by specialists with experience in the relevant field of law. All readers are advised to seek up-to-date legal advice from a qualified legal professional before they take any action whatsoever.

This final chapter is packed with ideas for other publications the reader may wish to read and where to get them. This may include information given on websites, and material in leaflets and booklets. It also gives contact details for the many specialist organisations mentioned in the course of this book, as well as many more. Website addresses need to be prefixed with 'www.'.

Accident Line *Insurance scheme endorsed by the Law Society specifically tailored for no-win no-fee claims.* The Law Society, 50-52 Chancery Lane, London WC2A 1PL; 0500 192939.

Action for Victims of Medical Accidents *Advice and practical support for those who believe they have been the victim of a medical accident.* Bank Chambers, 1 London Road, London SE23 3TP; avma.org.uk; 020 8686 8333.

Adoption Contact Register *To register your interest in contacting a birth-mother or a child given up for adoption.* Adoptions Section, General Register Office, Smedley Hydro, Trafalgar Road, Southport, PR8 2HH; statistics.gov.uk/registration/adoptions; 0151 471 4830.

Advertising Standards Authority *For complaints about inaccurate descriptions of goods and services in advertisements, or unsatisfactory* service from advertisers. 2 Torrington Place, London WC1E 7HW; asa.org.uk; 020 7580 5555.

Advisory Centre for Education (ACE) *Advice line for parents and information service for parents whose child is at risk of being excluded from their school.* ace-ed.org.uk. Advice line 0808 8005793; exclusion information 020 7704 9822. *For advice on discrimination and harassment in schools and colleges:* 020 7345 8321, Monday–Friday 2pm–5pm.

Advisory, Conciliation and Arbitration Service (ACAS) *Will help you to resolve an employment dispute with your employer, for example, in cases of discrimination.* acas.org.uk; 020 7210 3613.

Age Concern *Charity for older people. Among many other activities, it can provide information and practical advice on issues surrounding wills, administering estates, funerals,*

FURTHER READING AND USEFUL ADDRESSES

obtaining legal advice and crime prevention for older people. Astral House, 1268 London Road, Norbury, London SW16 4ER; ace.org.uk; 020 8765 7200.

Air Transport Users Council *Have an adviceline for consumers, open weekdays 9:00am-12:00 and 14:00-17:00.* CAA House, 45-59 Kingsway, London WC2B 6TE; caa.co.uk/auc; 020 7240 6061.

Alcohol Concern *Factsheets and leaflets with information on a wide range of subjects related to alcohol misuse in the UK.* Waterbridge House, 32-36 Loman Street, London, SE1 0EE. alcoholconcern.org.uk; 020 7928 7377.

Alzheimer's Society *Publish an excellent factsheet on powers of attorney and other ways in which a person can be authorised legally to look after another person's affairs.* Gordon House, 10 Greencoat Place, London SW1P 1PH; alzheimers.org.uk; 0845 300 0336.

Anti-bullying Campaign *Offer a helpline for those who are being bullied or their parents. Excellent website.* bullying.co.uk; 020 7378 1446 10:00am–4:00pm.

Association of Bonded Travel Organisers Trust 86 Jermyn Street, London SW1Y 6JD; travel-general.com; 020 7930 2388.

Association of British Travel Agents *Professional organisation for travel agents, operating a consumer complaints service.* 68-71 Newman Street, London W1P 4AH; abtanet.co.uk; 0901 2015050 (premium rate line).

Association of Independent Tour Operators 133a St Margarets Road; Twickenham, Middlesex TW1 1RG; aito.co.uk; 020 8744 9280.

Association of Personal Injury Lawyers (APIL) *Association of legal experts offering information on personal injuries claims and a list of professionals qualified to take on cases in this field.* 11 Castle Quay, Castle Boulevard, Nottingham, NG7 1FW; apilonline.com; 0115 958 0585.

The Association of Timeshare Owners Committees *Represents owners of timeshares across Europe.* Harmony House, 7/9 Church Street, Pershore, Worcester WR10 1DT; tatoc.co.uk; 0151 638 8239.

Bar Complaints Commissioner *Can handle consumer complaints against members. Complaints department:* Northumberland House, 3rd Floor, 303–306 High Holborn, London WC1V 7JZ; barcouncil.org.uk; 020 7440 4000.

Benefits Agency *Information on and access to all welfare benefits. You will find the address and telephone number of your local Benefits Agency office in the telephone book. Or check* dss.gov.uk.

British and Irish Ombudsman Association *Can provide information about all the bodies that handle consumer complaints in the UK and give contact details.* bioa.org.uk.

Chartered Institute of Arbitrators *Information on dispute resolution - alternatives to going to court.* arbitrators.org; 020 7421 7444.

FURTHER READING AND USEFUL ADDRESSES

Childline *24-hour helpline for children and young people.* 0800 1111.

Child Support Agency *Government agency which assesses and collects child support maintenance on behalf of those with absent parents. Very informative website.* PO Box 55, Brierley Hill, West Midlands DY5 1YL; csa.gov.uk.; 08457 133 133.

CIFAS *To register your personal details against identity theft.* cifas.org.uk; 0870 010 2091.

Civil Aviation Authority *Consumer protection for airline users.* CAA House, 45-59 Kingsway, London WC2B 6TE; caa.co.uk; 020 7379 7311.

Commission for Racial Equality *Action on race discrimination.* Head Office, St Dunstan's House, 201-211 Borough High Street, London SE1 1GZ; cre.gov.uk; 020 7939 0000.

Community Legal Service (CLS) *Run by the Legal Services Commission, the CLS provides information and ensures that ordinary people can be confident of the legal advice they receive. The CLS also runs a scheme to fund some civil court proceedings (formerly known as Legal Aid). You will find CLS information in local libraries and other public places, or you can ask them to send information in the post.* justask.org.uk; 0845 608 1122. *For information leaflets on a wide range of legal topics and in various languages:* legalservices.gov.uk; 0845 300 0343.

Consumer Credit Counselling Service *Free professional advice for those with debt problems.* Wade House, Merrion Centre, Leeds LS2 8NG; cccs.co.uk; 0800 138 1111.

The Consumer Gateway *Government website offering a wide range of advice and information to consumers.* dti.gov.uk/consumer_web

The Countryside Agency *Publishes free information on the law as regards leisure activities in the countryside.* John Dower House, Crescent Place, Cheltenham GL50 3RA; countryside.gov.uk; 01242 521381.

Court Service *All things to do with the courts, including local court addresses and forms for legal proceedings.* Sixth Floor, Southside, 105 Victoria Street, London SW1E 6QT; courtservice.gov.uk; 020 7210 2266.

Crime Reduction Service *Government advice on crime prevention.* crimereduction.gov.uk.

Crimestoppers *Organisation that enables the general public to give information about a crime, anonymously if they wish.* crimestoppers-uk.org; 0800 555 111.

Criminal Injuries Compensation Authority (CICA) *Information on personal injuries and how to claim for them.* Morley House, 26-30 Holborn Viaduct, London EC1A 2JQ; cica.gov.uk; 020 7842 6800.

Criminal Justice System Online *Information for those who have been called for jury service.* cjsonline.org.uk

Crown Prosecution Service *This organisation is responsible for deciding whether a person will be prosecuted.* 50 Ludgate Hill, London EC4M 7EX; cps.gov.uk; 020 7273 8152.

FURTHER READING AND USEFUL ADDRESSES

Cruse – Bereavement Care *Voluntary organisation that offers support, counselling and information to the bereaved.* 126 Sheen Road, Richmond, Surrey TW9 1UR; crusebereavementcare.org.uk; helpline: 0870 167 1677.

DEFRA *Information on protecting various flora and fauna, and on the PETS scheme.* defra.gov.uk/wildlife-countryside.

Direct Marketing Association *Consumer information on the best way to shop from home, including the leaflet 'Buying from Home'.* 70 Margaret Street, London W1W 8SS; dma.org.uk; 020 7291 3300.

Direct Selling Association *Trade Association that can pursue consumer complaints against its members.* 29 Floral Street, London WC2E 9DP; dsa.org.uk; 020 7497 1234.

Disabled Drivers' Association (DDA) *Information for disabled motorists.* Ashwellthorpe, Norwich NR16 1EX; dda.org.uk; 0870 770 3333.

Divorce, Conciliation and Advisory Service *Advice and help for anyone leaving a long-standing relationship.* 38 Ebury Street, London SW1W 0LU; 020 7730 2422.

Driver and Vehicle Licensing Agency (DVLA) *All things related to drivers' licences and vehicle registration.* dvla.gov.uk; 0870 240 0009.

Driving Standards Agency *All things related to training and testing of drivers.* Stanley House, 56 Talbot Street, Nottingham NG15GU; dsa.gov.uk; 0115 901 2500.

DrugScope *UK charity providing information on drugs and issues surrounding drug abuse. Aimed at both professionals and those with a personal interest. The website is possibly the most informative in this field.* drugscope.org.uk.

Equal Opportunities Commission *Information about rights under the sex discrimination and equal pay legislation.* Overseas House, Quay Street, Manchester M3 3HN; eoc.org.uk; 0161 833 9244.

Equifax *To request a copy of your credit record.* Credit File Advice Centre, PO Box 1140, Bradford, BD1 5US; equifax.co.uk; 0870 010 2091.

Experian *To request a copy of your credit record.* Experian Consumer Help Service; PO Box 8000, Nottingham NG1 5GX; uk.experian.com; 08702 416212.

Federation of Private Residents' Associations Ltd 113-115 George Lane, London E18 1AB; fpra.org.uk; 020 8530 8464.

Financial Services Compensation Scheme *Organisation that can help with compensation if a financial services company fails to pay its customers.* 7th floor, Lloyds Chambers, Portsoken St, London E1 8BN; fscs.org.uk; helpline 020 7892 7300.

Foreign and Commonwealth Office: Consular Division *Up-to-date government travel advice plus point of first contact for families whose members are in legal trouble abroad.* Consular Division, Foreign & Commonwealth Office, Old Admiralty Building, London SW1A 2PA; fco.gov.uk; 0870 6060290; BBC Ceefax p470 onwards.

FURTHER READING AND USEFUL ADDRESSES

The Free Representation Unit *Website gives information on where to look for free legal advice.* fru.org.uk.

The Gender Trust *Advisory organisation for transgender people.* PO Box 3192, Brighton BN1 3WR; home.freeuk.net/gentrust; 07000 790347.

General Medical Council *Professional association which handles very serious complaints against health care practitioners.* 178 Great Portland Street, London W1W 5JE; gmc-uk.org; 020 7580 7642.

General Register Office *All things related to registering births, marriages and deaths.* Family Records Centre, 1 Myddleton Street, London EC1R 1UW; statistics.gov.uk/nsbase/registration/ general_register.asp; 020 8392 5300; for certificates 020 7233 9233.

Health and Safety Executive *Information on health and safety legislation.* Broad Lane, Sheffield, S3 7HQ; hse.gov.uk; 01742 892345.

HM Customs and Excise *Up-to-date information on duty-free allowances and other information regarding importing goods from abroad.* hmce.gov.uk.

Home Education Advisory Service *Advice on educating your child outside the state system.* P.O. Box 98, Welwyn Garden City, Herts AL8 6AN; heas.org.uk; 01707 371854.

Home Office *Website gives details of government policy on controlled substances and alcohol-related offences, along with advice on* personal safety and crime prevention. homeoffice.gov.uk.

Immigration and Nationality Directorate *All things relating to staying in the UK and applying for British citizenship. Also, information for employers of foreign workers and information for asylum seekers.* Lunar House, 40 Wellesley Road, Croydon CR9 2BY; homeoffice.gov.uk/ind/hpg.htm; 0870 606 7766.

Immigration Law Practitioners Association *For a list of legal practitioners qualified to advice on immigration law.* Lindsey House, 40-42 Charterhouse Street, London EC1M 6JN; ilpa.org.uk; 020 7251 8383.

The Land Registry *Records ownership of land in England and Wales. Its website contains a mountain of information and forms that can be downloaded.* Headquarters: 32 Lincoln's Inn Fields, London WC2A 3PH; landreg.gov.uk; 020 7917 8888

Law Centres *A network of offices offering free legal advice to the general public. The website gives a list of local offices.* lawcentres.org.uk.

The Law Society *Contact details for solicitors and law firms in your area.* lawwsociety.org.uk; 020 7242 1222.

Leasehold Advisory Service *Information about leaseholds, including advice on the new legislation.* 70-74 City Road, London EC1Y 2BJ; lease-advice.org; 0845 345 1993.

Lesbian and Gay Bereavement Project *Support for gay men and lesbians in bereavement. Offer a free will model for those living with same-sex partners.* Vaughan M Williams centre,

FURTHER READING AND USEFUL ADDRESSES

Colindale Hospital, London NW9 5GH; 020 7403 5969.

Low Pay Unit *Information about a wide range of employment rights and issues, including information on the national minimum wage.* 10 Dukes Road, London WC1H 9AD; lowpayunit.org.uk; 020 7387 2910.

Mail Order Protection Scheme *Compensates consumers if they have lost money through the failure of a mail order company advertising in a national newspaper.* 18a King Street, Maidenhead, SL6 1EF; mops.org.uk; 01628 641 930.

Marie Stopes International *Family planning information and advice.* 153-157 Cleveland Street, London W1T 6QW; mariestopes.org.uk; 020 7574 7400.

Marine Environmental Protection Agency *For information on and permission for burial at sea.* 020 7 238 5872/5868

Mediation UK *For information on mediation services.* Alexander House, Telephone Avenue, Bristol BS1 4BS; mediationuk.org.uk; 0117 904 6661.

Mencap *Information on disability discrimination in schools, and the educational rights of children with learning disabilities.* 123 Golden Lane, London EC1Y 0RT; mencap.org.uk; 020 7454 0454.

Mental Health Act Commission *Safeguards the interests of those detained under the Mental Health Act (1983).* mhac.trent.nhs.uk; 0115 943 7100.

MIND *Mental health charity which offers a wide range of information factsheets and booklets on related subjects, including patients' rights under the Mental Health Act (1983).* 15–19 Broadway, London E15 4BQ; mind.org; 020 8519 2122.

Motor Accident Solicitors' Society *Contact details for solicitors who specialise in compensation claims after road traffic accidents.* Bridge House, 48-52 Baldwin Street, Bristol BS1 1QW; mass.org.uk; 0117 929 2560.

Motor Insurers Bureau *Can obtain details of a driver involved in an accident, including motorists from certain other countries, and may take up cases where the responsible party is uninsured.* 152 Silbury Boulevard, Milton Keynes MK9 1NB; mib.org.uk; 01908 240 000.

National Association of Bereavement Services *Support and information for the bereaved, including a National Directory of Bereavement and Loss Services.* 20 Norton Folgate, London E1 6DB; 020 7709 9090.

National Association of Citizens Advice Bureaux *For a list of local offices and a wide range of clear information online.* 115-123 Pentonville Road, London N1 9LZ; adviceguide.org.uk; 020 7833 2181.

National Debtline *Confidential advice for those in debt. The website has downloadable sample letters and useful information.* nationaldebtline.co.uk; 0808 800 4000.

National Drugs Helpline *Confidential helpline for drug users individuals concerned about somebody using drugs.* ndh.org.uk; 0800 776600.

National Family Mediation *Help for couples who are separating.* Star House 104–108 Grafton Road, London NW5 4BD; nfm.u-net.com; 0207 485 8809.

National Minimum Wage Helpline *For up-to-date information on the minimum wage.* dti.gov.uk/er/nmw; 0845 6000678.

The Natural Death Centre *Living wills, help with environmentally-friendly burials and woodland burial sites.* 6 Blackstock Mews, Blackstock Road, London N4 2BT; naturaldeath.org.uk; 020 7359 8391.

Neighbourhood Watch *For advice on organising a local Neighbourhood Watch scheme.* neighbourhoodwatch.net; 020 7772 3348.

Office of Fair Trading *Provide information to consumers and enforce trading regulations.* oft.gov.uk; Public Liaison unit 08457 22 44 99.

Office of the Immigration Services Commissioner *Ensures that all immigration advisors are suitably qualified and follow a code of conduct. Useful multilingual website.* Fleetbank House, 2-6 Salisbury Square, London EC4Y 8JX; oisc.org.uk; 020 7211 1500.

Organisation for Timeshare in Europe (OTE) *Professional association for companies developing and selling timeshares across Europe. Can offer advice on buying a timeshare and help to handle complaints.* 15-19 Great Titchfield Street, London W1P 7SB; ote-info.com; 020 7291 0901.

Patients Association *Information on patients' rights, support and advice.* PO Box 935, Harrow, Middlesex HA1 3YJ; patients-association.com; 020 8423 9111.

Patients' Charter *Health and literature line:* 0800 555777.

Parents Against Drug Abuse *Support and information for parents of drug-users.* 12-14 Church Parade, Ellesmere Port, Cheshire, CH65 2ER; btinternet.com/~padahelp; 08457 023867.

Passport Service *For new British passports and renewals. The service has several offices around the country. The website allows for e-mail applications and enquiries.* passport.gov.uk; 0870 521 0410 (24 hours); 0901 4700 110 (for a passport application pack).

Police Complaints Authority *Undertake investigations into serious police misconduct.* 10 Great George Street, London SW1P 3AE; pca.gov.uk; 020 7273 6450.

Prisoners Abroad *Practical help for those in prison abroad and for their families in the UK.* 89-93 Fonthill Road, Finsbury Park, London N4 3JH; prisonersabroad.org.uk; 020 7561 6820.

Probate Department Principal Registry, Family Division First Avenue House, 42-49 High Holborn, London WC1V 0NP; 020 7947 7000; personal applications 020 7936 6983.

Public Guardianship Office *Information on powers of attorney.* Archway Tower, 2 Junction Road, London N19 5RQ; guardianship.gov.uk; enduring power of attorney helpline: 0845 330 2963.

FURTHER READING AND USEFUL ADDRESSES

The Ramblers' Association *Provide leaflets and up-to-date information on a wide range of subjects to do with walking in the countryside.* 2nd Floor, Camelford House, 87-90 Albert Embankment, London SE1 7TW; ramblers.org.uk; 020 7339 8500.

Rape Crisis *The central helpline can put victims of rape or sexual abuse in touch with a local centre for free advice and counselling.* rapecrisis.co.uk; 0115 900 3560.

Refuge *24-hour domestic violence crisis helpline:* 0990 995443.

Registry of County Court Judgments *Compiles information on all county court judgements and passes it to credit reference agencies when required.* 173-175 Cleveland Street, London W1P 5PE; registry-trust.org.uk; 020 7380 0133.

Relate *Relationship counselling.* Herbert Gray College, Little Church Street, Rugby CV21 3AP; relate.org.uk 01788 573241.

The Rent Service *For information on how to contact a local Rent Officer.* 5 Welbeck Street, London W1G 9YQ; therentservice.gov.uk; 020 7023 6000.

Roadpeace *Charity for victims of road traffic accidents. Among other things can offer legal information and advice.* PO Box 2579, London NW10 3PW; roadpeace.org.uk; 020 8964 1021.

Royal Society for the Prevention of Cruelty to Animals (RSPCA) *Information on pet care and animal welfare.* Causeway, Horsham, West Sussex RH12 1HG; rspca.org.uk; 01403 264181.

The Samaritans *Nationwide organisation offering emotional support to those in distress or despair (including victims of crime).* samaritans.org.uk; 08457 90 90 90.

Shelter *Information and advice on housing issues, plus a network of Housing Aid Centres around the country.* shelter.org.uk; Helpline: 0808 800 4444 (24 hours).

Solicitors Family Law Association *Association of solicitors who specialise in family law.* PO Box 302, Orpington, Kent, BR6 8QX; sfla.co.uk; 01689 850227.

Survivors UK *Offer a helpline for men who have been the victim of a sexual assault.* survivorsuk.co.uk; 020 7357 6677.

Suzy Lamplugh Trust *Advice on personal safety.* 14 East Sheen Avenue, London SW14; suzylamplugh.org; 020 8392 1839.

TheSite.org *Website aimed at young people and providing up-to-date information about the law on controlled substances, plus a host of other information.* thesite.org.

Timeshare Consumers' Association Hodsock, Worksop, Nottinghamshire S81 0TF; timeshare.org.uk; 01909 591100.

Trades Union Congress *Advice on joining a union, plus information on a range of work-related subjects.* tuc.org.uk; 0870 600 4882.

Trashed *Website aimed at young people, offering information about controlled substances.* trashed.co.uk.

Treasury Solicitor's Department *Contact in cases where the deceased has no will* *and no relatives.* Queen Anne's Chambers, 28 Broadway, London SW1H 9JS; 020 7210 3034.

UKOnline.gov.uk *Gateway to all UK government websites, for information on a vast range of subjects, including current and new legislation and individual rights.*

UKVisas *For information on UK visas.* Visa Correspondence, UKvisas, London SW1A 2AH; ukvisas.gov.uk; general enquiries (answerphone service) 020 7008 8438; application forms: 020 7008 8308.

Victim Support *Information and support for victims of crime.* victimsupport.com; 0845 3030 900 (weekdays 9:00-21:00, weekends 9:00-19:00).

Voluntary Euthanasia Society

Campaigns for the legalisation of voluntary euthanasia; information on living wills. 13 Prince of Wales Terrace, London W8 5PG; ves.org.uk; 020 7937 7770.

Women's Aid

National organisation dedicated to co-ordinating and supporting a network of centres for victims of domestic violence, including women's refuges. www.womensaid.org.uk; national domestic violence helpline: 08457 023 468.

Index

Page numbers in **bold type** refer to contact details for organisations.

abatement notice 73, 77
abortion 99, 107
abuse, child 86–88
access, landlords' rights 9–10
Accident Line **307**
accidents and injuries 115–131
    abroad 215
    animals 254
    at work 126, 127–128
    traffic accidents 206
Action for Victims of Medical
    Accidents **307**
action plan order 300
active euthanasia 112
actual bodily harm (ABH) 151
additional maternity leave 185
administrator 144, 149
adoption 86, 187
Adoption Contact Register **307**
adversarial process 300
Advertising Standards Authority
    307
Advisory Centre for Education
    307
Advisory, Conciliation and
    Arbitration Service **307**
advocate 300
after-the-event insurance 129
Age Concern **307**
agency 110
age of consent 98
Air Transport Users Council **308**
air travel 240
Air Travel Organisers' Licence 247
alcohol and the law 224–230
Alcohol Concern **308**
alternative dispute resolution
    (ADR) 118, 297–298
Alzheimer's Society **308**

animals 249–257
animal welfare 250
annulment 65
Anti-bullying Campaign **308**
antisocial behaviour 75–77
antisocial behaviour order 300
appeal 300
appropriate adult 112
approved social worker 112
arbitration 297–298
arrest 286–289, 290
arson 151
assault 151–152
assisted suicide 112
Association of Bonded Travel
    Organisers Trust **308**
Association of British Travel
    Agents (ABTA) **308**
Association of Independent Tour
    Operators **308**
Association of Personal Injury
    Lawyers **308**
Association of Timeshare Owners
    Committees **308**
assured shorthold tenancies 14–15
assured tenancies 13–14
asylum-seekers 274–275
attendance centre order 96, 300
attorney 112
auctions 35, 43
au pairs 269
authorisation 110
babysitting 90
bail 300
balance of probabilities 162
banns 61
Bar Complaints Commissioner
    308
barrister 300–301
before-the-event insurance 129
beneficiary 149
Benefits Agency **308**

bequest 149
bigamy 62
binding over to keep the peace 96
boarding establishments 254–255
breach of contract 197
breach of statutory provision 188
breaking and entering 162
British and Irish Ombudsman
    Association **308**
British citizenship 258–263
burden of proof 163
burglary 152, 154
burial at sea 149
business visitors 269–270
buying and selling goods 39–45
camper vans 217
care order 88, 301
causation 116–117
caution 94
charge cards 53
Chartered Institute of Arbitrators
    308
child assessment order 87
child-friendly working 187
Childline **309**
child protection 87
children
    and the law 80–101
    arrangements for (divorce) 69
    neighbourhood problems 74
    registering births 276–277
Child Support Agency **309**
CIFAS **309**
Citizens Advice *see* National
    Association of Citizens
    Advice Bureaux
citizen's arrest 160
citizenship, British 258–263
Civil Aviation Authority **309**
civil law 301
civil wrong 301
claimant 301

claims assessors 121
claims managers 120–121
clean break settlement 68
clerk 301
clinical injuries 125–127
clocking 203
coaches 217
cohabitation 70–71
combination order 97, 301
Commission for Racial Equality **309**
commonhold 23–24, 36
common law 301
common travel area 282–283
Community Legal Services **309**
community punishment order 301
community rehabilitation order 301
community service order 97
compensation 130, 302
compensation order 96, 302
compensation recovery 130
Compensation Recovery Unit 123
complaints against the police 289–290
complaints procedures 298
completion 28, 36
compulsory maternity leave 184
conciliation 297
conditional discharge 303
conditional sale agreement 54
consent, age of 98
conservation 236–237
conspiracy 152
constructive dismissal 166
constructive manslaughter 156
Consular Service 244
consumer contracts 38–39
consumer credit 52–55
Consumer Credit Counselling Service **309**
Consumer Gateway **309**
consumer protection 56
contact order 85
contraception 98–99
contract of employment 166–172
contributory negligence 117
controlled drugs 230–234
conveyancing 34–35, 36
co-respondent 77–78

coroner 146–147
corporate manslaughter 184
council housing 17–18
Country Code 236–237
Countryside Agency **309**
countryside and the law 234–237
County Courts 292–294
Court of Appeal 295–297
courts 292–297
Court Service **309**
covenant (property) 18–19, 36
credit cards 52–53
credit sale agreement 55
cremation 149
Crime Reduction Service **309**
Crimestoppers **309**
criminal damage 152–153
criminal injuries 128–129
Criminal Injuries Compensation Authority **309**
Criminal Justice System Online **309**
criminal law 302
criminal record 298–299
criminal responsibility 94
Crown Court 295
Crown Prosecution Service **309**
Cruse – Bereavement Care **310**
curfew order 302
custodial sentence 302
custom and practice 197
damages 123, 303
dangerous dogs 253
death, registering 147–148
debit cards 52
debt 54
decree absolute 78
decree nisi 78
deductions, salary 174–175
deed poll 278
defendant 303
DEFRA **310**
dependants 143, 187–188
deportation (removal) 284
deposits (rented accommodation) 8–9
direct discrimination 192–193
Direct Marketing Association **310**
Direct Selling Association **310**

disabled access to restaurants 220–221
Disabled Drivers' Association **310**
discharge 303
    absolute discharge 299–300
    conditional 303
    young offender 96
discipline 91, 93
dismissal 165–166, 188–190
discrimination
    arranging a mortgage 33
    at work 192–196
    goods and services 55
    part-time workers 194
    renting accommodation 14
    school and college 93–94
    sex discrimination 193–194
disputes, neighbourhood 75, 76
disqualification from driving 208–209
District Judge (Magistrates' Court) 303
divorce 66–69, 85–86
Divorce, Conciliation and Advisory Service **310**
Divorce County Courts 293, 294
dogs 74, 251–254
domestic violence 71–72
domestic workers 269
door-to-door selling 50
drinking age 226–227
drinking and driving 211
drinking hours 226
Driver and Vehicle Licensing Agency (DVLA) **310**
drivers' licences 203–204
Driving Standards Agency **310**
DrugScope **310**
drug treatment and testing order 303
dual nationality 263
duty-free 245
duty of care 131
easement (property) 19, 36
eating out 219–224
education 91–94
emergency protection order 87–88
employee status 166–168
Employer's Liability Insurance 127

INDEX

employment agencies 169
employment contract 169–172
employment law 165–199
employment tribunal 197
encumbrance 36
endorsement, driving 208–209
enfranchisement 22, 36
engagement 59
entry clearance visa 283
Equal Opportunities Commission **310**
equal pay 194–195
Equifax **310**
estate 149
estate agents 29–31
European Convention on Human Rights 297
European Court of Human Rights 297
European Court of Justice 297
European Economic Area (EEA) 263–264
eviction 8, 36
    squatters 25
exclusion order 72
executor 138–139, 143
ex gratia payment 131
Experian **310**
express contract terms 170–171
express malice aforethought 163
false imprisonment 289
family law 303
faulty goods 44, 127
Federation of Private Residents' Associations Ltd **310**
film classification 246
Financial Services Compensation Scheme **310**
fine 96
fixed term contract 197
flexible working for parents 187
food hygiene 222–223
Foreign and Commonwealth Office: Consular Division **310**
freedom to roam 235–236
freehold 18–20, 36
Free Representation Unit **311**
funeral 149
gazumping 29

Gender Trust **311**
General Medical Council **311**
General Register Office **311**
godparent 138
going equipped 153
goods 57
goods and services 38–51
Green Card 214
grievous bodily harm (GBH) 153
gross misconduct 198
gross negligence manslaughter 156
guarantees and warranties 51
guard dogs 253
guardian 138
harrassment 153
    landlords 10
    sexual 196
    young people 99
health and the law 102–114
health and safety at work 182–184
Health and Safety Executive **311**
High Court 295
Highway Code 205
hire purchase agreements 54
HM Customs and Excise **311**
holidays 177–178
home brewing 224
Home Education Advisory Service **311**
Home Office **311**
home schooling 92
home shopping 48–50
homicide 163
hours of work 175–177
House of Lords 297
housing associations 17
indefinite leave to remain 283
identification 277–278
identity 276–282
identity theft 280–282
illegal employment contracts 171
illegal workers 270–271
illegitimacy 262
immigration 258–276
Immigration and Nationality Directorate **311**
immigration advice 275–276
Immigration Law Practitioners Association **311**

implied contract terms 170–171
implied malice aforethought 163
incitement 155
indecent assault 155
indictable offence 163
indirect discrimination 192–193
industrial tribunal see employment tribunal
infanticide 163
informed consent 102
inheritance tax 142
injunction 304
in lieu 198
International Driving Permit 215
intestacy 132–135
joint tenancies 16, 24
joy-riding 212–213
judicial review 304
jury service 296
knives 156–158
Land Registry **311**
Law Centres **311**
Law Society 291, **311**
lawyer 304
lay-offs 176
leasehold 20–23, 36–37
    extending 23
leave to remain 272
legal advice 291–292
legal system 285–306
legatee 150
license (accommodation) 15–16, 37
licensing laws 224–227
like pay for life work 194–196
livestock 257
Leasehold Advisory Service **311**
legal aid (public funding) 122
Lesbian and Gay Bereavement Project **311–312**
living will 105
Low Pay Unit **312**
Magistrates' Courts 294–295
Mail Order Protection Scheme **312**
maintenance (divorce) 68–69
malice aforethought 163
malicious prosecution 290
managing agents 21–22
manslaughter 155–156, 184
Marie Stopes International **312**

Marine Environmental Protection Agency **312**
marital rape 65
marriage 58–65
maternity rights 184–186
mediation 297
  accidents and injuries 119
  divorce 69
  neighbourhood disputes 75
Mediation UK **312**
medical accidents (clinical injuries) 125–127
medical records 106
medical treatment, refusing 104–105
Mencap **312**
mental health 108
Mental Health Act 108
Mental Health Act Commission **312**
mental illness 113
mental impairment 113
MIND **312**
minibuses 217
minimum wage, national 172–174
minor 101
miscarriage of justice 304
mistreatment of animals 250
mobile phones 213–214
mopeds 217
mortgage 32–33
Motor Accident Solicitors' Society **312**
motorcycles 217
motoring 200–218
  abroad 214–215
  buying a vehicle 200–203
  disqualification 208–209
  drinking and driving 211
  endorsements 208–209
  offences 208–214
Motor Insurers Bureau 204, **312**
multiple agency 30, 37
murder 156
name-changes 278–280
National Association of Bereavement Services **312**
National Association of Citizens Advice Bureaux **312**
National Debtline **312**

National Drugs Helpline **312**
National Family Mediation **313**
national minimum wage 172–174
National Minimum Wage Helpline **313**
Natural Death Centre **313**
naturalisation 261–262
nearest relative 109
negligence 115–116, 304
Neighbourhood Watch **313**
neighbours 72–77
noise 73
non-EEA family permit 272–273
non-molestation order 72
notice periods 180–181
no-win no-fee agreement 122
nuisance 73, 214, 304
occupation order 72
occupier's liability 131, 161
offensive weapons 156–158
Office of Fair Trading **313**
Office of the Immigration Services Commissioner **313**
ombudsman system 298
ordinary maternity leave 185
organ donation 106
Organisation for Timeshare in Europe **313**
out-of-court settlement 123–124
overstayer 283
package holidays 238–240
parole 305
Patients Association **313**
Patients' Charter **313**
parental leave 187
parental responsibility 84–85
Parents Against Drug Abuse **313**
partial intestacy 135
part-time workers 168
passports 242
Passport Service **313**
paternity leave, pay 186
payslip 174–175
permit-free 283
pets 249–257
PETS scheme 255–256
pet shops 249–250
physician-assisted suicide 114
plaintiff 79

police 285–290
Police Complaints Authority **313**
police detention 288
police interviews 287
police protection for children 87
polygamy 62
positive covenant 18–19
possession order 37, 72
power of attorney 111–112
pressure selling 51
primary identification 277–278
Prisoners Abroad **313**
probate 150
Probate Department Principal Registry, Family Division **313**
probation order 96, 305
prohibited steps order 85–86
property 7–37
pro rata 199
prosecution 305
protected tenancies 11–13
provisional drivers' licence 204
proxy marriages 62
psychopathic disorder 114
public funding 122
Public Guardianship Office **313**
public performances (children) 90–91
quarantine 256–257
quash 305
racially-aggravated offences 158
Ramblers' Association **314**
rape 65, 158
Rape Crisis **314**
reasonable doubt 162
reasonable force 160
receipts 42
reckless manslaughter 156
recreational drugs 230–234
recourse to public funds 283
redundancy 189–190
re-engagement (job) 166
references 173
referral order 305
Refuge **314**
refugees 274–275
refunds 41–43
registered social landlord 17, 37
registering a child's birth 276–277

INDEX

registration (citizenship) 261
Registry of County Court
    Judgments **314**
reinstatement (job) 166
Relate **314**
remand 289, 305
removal (deportation) 284
rental agreements 7, 10–18
renting accommodation 7–18
Rent Service **314**
repairs and renovations 9
reparation order 305
residence order 85
residue 139–140
restaurants 219–224
restrictive covenants 19
returning goods 41–43
right of abode 263
right of access (countryside) 235
rights of way 19, 234–235
right to buy 18, 22
right to die 114
right to roam 235–236
right to silence 288
Roadpeace **314**
road rage 213
road tax 204–205
robbery 158
rough camping 237
RSPCA **314**
sabbatical 199
salary deductions 174–175
Samaritans **314**
Schengen visa 284
school 91–94
school leaving age 89
seat belts 206
second-hand goods 45
secure tenancies 16–17
self-defence 159–161
self-employed 166–167
separation 66
service charges (property) 21–22
services, buying and selling 45–47
sex discrimination 193–194
Shelter **314**
shortage occupations 268
short-time working 176–177
sick leave and sick pay 179–180

small claims 293–294
smoking 183, 221
social housing 17
soldier's will 137
sole agency 30, 37
sole selling rights 30, 37
solicitors 291–292, 305
Solicitors Family Law Assoc. **314**
specific issue order 86
speeding 212, 217
sporting events and alcohol 229
squatters 25–26
stalking 77
statute law 305
statutory declaration 278–279
statutory maternity pay 186
statutory rights 199
sterilisation 105
stillbirth, registering 148–149
stolen vehicles 202
stop and search 285–286
store cards 53
stress at work 184
studying in the UK 266–267
subject to control 284
sub-letting 21
sue 306
summary offence 164
Sunday working 180
supervision order 97, 306
survey (property) 33–34
Survivors UK **314**
suspended sentence 306
Suzy Lamplugh Trust **314**
switching 267
Tailored Interactive Guidance on
    Employment Rights 184
temporary release 284
tenancies-in-common 24–25
tenancy agreements 10–18
testator 150
theft 158
TheSite.org **314**
timeshares 240–242
Timeshare Consumers' Association
    314
tort 306
totting up 208
trade union representation 181–182

Trades Union Congress **314**
Trading Standards 48
traffic accidents 206–207
trailers 217
Trashed **314**
travelling abroad 237–245, 255–257
treasure trove 25
trees 73–74
trespass 159, 236
triable either way 163
tribunal 306
UK ancestry status 269
UKOnline.gov.uk **315**
UKVisas **315**
unfair contract terms 50–51
unfair dismissal 166
unfit for human consumption 223
unlawful sexual intercourse 98
unsolicited goods 50
vehicles, stolen 202
verbal contracts 171
victimisation 165
Victim Support 161–162, **315**
visa national countries 264–265
visas 242–243, 265
visiting the UK 266
void 79
voluntary euthanasia 106
Voluntary Euthanasia Society **315**
warranties 51
whistle-blowing 190–192
wild animals 254
will 135–143
Witness Service 162
Women's Aid **315**
work 165–199
    alcohol 229
    injuries at work 127–128
    work permits 267–271
    work-related illnesses 128
    young people 88–91
wrongful arrest 289
wrongful dismissal 166
young offenders 96–97, 289
Youth Court 95
Youth Offender Panel 306